SALMAN RUSHDIE
A DELEUZIAN READING

SALMAN RUSHDIE
A DELEUZIAN READING

Søren Frank

Museum Tusculanum Press
University of Copenhagen 2011

Salman Rushdie: A Deleuzian Reading

© Museum Tusculanum Press and Søren Frank, 2011
Originally published in Danish as *Salman Rushdies kartografi*, 2003
Revised by the author and translated by Sten Pultz Moslund
Consultant: Frederik Tygstrup
Design, cover and typesetting by Pernille Sys Hansen, www.dampdesign.dk
Cover by Pernille Sys Hansen, www.dampdesign.dk
Set in Fresco sans and Relato sans
ISBN 978 87 635 3671 4

This book is published with financial support from
Humanioras Publikationsudvalg, University of Southern Denmark

Museum Tusculanum Press
126 Njalsgade
DK-2300 Copenhagen S
Denmark
www.mtp.dk

for Agnes and Marie
who, equal to all expectations,
were born around midnight

CONTENTS

    PREFACE — 9
    NOTE ON THE TRANSLATION — 10
    ABBREVIATIONS — 11

INTRODUCTION — 13
PROLOGUE: *GRIMUS* — 19
DELEUZE AND LITERATURE — 41

RUSHDIE'S CARTOGRAPHY — 71
    RUSHDIE'S CARTOGRAPHY: 1981–1988 — 73
    COMPOSITION AND ENUNCIATION — 84
    HUMAN IDENTITY — 118
    METAPHOR AND METONYMY — 164
    TOWARD A MINOR LITERATURE — 181
    HISTORIOGRAPHIC METAFICTION — 194
    THE OPENNESS OF TOTALITY — 239

EPILOGUE: *THE GROUND BENEATH HER FEET* — 251
CONCLUSION — 271

    BIBLIOGRAPHY — 275

PREFACE

This book is a translation of *Salman Rushdies kartografi*, published in Danish in 2003. However, before going through the process of being translated, I made a general revision of the original Danish manuscript. Besides modifying formulations here and there, the most significant changes are the omission of the Danish book's biographical chapter as well as the elimination of a few footnotes, sentences, and paragraphs, which I found redundant.

I wish to thank the following people for their various kinds of support: Julie Bjørchmar, Leif Bonderup, Johan Eckart Hansen, Anders Fogh Jensen, Jørgen Dines Johansen, Svend Ploug Johansen, Britta Timm Knudsen, Lars Ole Sauerberg, and Frederik Tygstrup. I also wish to express my deepest gratitude to Sten Pultz Moslund, the translator of the book, for his epiphanic appearance through an e-mail one day.

Søren Frank,
Copenhagen, November 2009

NOTE ON THE TRANSLATION

The cited works by the following writers and critics do not exist in English translation and have been translated from Danish only for the present purpose:

Lars Erslev Andersen; Pernille Bramming; Frants Buhl; Malene Busk; Jan Kjærstad; Martin Leer; Lis Møller; Claus Pedersen; Jacob Skovgaard-Petersen; Frederik Tygstrup; Hanna Ziadeh.

In addition, a footnote and a quote from the introduction to the Danish translation of the Koran have been translated into English.

ABBREVIATIONS

Salman Rushdie:
G   *Grimus*
MC   *Midnight's Children*
S   *Shame*
SV   *The Satanic Verses*
GB   *The Ground Beneath Her Feet*
IH   *Imaginary Homelands*
SA   *Step Across This Line*

Gilles Deleuze:
PS   *Proust and Signs*
DR   *Difference and Repetition*
LS   *The Logic of Sense*
N   *Negotiations*

Gilles Deleuze and Félix Guattari:
K   *Kafka: Toward a Minor Literature*
TP   *A Thousand Plateaus*
WP *What Is Philosophy?*

Gilles Deleuze and Claire Parnet:
D   *Dialogues*

INTRODUCTION

> "The writer returns from what he has seen and heard with bloodshot eyes and pierced eardrums."
> – Gilles Deleuze: "Literature and Life"

How to enter Salman Rushdie's body of works? It is a rhizome! Gilles Deleuze and Félix Guattari open their book on Franz Kafka with a similar question and assertion. This book will show that the concept of rhizome also characterises Salman Rushdie's works. In order to do so, I will analyse five of Rushdie's novels, namely the first four, *Grimus*, *Midnight's Children*, *Shame* and *The Satanic Verses*, and *The Ground Beneath Her Feet*, the seventh of altogether ten novels. Accordingly, the substance of this book is analytical and it provides the reader with thorough readings of Rushdie's novels in regard to themes, form and enunciation; but apart from this basically analytical disposition, the actual originality of the book consists in drawing up a general angle of entrance into Rushdie's writings based on the French philosopher Gilles Deleuze's conceptual apparatus. It is my intention with the book to show how Deleuze's combination of an empiricist "worldliness" and a conceptual constructivism that formalises specific processes of becoming corresponds to traits in Rushdie's artistic profile, just as I will try to incorporate a number of central concepts from Deleuze's writings into the analyses – concepts such as rhizome, simulacrum and lines of flight – in a way which is, hopefully, conducive to a further opening up of Rushdie's novels.

At one and the same time the novels comprise a linguistic tour de force, they are compositionally equilibristic, politically relevant, a bombardment of the senses, humorous fabulations, and intellectually stimulating. In the essay "One Thousand Days in a Balloon" Rushdie claims that his work has been fished out of a sea that reflects a fluid and transient world:

> Obviously, a rigid, blinkered, absolutist world-view is the easiest to keep hold of; whereas the fluid, uncertain, metamorphic picture I've always carried about is rather more vulnerable. Yet I must cling with all my might to that chameleon, that chimera, that shape-shifter, my own soul; must hold on to its mischievous, iconoclastic, out-of-step clown-instincts, no matter how great the storm. And if that plunges me into contradiction and paradox, so be it; I've lived in that messy ocean all my life. I've fished in it for my art (IH, 438-39).

According to Rushdie himself his writing arises from the experience that the ground beneath his feet is unstable and fragile, a *terra infirma*, where art and the novel continuously contribute to a re-writing of the world.

In Gilles Deleuze we find a similar perception of the world and art as process. Through the concept of simulacrum Deleuze characterises art and the novel in particular as anti-logos. The work of art is not created on the basis of any pre-existing model, on the contrary it ceaselessly breaks down fixed and closed systems, after which it reinvents the world anew through its differential perspective. Simulacrum is a force that undermines any thought of similarity in a way that makes it possible to conceive variety and diversity instead. Deleuze and Guattari's concept of rhizome, the heir to the abandoned concept of simulacrum, denotes an open system in constant movement and without any stable centre. The novel as rhizome becomes a cartography which does not copy the world, logos or doxa. Rather, it produces new maps of the world in a creative aesthetic of becoming. The rhizome is drawn by territories, segments, and stratifications as well as by deterritorialisations, reterritorialisations, and lines of flight. From this conceptual angle, focus is directed on the compositional strategies of the novel and the question of how the novel works becomes more important than what it means and why it has been written.

If one is to point to one concept which may legitimise the coupling of Rushdie's novels with Deleuze's philosophy, it must be metamorphosis. In Deleuze's aesthetic theory metamorphosis belongs to a plane of concepts which also includes lines of flight, meetings, metaphors, intermezzi and intensities. Deleuze understands the world as an open totality in an endless process of becoming, and renewal, or metamorphosis, is born in the meeting between two heterogeneous elements or through the actualisation of the virtual.

Rushdie's novels constantly attempt to seek out this virtuality, just as they constantly record collisions between heterogeneous elements, praising hybridity and eclecticism as catalysts of metamorphosis. In the words of the novelist himself: "No aesthetic can be a constant, except an aesthetic based on the idea of inconstancy, metamorphosis, or, to borrow a term from politics, 'perpetual revolution'" (IH, 418). I believe that Rushdie's poetics of the liquid work of art corresponds to Deleuze's characterisation of simulacrum and rhizome. But what Rushdie writes in his essays is one thing; it is quite another matter what he writes in his novels. Therefore my intention is to examine whether Rushdie's poetics, that is, his theorised intention and normative perception of art, as expressed primarily in *Imaginary Homelands* and *Step Across This Line*, but also in interviews, complies with his aesthetics, that is, with the practice of his writing as it unfolds in his novels? This book will show that there is a general agreement between Rushdie's poetics and his aesthetics. There is the exception, however, that his essays at times assume monological and unambiguous views which are differentiated and dialogised in his novels, among other things, through their aestheticised form.

*

This introductory chapter will be followed by a chapter on Rushdie's first novel *Grimus*. My analysis of *Grimus* is primarily intended as an anticipation of some of the themes and motifs that Rushdie expands and deepens in his subsequent novels, which this book will go on to examine in close detail. After this analytical appetizer, I shall attempt to draw a picture of Deleuze's literary theory, primarily through a presentation of the concepts of simulacrum and rhizome. The chapter will argue that there is an intellectual affinity between Rushdie, the writer, and Deleuze, the philosopher, which generally manifests itself on three levels: worldview, art, and subjectivity. The chapter will predominantly be dealing with Deleuze's philosophy, and I will try to explain Deleuze's unusual conceptual apparatus in order to make it comprehensible and applicable for my literary analyses.

The next chapter, "Rushdie's Cartography: 1981-1988," is the weightiest chapter of the book and comprises readings of *Midnight's Children*, *Shame*, and *The Satanic Verses*. The chapter opens with a brief thematic summary of each of the three novels after which I go on to examine the novels' compositional and enunciatory strategies. This will, together with my analysis of human identity, make up the foundation for an estimation of whether it is reasonable to ascribe a rhizomatic character to the novels. What does it mean, one may ask, that a novel combines a linear plot with digressions? Why is a novel composed of three heterogeneous lines? Who is speaking and from where does he or she speak? Who is the observer and from where does he or she make observations? What does it mean that the narrator exposes his or her own principles of construction? Generally, one can say that the compositional strategies of the novels undermine established concepts like beginning and end. Instead they open the possibility of viewing the novels as intermezzo, which means that the novels spread out from the middle, preventing one person, one narrative strand, or one story from forming a centre. Enunciation varies a lot in Rushdie's writings, but generally speaking, Rushdie rarely allows one voice to take possession of the of the fictive universe as an ultimate authority.

What is an individual? Is it homogeneous or heterogeneous? Is it continuous or discontinuous? Human identity is a key issue in Rushdie, who sees the migrant, and the ontological and epistemological potential of the migrant, as a crucial figure and, indeed, a metaphor of humanity; man is a wanderer, a nomad, who is constantly situated in-between two points. Metamorphosis plays a key role in Rushdie's characterology, inasmuch as he never sees man as a homogeneous entity, but rather as a flux of heterogeneous lines. Accordingly, any attempt to establish a traditional subjective centralism in the aesthetics of the novels is made impossible.

In the subsequent theoretical and analytical subchapter about metaphor and metonymy I examine what I call the assembling and distributive forces at work in the novels. This is not intended as a comprehensive study of the distinctions between the two tropes. My purpose is another one, namely to try to describe the central ploy in Rushdie's way of writing. Hence, the subchapter will carry the overall argument that Rushdie uses both tropes simultaneously as principles of structuring. What happens when details are accumulated fragmentarily? Why does the narrator establish connections between distant spheres? The metaphor has two purposes. It assembles diversity through a relation of similarity and it catalyses the metamorphoses of the novel through a relation of difference, thereby giving birth to the new. Metonymy works as a distributive force as it operates in terms of fragmentation, and, because of that, it makes any totalisation of the fictive universe difficult. The most distinguishing feature in Rushdie is that he writes conjunctively, which is to say that his novels progress through "and... and... and...," rather than through the fixed distribution of "is" or "are." The world is both this and this and this. The analysis of the conjunctive style may be taken a step further as it results in what Deleuze calls the (inclusive) disjunctive synthesis, that is, an aesthetics of complementarity in which seemingly incompatible elements are brought to communicate in a transversal dimension without synthesising the elements for that reason. The ruling logic here is an inclusive logic of either-or. In addition, an aesthetics based on complementarity through the logic of both-and and the inclusive logic of either-or is significant for the ethics of Rushdie's writings. Quite simply, there is an ethical point in the construction of a processual and nomadic universe where incompatible worlds may co-exist, and where it is impossible ever to monopolise truth, as truth is reinvented incessantly. An ethics like this includes rather than excludes and, with that, it assumes a conspicuously democratic and anti-authoritarian physiognomony.

In the succeeding subchapter I will discuss Rushdie's novels in relation to their use of language, their relation to politics, and their status as a collective enunciation by means of Deleuze and Guattari's concept of a "minor literature." What role does language play? Is language transparent? Should literature be quietic or engaging? In the last subchapter of chapter four I will read Rushdie's novels as historiographic metafiction, which is the paradoxical poetics of postmodernism Linda Hutcheon arrives at. The paradox issues from the simultaneous movement in the novels of an extrovert referentiality to a past discourse (the extratextual dimension) and an introvert, self-reflective, "navel-gazing" activity (the intratextual dimension). What status does the past have in Rushdie? What tools does he employ in recreating the past? In Hutcheon these questions indicate both an ontological and an epistemological point. Moreover, it is in this subchapter that I will discuss the Rushdie Affair, firstly by explaining the "historical" event of the satanic verses in 616, secondly by examining Rushdie's use of this much disputed episode in order eventually to provide an informative insight into the Affair in 1988-89.

Finally, the last chapter before the conclusion will deal with the millennium novel *The Ground Beneath Her Feet*. The function of this chapter echoes the first chapter on *Grimus* as it summarises some of the most important themes and techniques in Rushdie's body of writing, and, lastly, the chapter will wrap up the affinity between Rushdie and Deleuze.

PROLOGUE: *GRIMUS*

> "A novel examines not reality but existence. And existence is not what has occurred, existence is the realm of human possibilities, everything that man can become, everything he's capable of."
> – Milan Kundera: *The Art of the Novel*

Rushdie's first novel, *Grimus*, was released in 1975, after entering a competition of the best new science-fiction novels at the publishing house Victor Gollancz. In my opinion *Grimus* is worth a close examination, firstly because it can be said to contain the seeds of Rushdie's succeeding novels, and, secondly, because it has received a rough and rather unfair treatment which I intend to problematise. My main purpose in that connection is to show that the negative criticism of *Grimus* fails to allow the amount of autonomy that the novel deserves, regarding the characteristics of its genre. The problem is, in short, that its critics pass sentence on the novel based on hindsight, in the sense that the novel, which sets itself apart from Rushdie's other works by leaning against the science-fiction genre, is assessed in view of the success of the following novels and the characteristics of their styles and genres. After a short summary of the novel, this chapter will start out with an introduction and a problematisation of the criticism of the novel. After that, I will introduce Mikhail Bakhtin's explanation of the Menippean satire which will serve as a framework for the reading of the novel that follows.

Grimus is based on a Persian Sufi poem by Farid ud-Din Attar, *The Conference of the Birds*, in which thirty birds set out to find the bird god Simurg (Grimus forming an anagram of the bird god's name). The point of the poem is that the name "Simurg" actually means "thirty birds", and, with that, the Grand Tour of the thirty birds serves to make them conscious of the fact that they are Simurg themselves. In *Grimus* it is the main character, Flapping Eagle, who sets out to find Grimus. Flapping Eagle grows up with his sister, Bird-Dog, among the Axona Indians who live in isolation from the surrounding world. Bird-Dog decides to leave the tribe when she meets the mysterious Sispy (who turns out to be Grimus), and he offers her a yellow liquid that will give her eternal life. As a consequence of Bird-Dog's violation of the law and his own otherness (fair skin, born by a dead mother, hermaphrodite), Flapping Eagle is banished from the tribe. He drinks the yellow liquid, too, and proceeds to spend 743 years, four months and three days on finding his sister. He finds her with Grimus on the mountain island, Calf Island, where the main part of the novel takes place. The island exists as one among many possible worlds and is conceptualised by Grimus by the use of a Stone Rose: "I think, therefore it is" (G, 230). Flapping Eagle is washed ashore on the island after a mysterious fall where the ocean opens itself and swallows him (he is moved from one dimension to another), and the friendly and intelligent Virgil helps him recover. Virgil becomes Flapping Eagle's Dantean guide up the mountain on the way to the city K and to the summit where Grimus rules in his Grimus-home, which, via his Stone Rose, Ion Eye, Water Crystal, and Crystal of Potentialities, comprises a panopticon, surveying Calf Island along with an infinite number of other dimensions. In this way *Grimus* is affiliated with the *Bildungsroman*, insofar as Flapping Eagle's intra- and interdimensional journeys finally enable him to confront the demiurge, Grimus.

Grimus did not win the competition at Victor Gollancz's and, in contrast to Rushdie's later novels, it was no runaway success in terms of sales either. Nor was it a success with the critics. What are the reasons for this? At a number of occasions, Rushdie himself has expressed his disapproval of the novel: "I was trying to take a theme out of eastern philosophy or mythology and transpose it into a western convention, and I think it didn't really work. I find the book difficult to read now: the language in it embarrasses me" (Haffenden, 43). Moreover the novel's fantastic design does not seem to comply with the method that Rushdie attaches to his concept of imagination later on. In *Grimus* the imagined is not rooted in the real world, says Rushdie, "whereas I now think of it as a method of producing intensified images of reality – images which have their roots in observable, verifiable fact" (*ibid.*, 43). Rushdie concludes: "I think *Grimus* is a clever book. But that's not entirely a compliment. It's too clever for its own good" (Durix, 2000, 15).

For the most part, the critical literature on the novel bases itself on comments like these, launched against the novel by Rushdie himself. Hence, the author is, in a way, employed by the critics with the purpose of legitimising their own verdict. Surely, supporting one's commentary with the author's observations on his or her own work may be very informative and instructive, yet the question is whether the case of *Grimus* calls for greater consideration. The objections to the novel may be grouped under the following two points: 1) the novel fails to create an organic whole from the heterogeneous elements it incorporates; 2) the novel is not anchored in any concrete, recognisable reality, which makes it abstract and laboured.

As to the supposed failure in organicity and synthesis, this critique is raised by D.C.R.A. Goonetilleke and Catherine Cundy, the latter stating that the novel's various elements are "insufficiently blended to make the novel appear a skilfully amalgamated whole" (Cundy, 1992, 128). She continues: "*Grimus* is clearly a novel of a period when Rushdie had not yet achieved the synthesis of diverse cultural strands and narrative forms. He rightly attributes the novel's failure to this lack of a defined voice at its heart, or even, to borrow from Sufism, a unified voice which expresses its own diversity" (*ibid.*, 137). Joel Kuortti is more nuanced, yet evasive: "the question remains how successfully the various components are amalgamated to create a new whole. In the case of *Grimus*, the answer seems to be that it did not succeed. It demands such an amount of concentration and effort to make anything of the allusions. And most of the time they seem to evade or confuse readers, if one can judge by the scant criticism of the novel. (...) In being too demanding and enigmatic, the novel has resisted readings" (Kuortti, 36, 50). Margareta Petersson, who in her book *Unending Metamorphoses* puts forward several points in line with mine, offers the most positive consideration of *Grimus*: "Several scholars suggest that the myths are sidelined and lack inner coherence. I, on the contrary, see them as subordinated to a myth or a symbolic language, that of alchemy, which plays an important part in Rushdie's later works as well" (Petersson, 61). In this way Petersson traces an underlying alchemist structure and thematics in the novel's heterogeneous fabric of intertextuality, suggesting alchemy as the novel's synthesising factor.

Moving to the second objection, the novel's abstract topographical construction is its greatest mistake according to Timothy Brennan and Catherine Cundy. Cundy says that "*Grimus*'s lack of a specific and identifiable geographical location is its chief failure" (Cundy, 1992, 128). Damien Grant is reserved, but also more balanced and positive: "*Grimus* is a young man's novel; it is ambitious, over-literary, philosophically overheated; a 'novel of ideas' in the doubtful sense that it is the ideas that run the show. It is in this sense that it may be considered 'premature.' But it is also brilliant in its design and successful in many of its devices; and if the ideas run the show they are at least absorbing ideas" (Grant, 37). With this Grant seems to acknowledge the composition of the novel as well-shaped and its use of literary techniques as intelligent, and if the novel is an abstract "novel of ideas," it at least gives the reader something to think about. Ib Johansen and Mujeebuddin Syed both grant the novel a formal autonomy: "Combining mythology and science fiction, mixing Oriental thought with Western modes, *Grimus* is in many ways an early manifesto of Rushdie's heterodoxical themes and innovative techniques" (Syed, 135), says Syed but goes on to support the view that the novel lacks rootedness in reality and, for that reason, fails to express postcolonial matters in any convincing way: "In spite of its brilliant attempt at creating an ironic *meta-histoire*, a sardonic *philosophia perennis*, *Grimus* falters in its failure to countenance postcolonial concerns" (*ibid.*, 148). However, who says that postcolonial concerns were ever in Rushdie's plans?

If one chooses to accept Rushdie's own distance to the novel by adopting the reservations he expresses himself, then it is noteworthy that he, in another interview, resorts to ascribe a more potent and warranted position to *Grimus*: "I have begun to see the novels as a body of work. I also see my first novel, *Grimus*, as part of this" (Appignanesi and Maitland, 30). The critics also seem to recognise the novel's importance for the later novels, which may be expressed as follows: 3) the novel is appreciated to some extent, inasmuch as it carries the seeds of the greater success of the subsequent novels in regard to themes, style and composition. On the thematic level Cundy identifies "ideas of personal and national identity, the legacy of colonialism, the problems of exile and even the first signs of a tendency to demonize female sexuality" (Cundy, 1992, 128); as for the stylistic level she notes the following: "*Grimus* represents the beginning of a conception of literature as an orchestration of voices – one in which the art of the oriental story-teller is blended with a diversity of literary techniques to form something entirely individual" (*ibid.*, 137). Nevertheless, she retains the conviction that *Grimus* does not manage to integrate diversity into any artistic synthesis. Likewise, Goonetilleke recognises the seeds of the later works in *Grimus* and thinks that Rushdie's mistake in the novel actually functions as a catalyst to his later success: "his failure in *Grimus* remains the pillar of his success" (Goonetilleke, 15).

Grant's predominantly positive approach to the novel includes the following observation: "the transgression of genre categories has remained a consistent feature of Rushdie's fiction, and this is due both to the eclectic traditions from which he has drawn and the desire – traceable to the novel's origins – to make something *new* in the world" (Grant, 27). Accordingly, Grant identifies an already accomplished eclectic technique on the compositional level of *Grimus*, which causes a transgression of boundaries of genre and is motivated by a desire to turn the novel into a generator of "the new." Kuortti recognises the novel's focus on the status of history in relation to language and fiction and interprets this constellation in relation to the exercise of colonial power: "Clearly, one of the strengths of Rushdie's writing is the insistence on the power of language in governing and defining people. He shows time after time that the powerful fictions created by the religious, patriarchal and colonial authorities become the reality people live by and within" (Kuortti, 48). In this way *Grimus* launches some of the themes that I intend to pursue all the way through this book: the power of language to construct fictions and distort history as well as the status of epistemology and ethics in fiction. In connection with the issues of identity, Kuortti proceeds to note: "there is a resistance to genealogy, which means simultaneously recognising and fighting one's origins, history, roots" (*ibid.*, 59). Thus, anti-genealogical tendencies are present in Rushdie's first novel and he retains a consistent interest in problems of genealogy throughout the body of his work. Petersson registers both thematic and structural facets in *Grimus* that are later developed on a greater scale: "On a very general level Rushdie can be said to anticipate what will become fundamental factors in the following works, structurally as well as thematically: the nature of reality and different ways of portraying it, the role of perspectives for what one sees. When Rushdie turns from abstract symbolic language to concrete historical application, the questions become politically charged, too" (Petersson, 87). In addition, Petersson appears to be the only one, apart from Kuortti, who unwraps the metafictive aspect of the novel, insofar as they both read the novel as an analogy of the possibilities and necessities of fiction and creative forces.

*

In the following I will carry out a reading of the novel with the purpose of introducing some of the themes to be pursued in greater depth later in this book. In *Problems of Dostoevsky's Poetics* Bakhtin extrapolates a genealogy of the Menippean satire whose antique representatives comprise Lucian, Petronius, Varro, and Apuleius, among others. The interesting thing for our purpose is that *Grimus* may be said to continue and renew this genre. By considering *Grimus* in terms of Bakhtin's delineation of the Menippean satire, I may, first, draw a relatively precise picture of the novel, and, secondly, I will create an opportunity to take a critical stance to the unfavourable criticism of the novel mentioned above.

According to Bakhtin the comic element has a strong place in the Menippean satire. Another typical feature is an unusual liberty in regard to plot and philosophical invention. With that, the genre is not tied to any requirements of feasibility in relation to reality. A third characteristic is a bold and unrestrained use of the fantastic and the marvellous, a use which is internally motivated, legitimised by and solely committed to the philosophical purpose of exploring ideas. The fantastic functions exclusively as a vehicle of thought that provokes and tests a given truth. In this way the ideas become more important than the hero; the abstract is favoured over the concrete and the tangible. In addition, the testing of truths often takes place in strange situations, unfolding in heaven or hell-like spaces. Furthermore, the genre is characterised by an organic fusion of unrestrained elements of the fantastic, symbolic elements and, at times, even mystic-religious elements with an extreme and crude slum naturalism: "The organic combination of philosophical dialogue, lofty symbol-systems, the adventure-fantastic, and slum naturalism is the outstanding characteristic of the menippea" (Bakhtin, 1984, 115).

In addition, audacious creativity and fantastic elements are combined with an extraordinary philosophical universalism along with an ability to contemplate the world at the greatest possible scale. The genre poses ultimate questions that are cut to the bone as a *pro et contra* and presented paratactically as a "grand buffet." The topography of the Menippea is a three-step construction, Bakhtin continues, where the plot has been moved from the world to the Olympian stage and the Underworld. Also, unusual perspectives on the world are produced by an experimental fantasticality, and moral-psychological experimentation gives rise to a representation of man's abnormal morality and psychological conditions (insanity, split personalities, uninhibited daydreaming, passion bordering madness, suicide). This is not only significant on the thematic level, but also on the formal-generic level: daydreams and madness may ruin a character's epic and tragic unity, which causes him to realise the possibility of becoming another person leading another life.

Furthermore, scandalous scenes, eccentric behaviour, and untimely utterances and conduct are common in the genre, says Bakhtin. These features break with norms and may liberate man from predetermined conventions and motivations. The untimely is inappropriate due to a cynical forwardness, a profane de-masking of the sacred, or a rude violation of etiquette. Finally, the last traits Bakhtin mentions are sharp contrasts and oxymoronic combinations (e.g. the virtuous hetaerae), elements of social utopia, genre-pluralism, a multi-stylistic and multi-voiced quality, and a concern with current issues, the latter being an influence from the journalistic genre.

Reading *Grimus*, it is obvious that the novel corresponds very well to the characteristics Bakhtin identifies in the Menippean satire. In fact, the same can be said about Rushdie's other novels. I will now move on to a discussion of the most important points of correlation.

*

We find the kind of humour that Rushdie is known for already in *Grimus*, that is, a humour expressed primarily in situational comedy and in his linguistic playfulness, for example in the portrayal and the naming of the novel's characters. Another characteristic feature of *Grimus* is its philosophical creativity and loose plot structure, noticeable in its insistence on a technique of digression, among other things. In this respect Grant notes Rushdie's "willingness to be distracted from the narrative by any stray idea that seems to offer discursive possibilities" (Grant, 30). Moving on with Bakhtin, the novel's anti-naturalistic aspects represent one of the elements constituting the Menippean satire. Accordingly, a genre ontology seems to offer itself as an explanation of the novel's abstract and fantastic chronotope. In regard to this particular aspect, the novel's critical reception may be said to be problematic. In my opinion, the criticism of the novel partly lacks a motive and an inner logic. It uncritically adopts Rushdie's own reservations against the novel's contravention of any recognisable reality, and this kind of inference seems to be based more on personal taste and preference than forming an objective assessment of the novel's space based on the inner premises of its literary genre. Needless to say, the science-fictional quality of *Grimus* lends an inner logic to the novel's abstract universe. My point is that the criticism of the novel in this regard is based on wrong standards of evaluation which are established, firstly, by reference to Rushdie's subsequent comments on his inclination to employ a methodology of the fantastic, and, secondly, by reflections on the aesthetics of the successive novels.

The novel's own narrative method is discussed explicitly in its dialogues. The two objects of Flapping Eagle's obsession, Elfrida and Irina, seem to contain two oppositional poetics. In Elfrida's case there is an obligation to depict life as it is, and since she perceives life as fraught with contingency, tattered margins, and inconclusiveness, her poetics is expressed through such notions: "I do not care for stories that are so, so tight. Stories should be like life, slightly frayed at the edges, full of loose ends and lives juxtaposed by accident rather than some grand design. Most of life has no meaning – so it must surely be a distortion of life to tell tales in which every single element is meaningful?" (G, 141). To Irina stories are not of vital importance. Therefore, she does not obligate herself to a 1:1 scale between life and art the way Elfrida does. Irina does not mind the deceptive quality of art as something that is carefully composed, spoiling people with the illusion of order: "Tales are really very unimportant things. So why should they not bring us a little innocent pleasure by being well-shaped? Give me shapeliness over the *lumpen* face of life, every time" (G, 141-42). Whereas Elfrida speaks of an all-embracing aesthetics, Irina speaks of compression and condensation. According to the philosopher of empirical positivism, Ignatius Quasimodo Gribb, Elfrida's husband, the poetics of both ladies contain a contradiction, because both conceptual pairs of "important"-"less-full-of-meaning" (Elfrida) and "unimportant"-"well-shaped" (Irina) form paradoxes or oxymora in his semantic universe:

> The crux is this: the word importance means "having import." That is to say, having meaning. Now Elfrida, who believes tales to be important things, says she would prefer them to be less full of meaning, that is to say, less important. Whereas the Countess, for whom these same tales are very unimportant things, likes them to be well-made, that is to say, important selections, or important. Thus both ladies contradict themselves. A simple matter of semantics, you follow. If tales are important, they must be well-shaped. If they are not, they cannot be. And vice versa (G, 142).

Gribb's argument excludes flexibility and a dialogic semantics as he focuses only on one lexical meaning of the word "importance," which may mean "having import" as well as "having meaning." To Gribb "importance" only means "having meaning," which rules out the possibility of a worldview that sees the absurd as important and the well-composed as unimportant.

Grimus and Rushdie do not position themselves unambiguously in this tirade of poetics. On the contrary, they may be said to pick a little of this and a little of that. There seems to be a great deal of potentiality in Elfrida's poetics of loose ends, contingency, paratactics and, of course, the importance of the stories, but contingency and loose ends do not exclude the idea that everything in a novel "has meaning," insofar as textual "holes" are also meaningful. The solid opposition between Elfrida and Irina is only a seeming opposition: the conceptual levels of their respective poetics may cross each other, as the concepts are not unequivocal, but contextually determined. What is carefully conceived does not necessarily exclude playfulness, what is well-composed does not necessarily exclude frayed edges, the meaningful does not necessarily exclude the absurd. Everything depends on the poetic paradigm through which these features are assessed.

In *Grimus* the narrative engine often seems to have been put on stand by. This does not mean that the novel does not have a narrative drive. Rather, it shifts between fantastic occurrences and philosophical monologues and dialogues. The fabulous universe, the fantastic occurrences, and the fictive characters all serve a higher purpose; they form a backdrop to and lend themselves as tools for the testing of philosophical ideas. In *Grimus* Rushdie is obsessed with the same questions that enthral him later in his writing career, but they evolve within a speculative frame rather than within a frame of "flesh and blood." Once again it must be pointed out that this feature is typical for the genre, which relativises the critics' disapproval of *Grimus* as a novel of ideas and its disposition as laboured.

As it happens, *Grimus* combines the discourses Bakhtin mentions. The novel incorporates an abstract and imaginary universe (multi-dimensionality, time travels), the symbolical-allegorical (numerology, meta-fictional games, the Grand Tour), the mystic-religious (eternal life, ritual), and finally a slum naturalism (the bordello, the cabin on the beach, Livia Cramm). One of the two cardinal issues of the novel's negative reception is exactly the question of the organicity of its discursive pluralism. However, whether one is dealing with *Grimus* or Rushdie's later novels, their comprehensive intertextual baggage is inexhaustible, and something regressive, and rarely fruitful, may lie at the heart of readings that are too strongly orientated towards intertextuality alone. This is not to say that intertextuality is only a matter of ornamentation and intellectual show-off. Surely it contributes with meaning to the text, and it may even be considered as a strategy with the direct aim of invigorating the relations between tradition and renewal. To me, however, the difficulty of *Grimus* is more a matter of its high level of abstraction, but, as I have argued, this is an inherent element of its genre. As I see it, the critique of the novel as not being sufficiently lodged in reality is based on subjective preferences. As concerns its organicity, I tend to follow Petersson, although I do not agree entirely with her angle of alchemy.

As indicated before, *Grimus* is a novel in which the world is reflected at the greatest possible scale. One example of this is the discussion of poetics I have already cited, which precisely presents questions of the status of life and stories as a form of "grand buffet" in a paratactical logic. The novel and the narrator never make any unequivocal suggestion as to which of the poetics is most adequate. Besides, philosophical universalism is predominantly represented by the intelligent and speculative Virgil Jones (the relativist and the doubter), the philosopher I.Q. Gribb (the positivist and the windbag), and Grimus (the idealist). Here is an example of Virgil Jones challenging the reader:

> The simple fact, said Virgil Jones, is that Grimus is in possession of a stupendous piece of knowledge: that we live in one of an infinity of Dimensions. To accept the nature of the Dimensions involves changing, entirely, our ideas of what we are and what our world is like. Thus rewriting the book of morality and priorities from the beginning. What you must ask yourself is this: is there such a thing as too much knowledge? If a marvellous discovery is made whose effects one cannot control, should one attempt to destroy one's find? Or do the interests of science override even those of society, and, indeed, survival? Is it better to have known, and die, than not to have known at all? (G, 189-90).

This is the type of questions that the novel confronts its reader with over and over again. In this case the only answer that is provided is Flapping Eagle's choice of kinesis over stasis: he vigorously seeks a showdown with Grimus, who is the person alluded to in the quotation, as Grimus has lost control of the effect of the Stone Rose.

Another example of the novel's ambitiousness and high level of abstraction may be found in Grimus's triangular, labyrinthine stone house: "It is the Crystal of Potentialities. In it I can examine many potential presents and futures and discover the key moments, the crossroads in time, which guide us down one or the other *line of flux*" (G, 235). Grimus's panoptical perspective introduces us to a deterministic condition of existence which we, as readers, have difficulties accepting without question: "Free will really is an illusion, you know. People behave according to the flux-lines of their potential futures" (G, 239).

Grimus thematises human identity and incessantly questions the status of subjectivity. Here Rushdie touches upon the themes of exile and translocation that are so carefully expanded in his later writings where they engage both possibilities and problems. Flapping Eagle is the protagonist in *Grimus*, but the novel introduces a varied and interesting gallery of characters, stretching between the poles of rootedness and flux. Flapping Eagle introduces himself in the following way: "I was the boy. I was Joe-Sue, Axona Indian, orphan, named ambiguously at birth because my sex was uncertain until some time later, virgin, young brother of a wild female animal called Bird-Dog, who was scared of losing her beauty, which was ironic, for she was not beautiful. It was my (his) twenty-first birthday, too, and I was about to become Flapping-Eagle. And cease to be a few other people" (G, 16). The passage is dense with typical Rushdian themes: in regard to human identity it touches upon minority questions, the evanescence of hermaphroditism, problems of lineage, sexuality, and relations between siblings. In terms of enunciation Rushdie introduces the characteristic playfulness and self-consciousness of his narrative voices.

As mentioned, Flapping Eagle is exiled from the Axona tribe after Bird-Dog has fled. The Shaman of the tribe justifies Flapping Eagle's ostracism with the community's motto: "'All that is Unaxona is Unclean.' I'm afraid we really can't have contamination around here, you know" (G, 24). The inhabitants of K harbour the same fear of contamination, and, whereas the Axona Indians use religious rituals in their strive for health and purity, K's inhabitants defend themselves by means of individual obsessions in their attempts to avoid the Grimus-effect and the chaos of identity it entails. Life in K is marked by repetition and stasis: "Often they fix themselves a time in their lives to mull over. Live the same day over and over again. Displaced persons are like that, you know. Always counterfeiting roots. Still. If a false front's thick enough, it serves. To protect" (G, 81-82). Virgil seems to think that migrants, in order to protect themselves against their new environment, constantly wallow in a regressive search for roots and solid foundations. They shield themselves through rituals which are often intensified by exile, as these are far more important in a state of displacement. The need for shields and the endless confirmation of identity is the reason why I.Q. Gribb's thoughts are accepted by all of the town's inhabitants. His philosophy functions as a kind of protection by offering a closed totality of eternal categories: "The All-Purpose Quotable Philosophy. A quote for all seasons to make life both supportable and comprehensible. A framework of phrases to live within, pregnant with a truly universal meaning" (G, 129).

Having travelled for 743 years, four months and three days, Flapping Eagle reaches Calf Island at the age of 777, seven months and seven days. His body, however, is only thirty-four years, three months and four days old, as that was the age at which he drank the yellow liquid. Tired and exhausted by the journey, Flapping Eagle wants to settle down: "You must understand that I have been rootless for a very long time now" (G, 143), and he hopes that K may be a new home: "Home is the sailor, home from the sea, and the hunter home from the hill. Flapping Eagle was coming home, to a town where he had never lived" (G, 106). Here, K represents an element of social utopia which Bakhtin mentions as one of the characteristics of the Menippean satire. Initially, K represents the aspiration to paradise, but the illusion bursts as Flapping Eagle catches the eye of an indigenous K dweller through a window: "The eyes had done it: they had told him that he was still pariah. The untouchable" (G, 107). And it goes on: "A glimpse through another window: an old woman gazing at a photograph album, immersed in her past. It is the natural condition of the exile – putting down roots in memories" (G, 107). The inhabitants of K are exiles themselves as they have been brought to the island from other dimensions. Once again the narrator calls attention to the exile's obsession with genealogy, insofar as the photo album represents a longing for the long lost past. To look at old photos is to consolidate one's roots, but this happens on false premises as the past in the photo album is "dead."

Flapping Eagle decides to adjust to the life in K despite the resistance he meets, and the two people who make it easy for him are Elfrida and Irina. The two beauties complement each other, one is chaste, the other seductive. Flapping Eagle falls in love with both of them: "he too was gradually becoming obsessed, and they were to be the objects of his obsession" (G, 154). In spite of his search for heavenly stasis and perfection, Flapping Eagle is still haunted by constant doubt and thereby "ceases to coincide with himself" (Bakhtin, 1984, 117). He seems to shift between the need of Elfrida's light, compliant nature and the need of Irina's dark, dangerous, and assertive temperament: "There were too many fluctuations within him" (G, 154). During a séance of lovemaking with Irina, Flapping Eagle reaches a climax where the two beauties melt together in his mind, so to speak, and a fusion of their names accidentally slips his tongue: "Elfrina", he burstsd out (G, 172).[1] Naturally, Irina is furious and decides to leak the secret about Elfrida and Flapping Eagle's love to Elfrida's husband. Flapping Eagle realises that his moment of completion turns out to contain its own inevitable dissolution: "The moment of perfection had spawned its own destruction" (G, 172). One of Rushdie's most recurrent themes is represented in this passage: the relation between stasis and kinesis, between stagnation and processuality. However, Elfrida forestalls Irina by confessing to her husband, the prosaic and judicious philosopher, that she loves Flapping Eagle. The confession proves to have catastrophic consequences for K.

Hearing the news, I.Q. Gribb dies on the spot: "Elfrida's withdrawal had removed the cornerstone of the persona he had built; and in that instant, when everything which had seemed sure was suddenly flung into a state of flux, the fever of the Inner Dimensions had swarmed over him" (G, 177). The core of Gribb's identity dissipates as his anchor and support, the faithful Elfrida, withdraws from the accustomed solid bell jar of their married life. The inhabitants of K do not abide disturbances, and, as the Axona tribe, they try to avoid contamination through their monomania. Gribb's death causes more deaths and Flapping Eagle and Elfrida are banished from K, but they take refuge with Madame Jocasta and Virgil in the bordello, The House of the Rising Son. Virgil persuades Flapping Eagle to confront Grimus, as Grimus has lost control over Calf

---

1   Petersson notes: "Opposites and their union are central motifs in the novel, as in the mono-myth and in alchemy" (Petersson, 74). Petersson makes the mistake, however, of focusing too much on the unifying propensity of alchemy: "The way goes through dissolution to chaos, which could lead to a new union" (*ibid.*, 80). *Grimus* does not support the idea of "union," an idea which constantly proves to be an illusion. Rather than union, the novel contends with collision or vibration, which causes continuous processuality. The same thing can be said about the dichotomy in *The Satanic Verses* between the satanic and the angelic. If language, as such, inescapably produces punctures in life as process, then it is precisely through oxymoronic (vibrating) constellations like "Elfrina" that Rushdie tries to infuse a little "Dionysian blood" into the "Apollonian veins" of language.

Island. That is, Grimus's tool of conceptualisation, the Stone Rose, has been partially ruined by Nicholas Deggle (Devil) who found the Stone Rose with Virgil and Grimus long ago.[2] Deggle was against Grimus and Virgil's experiments with the Stone Rose and he made an attempt to destroy it as Virgil's intradimensional travels drove the latter insane. Virgil explains to Flapping Eagle that the inhabitants of K will face their inevitable annihilation as the Grimus-effect is getting stronger and stronger. If Flapping Eagle defeats Grimus, the inhabitants have a theoretical chance of surviving. Flapping Eagle chooses to take action: "The brothel air was heavy with the scent of solace. But sanctuary was not for him, or at any rate not for long. If he had failed to achieve stasis – failed, that is, to ingrain himself into the way of K – he would have to revert once more to kinesis" (G, 187).

As has been shown, questions of human identity play a great role in *Grimus*. The main condition of the characters is that of exile which is examined in various modalities between obsession and fluctuation, stasis and kinesis, and roots and contamination. Obsession works as a centripetal force and helps the inhabitants of K keep hold of a stable identity, sustained by an everyday logic of repetition and memories of a dead past. However, as the Grimus-effect runs wild, several of the characters succumb as they are overwhelmed by an irrevocable fluctuation of consciousness breaking down their identity cores. As indicated, Flapping Eagle also seems to exist in a perpetual schizophrenic process, adapting himself to his environments like a chameleon.

On his way to Grimus-home, Flapping Eagle pays a visit to Liv, Virgil's previous wife, who is the first one to draw his attention to the fact that he resembles Grimus: "Your face is as like the face of Grimus as his own reflection" (G, 205). In one of the novel's numerous scenes of sexual intercourse, Flapping Eagle is seduced by Liv, "*Liv, ice-peak of perfection.*

---

2   The Stone Rose has a remarkable semblance with the spindle in Plato's *The Republic*. The spindle features in a myth and is used by Plato to illustrate the coherence of the universe from a geocentric perspective. The myth is employed with the purpose of founding and legitimising a cosmic perception of the world where everything revolves in a circle. Accordingly, the allusion of the Stone Rose to Plato reinforces the novel's status as a novel of ideas.

Virgil had overstated nothing" (G, 219).³ For the first time he surrenders unconditionally to Liv's control and just as he reaches climax, Liv pulls away as a circuitous act of revenge against Grimus, whom she used to be in love with. Through Grimus's spectrum, Flapping Eagle, Liv revenges herself against Grimus.

Grimus-home turns out to be a triangular, labyrinthic stone house and, as a symbol of Grimus's divine status and the ruling order, a giant ash grows outside the house: "Flapping Eagle remembered Virgil Jones' description of the Ash Yggdrasil, the mother-tree which holds the skies in place. And wondered what monsters were gnawing at its roots" (G, 225). The Ash Yggdrasil, from Nordic mythology, is a symbol of the axis of the world, and as a tree-figure, it is a recurrent motif in Rushdie. In *Grimus* we find an additional ash in I.Q. Gribb's garden, where the tree also serves to represent the philosopher's conviction of the rootedness of the world and its harmonious rotation around a centre full of universal clichés. However, as Flapping Eagle insinuates, the idea of cosmos is undermined by monsters gnawing at its roots.

It transpires that Grimus is the great producer of virtually the

---

3   The scenes of sexual intercourse are primarily "scandal scenes" in Bakhtinian terms. Flapping Eagle has intercourse with his sister twice, and incest is a returning theme in Rushdie (cf. Jocasta and The House of the Rising Son, which are great examples of Rushdie's humour, intertextual resourcefulness, and ingenious use of language). When Flapping Eagle, wrestling with his inner dimensions (demons), rapes the god of the Axonas, who turns out to be a woman: "The god Axona was an old, dark, hawknosed, feathered woman" (G, 87), he does it to liberate himself from his roots: "To free myself, I must render Axona unclean" (G, 89). Flapping Eagle and Nicholas Deggle's intercourse with Livia Cramm, the ancient "clutching woman," is also worth mentioning. Similarly, the description of the intercourse between Virgil and Dolores manifests the grotesque, "a hunchbacked crone." What these scenes have in common is their quality of transgression and breach of conventions, and the style belongs to the kind of slum naturalism Rushdie blends with the elevated styles of philosophical and religious discourse. An incessant challenge of conventions, strong in communities like those of the Axonas and K, is at issue; the novel ceaselessly extrapolates antagonistic lines which lead to collisions and, with that, rifts are made in the segment formations of the fictive universe: "The novel is on the whole structured so that the opposites face each other at all levels" (Petersson, 74).

entire story line of the novel. He has piloted Flapping Eagle to the showdown himself, and Grimus's desire for his own obliteration owes to the fact that he has achieved perfection: "To be wise and powerful is to be complete. *That which is complete is also dead*" (G, 232). Hence, it would be erroneous to perceive Grimus as a conservator through and through, as he endorses the idea of process. The antagonism between Flapping Eagle and Grimus evolves on another level as it relates to the nature of process itself: will the new creation arising from deconstruction be a creation of sameness or newness? In other words: is the process locked within a mono-centered circle or will it elapse like eccentric circles? Grimus believes the former is true: "The period of stability containing the seeds of its own downfall. The cataclysm being followed by a new and very similar order. It is aesthetic. It is right" (G, 240).

On the last pages of the novel, Grimus tries to defeat Flapping Eagle's resistance by letting them melt together and in that way instil so much Grimus-consciousness in him that he will give in: "*You swallow me, I swallow you. Mingle, commingle. Come mingle. Grow together, come. You into me into you*" (G, 242). Their personalities merge chiasmatically in a surrealistic passage, "*I have become you, I have become you are me*" (G, 243), but we end up with four consciousnesses rather than two: "There is still an *I*. An *I* within me that is not *him*" (G, 243). Flapping Eagle's consciousness is doubled to an "I" and a "him" which now enter a dialogic struggle, but Grimus's purpose with the fusion, to win over Flapping Eagle from the inside through "him," is now turned against himself as Grimus is invaded himself by Flapping Eagle's consciousness, but also because Flapping Eagle is now capable of seeing Grimus's doubts and motives. Flapping Eagle's perspective turns stereoscopic: "I can see his whys" (G, 243). By imagining Calf Island without the Stone Rose, the one half of Flapping Eagle's consciousness ("I") defeats the other ("him"). In the meantime, a trio from K, Flannery Napoleon O'Toole, One-Track Peckenpaw, and P.S. Moonshy, has reached Grimus-home where they, in keeping with Grimus's plan, kill Grimus by lynching him in the ash-tree.

The novel ends with the slow disintegration of the island while Flapping Eagle and Media, who has been allowed to accompany him to Grimus-home, are making love. It is indicated that the new order is not the same as the old one: "A fascinating new status quo" (G 250), and: "The peak implies no kind of superiority now" (G, 250).[4] What happens is that Grimus ("the Simurg, bird of paradise") and Flapping Eagle ("the Eagle, prince of earthly birds") in their fusion point to a collapse of the vertical axis between heaven and earth. Hierarchy and cosmos are subverted through Flapping Eagle's deed. The straight line between the Father and the Son, between Grimus and Flapping Eagle, is distorted: "Like, and yet unlike" (G, 228), and, in another place, Grimus asks: "My son, my son, what father fathered a son like this, as I do in my sterility" (G, 243).[5] To anticipate Deleuze, we might say that Flapping Eagle constitutes a simulacrum of Grimus as a difference has been inserted into his identity, and this inexorable ontological difference brings about the renewal of process.

Rushdie provides a breeding ground for the continued development of process, and, at the same time, he seems to advocate a rebirth containing the seeds of the New: "Deprived of its connection with all relative Dimensions, the world of Calf Mountain was slowly unmaking itself, its molecules and atoms breaking, dissolving, quietly vanishing into primal, unmade energy. The raw material of being was claiming its own" (G, 253). What we witness here is the meltdown of forms, leaving a kind of primeval substream of vital energy. The disintegration of the island is not supposed to be interpreted negatively because this kind of destruction always contains the seeds of a new creation.[6] This appears to be a

---

4   As Petersson points out: "In the Idea of process is the insight that a goal can be nothing but a starting point for a new process" (Petersson, 68). Despite her correct emphasis on processuality, she misunderstands the nature of process: "a period of stability carries the seed of its own destruction, the upheaval is followed by a similar new order. These episodes show that the dissolution stage of the novel is over. It is followed by union, coagula" (*ibid.*, 82). The passages from *Grimus* I have cited do not suggest a "similar new order," but a new order altogether.

5   For that reason, I do not agree with Kuortti who says: "Ultimately he ends up becoming one with Grimus, in the same way as the thirty birds of Attar's poem find themselves to be Simurg" (Kuortti, 36). Rather, Rushdie turns Attar's poem, and with that the myth of the thirty birds, upside down, which is Goonetilleke's point precisely: "The novel reverses both the name (Simurg) and the aim of Attar's The Conference of Birds" (Goonetilleke, 13).

6   This interpretation corresponds with Syed's: "The novel ends on an apocalyptic note, with the Grimus effect destroyed, the Stone Rose demolished, the ash-tree

basic existential condition which Rushdie continually draws attention to in his works.

Fundamentally the novel's idea of processuality corresponds to Bakhtin's concept of the carnivalistic: "Carnival celebrates the shift itself, the very process of replaceability, and not the precise item that is replaced. Carnival is, so to speak, functional and not substantive" (Bakhtin, 1984, 125). Bakhtin prefers the pragmatic to the essential which for its part may be said to represent an illusionary metaphysics. Another way of putting it is that functionality corresponds to the processual and dynamic character of verbs, whereas nouns and substantivising verbs ("be" and "have") grind reality to a halt. What is important is not what the process changes, but that it inescapably causes change. As for organicity, this is to be understood precisely according to the principle of carnivalistic becoming: "We have uncovered in the menippea a striking combination of what would seem to be absolutely heterogeneous and incompatible elements: philosophical dialogue, adventure and fantasticality, slum naturalism, utopia, and so forth. We can now say that the clamping principle that bound all these heterogeneous elements into the organic whole of a genre, a principle of extraordinary strength and tenacity, was carnival and a carnival sense of the world" (*ibid.*, 134). To accept processuality where unification can only be said to contain its own dissolution is to accept a carnivalistic view of the world. Accordingly it may be argued that the synthesising impulse in *Grimus* is comprised by a carnivalistic worldview with all that it involves of intimacy, mésalliances, masquerades and mystifications, contradictory pictures, scandals, eulogies, and denigrations. The central function of carnival is a de-hierarchisation of the world, where high and low, king and peasant, are levelled. In that respect, the carnivalistic constitutes a line of flight out of the stratified, institutional

---

burnt, and Grimus's power over the Island broken. Nevertheless, there is a sense of regeneration" (Syed, 143). As concerns the novel's metaphysical skeleton, Syed goes on to say: "Rushdie, however, has a different use for metaphysics in *Grimus*; he sets up a fictional universe that deliberately partakes of a variety of metaphysical and mythological discourses in order to, ultimately, demolish them all symbolically, in one swift, last stroke" (*ibid*, 142). Accordingly, Rushdie's use of myth and metaphysics is characterised by distortion and parody.

categories and categorisations established by society through normative genus-subgenus conventions of possible encounters and collisions.

As the above illustrates, *Grimus* may benefit from a reading that follows Bakhtin's delineation of the Menippean satire. However, the novel also contributes with a new element of metafiction which should be taken into account as well. The philosophical universalism that seeps through the novel challenges the reader with questions of the status of fiction and reality. *Grimus* may be read, accordingly, as an allegory of its own pragmatics; that is, as an allegory of the principles of its own construction and techniques: how does a novel work?

By use of the Stone Rose, Grimus is able to think worlds into existence and that is exactly what the author does when he writes a novel. With imagination as his tool, the novelist examines the range of human possibilities. He carries out experiments in his anthropological laboratory, the way Grimus experiments in Grimus-home. He is the creator and director of a possible world: Virgil explains to Flapping-Eagle that "[t]here are a million of possible Earths with a million possible histories, all of which actually exist simultaneously. In the course of one's daily life, one weaves a course between them, if you like, but that does not destroy the existence of pasts or futures we choose not to enter" (G, 53). In this way it is possible to create corporeal, exterior worlds in which people may be able to live: "With sufficient imagination, Virgil Jones had found, one could *create* worlds, physical, external worlds, neither aspects of oneself nor a palimpsest-universe. Fictions where a man could live" (G, 75). Evidently, Rushdie touches on an idea that he is to develop later on, that is, that the languages in art, historiography, and politics are all joint creators of reality which may be said to be fictional to a greater or lesser degree. Fictions create new maps of reality which, just like Calf Island, have to be endlessly reinvented and re-conceptualised: "The truth is, Flapping Eagle, a Conceptual Dimension like Calf Island needs constant fostering and Re-Conceptualizing at regular intervals, in order to preserve its existence. If I am to die without a successor the island will crumble. You have to take my place" (G, 237).

Grimus emerges as a complex palimpsest of various interweaving fictive levels, making it impossible to ascertain one true reality. Grimus seems to be the demiurge or the God of Calf Island by virtue of his role as its creator, but there is also another dimension which is "higher" than Grimus's world. On the planet Thera (Earth) live Gorfs (Frogs) which form the ultimate links between the dimensions as they were the ones who created the Stone Rose with which one may travel intra- and interdimensionally. The author may be said to be a Gorf and the Stone Rose his tool, his imagination. In *Grimus* the role of the creator is not divine in the usual sense of the word, since the dimensions are allowed a degree of autonomy, depriving the creator of full control with his creation. Likewise, fiction acquires a life of its own, spelling the author's loss of complete authority.

*

Grimus is a work which carries the seeds of Rushdie's successive novels in regard to themes, composition, and style. Themes and motifs like hybridity, exile, imagination, processuality, metamorphosis, human identity, and sexuality are launched in *Grimus*. On the level of composition, Rushdie stages an early attempt at a polyphonic architecture qua the incorporation of heterogeneous elements in a paratactic logic. In terms of style, the novel employs a number of divergent literary techniques, for instance fluctuation in the narrative position, a strategy which is definitely far more successful in Rushdie's later novels. *Grimus* seems to contain a perception of literature as a polyphonic orchestration of voices, combining the Oriental art of storytelling from *Arabian Nights*, for instance, with various Western literary techniques with the purpose of creating an utterly distinctive, individual style. The incorporation of cultural diversity within an artistic entity, says Cundy, is a central motive in Rushdie's works (see Cundy, 1992, 133). *Grimus* is markedly different from Rushdie's other novels, primarily because of the overriding fact that it is completely detached from any recognisable geographical location. Furthermore, the characters are subjected to examinations of ideas, whereas much more "life" is put into the characters in the later novels, projected, to a far greater extent, in "flesh and blood." Both features, the abstract topography and the preponderance of ideas, correspond to typical characteristics of the Menippean satire as a genre and, as such, they are not "errors." With this, *Grimus* may be said to differ from the rest of Rushdie's works by resting significantly against the anti-naturalistic element of the Menippean satire (yet anti-naturalism is strong in both *Midnight's Children*, *The Satanic Verses* and *The Ground Beneath Her Feet*). In *Grimus* we find "a tendency to adopt the speaking style and speech patterns of others" (G, 39), and the novel even provides us with a sentence that may summarise this chapter, and which may very well be Rushdie's own words: "I am looking for a suitable voice to speak in" (G, 32).

DELEUZE AND LITERATURE

> "The novel form is, like no other, an expression of this transcendental homelessness."
> – Georg Lukács: *The Theory of the Novel*

In a way the French philosopher Gilles Deleuze (1925-1995) has always been regarded as an outsider in relation to the generation of French thinkers that he belongs to, but this peripheral position seems to be changing as the interest in his writings has increased remarkably within the last two decades, to the extent that Michel Foucault's often cited prophecy of a Deleuzian century may turn out to come true. Deleuze's role as an outsider appears to be both confirmed and disproved by Foucault's comment insofar as it suggests that the world, in 1970, was not yet mature for Deleuze's philosophy, but, on the other hand, the prophecy also points to the fact that Deleuze was regarded as a significant source of inspiration among his contemporaries. The latter is also emphasised by Jacques Derrida. In his obituary for Deleuze he writes that among their peers, who apart from Deleuze, Foucault, and Derrida also include Roland Barthes, Jean-François Lyotard, and Louis Althusser, Deleuze was without a doubt the person he felt he had the closest affiliation with intellectually. What these thinkers can be said to have in common is an attempt to reverse the Platonic metaphysics of similitude. One also finds in their thinking a distrust of rationalist philosophy which arrives at truth through human consciousness. In a certain way they are all Nietzschean and share a firm, yet critical rooting in Freud and Marx. Finally, one may identify a revolutionary mould in their thinking which, among other things, is anchored in the 1968 revolt and its anti-dogmatic ideals.

Gilles Deleuze left behind a versatile body of writing of almost thirty books, covering 1) philosophical monographies, on Hume, Nietzsche, Bergson, Spinoza, and Leibniz, among others, 2) a number of works on aesthetics and artists, for example on Proust, Lewis Carroll, and Kafka as well as on the painter Francis Bacon and two books on cinema, and finally 3) what one may term more autonomous works of philosophy, for instance *Difference and Repetition* and the three books co-written with the psychoanalyst Félix Guattari, *Anti-Oedipus, A Thousand Plateaus*, and *What Is Philosophy?* It is symptomatic of Deleuze, however, that this is only a seeming categorisation, as his writings are characterised by a continuous dialogue across the three "genres" he spans. As a result, the history of philosophy is always embedded as a horizon of discussion in his more autonomous philosophical books as well as it prolifically pollinates his portraits of artists; his aesthetics spawns autonomous philosophical thinking and the invention of new concepts as well as it is a concretising element in his monographies on other philosophers; finally, one always senses a distinctive and noticeable Deleuzian contour in the portrait of a novelist, painter, or philosopher.

As already mentioned, my motive for a Deleuzian reading of Rushdie's novels is based on what I see as a triple affinity between the two of them: first, they seem to share more or less the same worldview, which may be described as an ontological affinity; secondly, their perception of art seems to be revolving around the same maxims and basic ideas; thirdly, they both propose a new and radical formulation of subjectivity. This chapter will deal mainly with Deleuze's ideas in regard to these three levels in order to chart the ways in which the conceptual framework of his philosophy may be applied in an analysis of Rushdie's novels. In other words, the chapter will give off a number of analytical frames and explain a number of concepts with a forward and partially hypothetical thrust to be followed up in the successive chapters of specific analytical concretisations. Hopefully, the analytical chapters will then legitimise my use of Deleuze through a backward-looking reciprocity, perhaps even refining the portrait I will sketch of him now.

*

Deleuze belongs to the generation of French thinkers who have been called the philosophers of difference and whose joint project has often been summarised as an inversion of Platonism. By concentrating on difference and disclosing the illusionary character of similarity, Deleuze makes an attempt to unleash diversity. To Deleuze the world is a matter of becoming, and constant change is the product of an uninterrupted line of singular events which, by virtue of their singularity, cannot be subordinated to or seized by a logic of identity. Accordingly Deleuze proposes the annulment of essences by events as the crucial point in overturning Platonism: "To reverse Platonism is first and foremost to remove essences and to substitute events in their place, as jets of singularities" (LS, 53). In a world of processuality which is ceaselessly discharged as a new world, it becomes impossible to sustain a belief in absolute truths, and, with that, the philosopher's task becomes one of creating concepts that may capture the concrete expression of movement: "Everyone knows that philosophy deals with concepts. A system's a set of concepts. And it's an open system when the concepts relate to circumstances rather than essences" (N, 32). Here, Deleuze rejects neither that philosophy is metaphysical nor that it is a generator of systems. It is only the nature of the system which has changed from being a closed to an open totality. In this way Deleuze may be said to represent a constructivist imperative. Firstly, because the world as becoming ceaselessly expresses itself in new ways, and, secondly, because the natural connection between the world and representation has ruptured: "In every respect, truth is a matter of production, not of adequation" (DR, 154). The world is tangled up in man-made languages and representations which cause a (partly necessary, partly sad) slowing down of life as a process of becoming. Therefore the point is to liberate life by constantly re-inventing the world anew, and this creative activity (pragmatics) may be staged exactly through an intense and unending creativity in language: "It is language which fixes the limits (...), but it is language as well which transcends the limits" (LS, 2-3).[7]

---

7   The constructivist imperative means that the philosopher's focus is directed towards a creative questioning. Rushdie shares this view on the relation between question and answer in regard to the modern novel: "It tells us there are no rules. It hands down no commandments. We have to make up our own rules as best we can, make them up as we go along. And it tells us there are no answers; or, rather, it tells us that answers are easier to come by, and less reliable, than questions. If religion is an answer, if political ideology is an answer, then literature is an inquiry; great literature, by asking extraordinary questions, opens new doors in our minds" (IH, 423).

Deleuze' vitalistic ontology of power is inspired by Nietzsche and Bergson who offer elaborate philosophies on imbalance and becoming. The world consists of two kinds of forces, the active that want change and the reactive that want sameness, and it is precisely the imbalance between the two of them which guarantees becoming. For this reason, Deleuze does not reject the existence of similitudes or dichotomies; in fact, newness is created through a continuous disturbance of dichotomies and a persistent act of sneaking in between them. Deleuze considers the creation of newness as both the raison d'être of art and as an obligation to confirm the multiplicity of life: "For the new – in other words, difference – calls forth forces in thought which are not the forces of recognition, today or tomorrow, but the powers of a completely other model, from an unrecognised and unrecognisable *terra incognita*" (DR, 136). In Plato cognition and recognition are inseparably connected within the reign of ideas and identity in their pursuit of an a priori truth, a truth, that is, which exists independently of experience, whereas truth and meaning in Deleuze always arise through an a posteriori effect based on creativity, obscurity, and chance rather than recognition, always emerging from an experience-based, empirical "worldliness."

Likewise, the opposition between difference and similarity, or between the active and reactive forces, is an opposition between a vital impulse and a formalistic articulation, or between a chaotic primal soup (the molecular) and a stagnated (cultural) form (the molar). As Frederik Tygstrup remarks: "there is a barrier between them, between the fascination of the chaotic, microphysical, and vitally disruptive processes, on the one hand, and the culturally useful world of forms on the other" (Tygstrup, 2001, 272). As mentioned, both of these elements are inescapable conditions in the world, but Deleuze's focus is directed towards the unstable balance which occurs between the conceptual pair of dualism (in this case, chaos-form); towards morphogenisis itself or the becoming-form, to be exact. Accordingly, Deleuze is not so much interested in sheer chaos (an inescapable undercurrent, but in which we would drown and dissolve) and in hardened forms (indispensable for strategies of survival, but they would bring life to an artificial halt). One senses a fascination with a Dionysian force combined with an Apollonian ethos in this complementary constellation: "In short, it is a question of causing a little of Dionysus' blood to flow in the organic veins of Apollo" (DR, 262).[8] Consequently, Deleuze's focus – to borrow a concept from James Joyce – is on chaosmosis which arises or is created in the anarchistic or violent clash between heterogeneous elements, where cosmos and logos are merely effects and no longer foundations or causes: "making a line or bloc shoot between two people, producing all the phenomena of a double capture, showing what the conjunction AND is, neither a union, nor a juxtaposition, but the birth of a stammering, the outline of a broken line which always sets off at the right angles, a sort of active and creative line of flight? AND... AND... AND..." (D, 10). Deleuze's vitalistic impulse is thus formally articulated in a conjunctive both-and logic where dynamism and the process of becoming are ensured by the transversalising thrust or the transverse connection that this logic activates. Another term for this logic is "assembling, being in the middle, on the line of encounter between an internal world and the external world" (D, 52). These transversal and a-parallel communications are occurrences or intensities in which all elements, for example man and the world, are "matured" in a constant process of becoming. At the same time transversalism launches a critical stance against the logic of vertical provenance which one finds in for instance Plato's methods of selection and classification. In Plato communication does not take place horizontally, but vertically, from the level of the idea down into the sphere of phenomena by virtue of the similarity-governed logic of representation.

But how does a worldview like that fit with perceptions of art? How may literature as form give expression to vitalism? How may we arrive at a possible novel-ontology? These are questions to be addressed in the following.

---

8   We find a similar poetic decree in Rushdie's *The Ground Beneath Her Feet* where the motion and imbalance between dichotomies are in focus: "The reconciliation of the conflict between the Apollonian and the Dionysiac we may call harmonia. Where reason and light meet madness and darkness, where science meets art and peace meets battle; where the adult meets the child, where life faces death and scorns it, make your music there" (GB, 392). The novel's consummate enunciation does not show, however, that a harmonious state of ease may be accomplished between the Apollonian and the Dionysian; harmony is always short-lived; epiphanic.

*

The focus in my presentation of Deleuze's perception of art will primarily be directed at his ideas of literature and in that connection I will primarily concentrate on two of his philosophical concepts: simulacrum and rhizome. However, these two are not only relevant in regard to Deleuze's theory of literature. In fact they relate to each of the three levels I have delineated. Hence the nature of the concepts allows them to serve as models in a typology of the work of art while at the same time they relate to Deleuze's ontology and view on human identity.

Deleuze rehabilitates the concept of simulacrum through a new reading of Platonism. The traditional understanding of Plato may be summarised in the dichotomies between idea-image, essence-appearance, intelligibility-sensibility, original-copy, and model-simulacrum, but in Plato's *The Sophist* Deleuze finds an opening which makes it possible for him deconstructively to drive a wedge between Plato's systems via Plato himself. Surely, Plato's immediate motivation is the division of the thing itself and the image of the thing, but Deleuze traces a deeper motivation which states a distinction between the images that look like the idea (copies) and those that do not (simulacra). Consequently, the adequation that existed between the copy and the simulacrum before, both of them being images of the idea, now shifts to become an opposition:

Traditional reading of Plato: $\frac{\text{Essence}}{\text{appearance}} \Leftrightarrow \frac{\text{Idea}}{\text{image}} \Leftrightarrow \frac{\text{Original}}{\text{copy}} \Leftrightarrow \frac{\text{Model}}{\text{simulacrum}}$

Deleuze's reading of Plato: $\text{image} \Leftrightarrow \frac{\text{Idea}}{\frac{\text{copy}}{\text{simulacrum}}} \Leftrightarrow \frac{\text{resemblance}}{\text{difference}}$

Hence, Platonic classification is not neutral. On the contrary, it is moral and concerned with the authentification of ideas and a selection of line or lineage, and usually it is the function of myth to secure the basis of judgement on which an image may be determined as good or bad. What is special about *The Sophist* is that Plato does not present any founding myth which may serve as a guarantee for the selection because the purpose of the dialogue is precisely to determine what characterises the bad image, the simulacrum, that is. With this Deleuze's analysis of Plato shows that Plato's motivation is to rid his metaphysics of simulacra and differences, yet at the same time it also shows that Plato, by persistently pursuing the nature of the simulacrum, actually allows an entry of inconsistency into his own system.

Plato's ideas have an essentialist nature and do not refer to anything but themselves. Thus, goodness is good, beauty is beautiful, and truth is true. They are absolute and non-relational concepts, and it is this qualification Deleuze opposes. In his thinking, the event, with all its relational elements and its consequent singular nature, replaces ideas: "The event must be considered as a *singularity*, and as a process that organises singularities. The manifestations of life in an event actually emanate from real relations, exchanges, interactions" (Tygstrup, 2001, 273), is how Tygstrup explains it.

It is also a central concern in Plato to estimate the relation between the image and the absolute and general idea: is there a derived, hereditary resemblance in the image, or does the image fail to live up to the transcendental definition of the idea? Plato's copies are successful images because they, through an internal connection with the idea, are equipped with the constitutional proportions that endow the idea with its inner essence: "In short, it is the superior identity of the Idea which founds the good pretension of the copies, as it bases it on an internal or derived resemblance" (LS, 257), Deleuze says in the important appendix in *The Logic of Sense* entitled "Plato and the Simulacrum." As mentioned before, a worldview like Plato's is based on the establishment of similarity as an ontological mainstay, given the presupposition of a superior layer of absolutes that images strive to resemble, whereas the foundation in Deleuze is pure difference. Deleuze summarises this in the following way:

> Let us consider the two formulas: "only that which resembles differs" and "only differences can resemble each other." These are two distinct readings of the world: one invites us to think difference from the standpoint of a previous similitude or identity; whereas the other invites us to think similitude and even identity as the product of a deep disparity. The

> first reading precisely defines the world of copies or representations; it posits the world as icon. The second, contrary to the first, defines the world of simulacra; it posits the world itself as phantasm (LS, 261-62).

Actually, this is a rather simple summation of two opposing ontologies: in the first one, similarity is recognised as the basis of the world which is always perfectly contained within itself in a representational 1:1 logic, whereas the other one sees difference as the basis of the world which always appears as a remainder or a fraction that does not come out evenly, but remains in a state of imbalance and differentiation.

Plato aims to obscure simulacra, or even to prevent them from surfacing from the muddy abyss of the material world and break the illusion of balance and harmony (between ideas as absolute entities and sensibility as becoming and pure difference) which is sustained by the idea of similitude: "It has to do with selecting among the pretenders, distinguishing good and bad copies or, rather, copies (always well-founded) and simulacra (always engulfed in dissimilarity). It is a question of assuring the triumph of the copies over simulacra, keeping them completely submerged, preventing them from climbing to the surface, and 'insinuating themselves everywhere'" (LS, 257). In contrast, Deleuze aims to liberate simulacra, and, with them, differences, in order to confirm their justification among copies. Consequently, Deleuze does not recognise successful images in the Platonic sense, given that they represent an illusory metaphysics to him, founded on universal, essentialist concepts. The result is a severe assault on representational thinking, where something always represents something else, and where the relation of similarity always functions as the foundation of judgement and thus as a criterion of truth. Rather, Deleuze wants to grant a status of precedence to difference in a logic where similarities only occur as a posteriori effects rather than a priori causes. Only by focusing on and acknowledging the singularity in each and every phenomena may we liberate life from being trapped in the logic of identities in representational thinking which inevitably misses out on the opportunity to think or trace newness. If we still seem to be within the area of ontology, then, as I have said before, this is due to the fact that simulacrum is not only relevant to the field of aesthetics, but is also to be understood as carrying a distinct perception of the world. However, it is now time to ask what relevance the concept has for the field of aesthetics.

Deleuze writes that catechism, inspired by Platonism, lectures us on the difference between copy and simulacrum: God created man in His own image and likeness (copy), but with the Fall man has lost his semblance with God, yet without ceasing to be an image of Him (simulacrum): "We have become simulacra. We have forsaken moral existence in order to enter into aesthetic existence" (LS, 257). In Rushdie's *Grimus*, Grimus creates Flapping Eagle in his own image, but Flapping Eagle turns out to be a simulacrum, "against the father," as he is fundamentally different from Grimus. Similitude is a metaphysical abstraction and illusion, whereas difference, falseness, and the singular, as subversive forces, constitute the basic ontology. Difference is inescapably the primary relation in *Grimus*. It functions as a catalyst of the continuation of process and the transgression of the monocentric circle which can only serve as a model for the eternal return of the same. Oppositely, the eternal return of the different may best be expressed with an eccentric circle as a model where the axis of rotation is in constant movement, incessantly causing the circle to off-track.

Deleuze invents an oxymoronic concept as a synonym for simulacrum, namely the concept *effondement* which is a contraction of *fondement* (foundation) and *effondrement* (breakdown). Accordingly a simulacrum-literature is characterised by an imbalance between the creation of a foundation and the instantaneous collapse of this foundation. So, simulacrum-literature is both earth and earthquake. To put it another way, the modern novel is both form and vitalism, it is *vitalistic form*, in constant movement and without a fixed centre or central perspective. A literature like that is not based on any pre-existing model to be represented in a copy-based relation. On the contrary, it constructs the world anew through a cartographic activity: in art the world always starts over again.

Along with processuality and constructivism, Deleuze opens up doors for a new form of art where heterogeneous lines may coexist, as concepts like cosmos, logos, and convergence are replaced by concepts like chaos, anti-logos, and divergence: "It is not at all a question of different points of view on one story supposedly the same; for points of view would still be submitted to a rule of convergence. It is rather a question of different and divergent stories, as if an absolutely distinct landscape corresponded to each point of view" (LS, 260). One senses here the contours of an aesthetics of complementarity which I will elaborate on at a later point in connection with the concept of rhizome.

Meanwhile, we may take a look at the philosophical and historical background of the development of the concept of perspectivism. As it is, an ontological slippage occurs between Leibniz's perspectivism, as expressed in his monadology, and the perspectivism expressed in Nietzsche's philosophy. Leibniz works with a "pre-established harmony" assured by God, which has the effect that every monad, despite his or her closed doors and windows (the problem of communication), despite his or her singularity, gives expression to the same world, only the degrees of the expression may vary. In Nietzsche on the other hand, where God is dead, incompossibility has become the means of communication itself, guaranteeing the process of becoming. Here heterogeneity and incompatibility prevail as positive, inclusive circumstances.

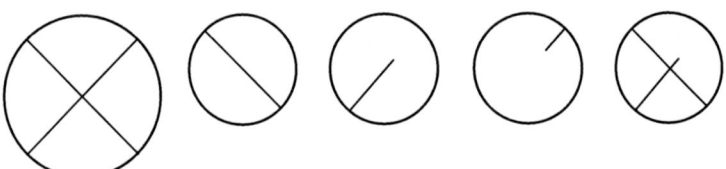

Leibniz's cosmos and convergent series (monads).

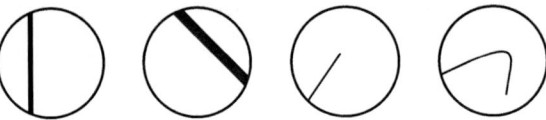

Nietzsche's divergent series.

In the Leibnizian model of the world, every monad or every perspective of the world is singular, but as humans we can be certain that we speak of the same world because God has made sure that every monad contains the same fundamental holding or the same basic structure. The relation between the world as cosmos and the monad as a perspective on the world corresponds to the relation between a macro- and a microcosm. The monad only gives expression to a part of the world, but this part converges with the cosmic world picture. In the Nietzschean model of the world, there is no cosmos any longer which may be implanted in singular perspectives on the world; in Nietzsche the world has no superior guardian who ensures the unity of the world, and, for that reason, Nietzsche opens up the possibility of a more radical perspectivism as there is no guarantee of convergence between the different series anymore. In this way a perspective forms its own unique version of the world, making it difficult to judge which versions of the world are right and which ones are wrong.

*

The concept of rhizome is introduced in connection with Deleuze and Guattari's *Kafka: Toward a Minor Literature* (1975) and, in extension of this book, they published the small text *Rhizome* (1976), the contents of which were later revised a bit into the manifesto-like introductory chapter of the main work *A Thousand Plateaus* (1980). The chapter can (and must) be read as a normative poetics in which the two authors launch a triadic typology of the work of art, involving characterisations of the root-book, the radicle-book, and the rhizome. However, as with the concept of simulacrum, the concept of rhizome does not relate to perceptions of art only. The rhizome also articulates significant characteristics of Deleuze's view of the world as well as of his idea of the subject.

Rhizome is a botanical term, etymologically it is Greek (*rhizoma*), meaning "root," and in botany it refers to a creeping rootstalk or rootstock, specifically the continuous part of perennial plants which serves the purpose of vegetative reproduction. Deleuze and Guattari bend the term a bit as in their terminology it acquires the meaning of a root system; grass, for instance, may be characterised as a rhizome. With rhizome Deleuze and Guattari launch an alternative to the traditional metaphysics of Western thinking, of which the predominant metaphors have been those of the tree and the root. Rhizome forms a new image of thought which is irreconcilable with representational thinking. In Deleuze and Guattari's triadic classification of the book, the first type is characterised by a representational logic, while the second type is partially retained within such a logic.

The root-book represents the classical work in which the tree forms an image of the world and the root an image of the world-tree. The classical work, according to Deleuze and Guattari, is characterised by an organic (that is, harmonious, a priori), significant (that is, each element occupying a meaningful position within the whole), and subjective (that is, the possibility of tracing the meaning of the work back to a subject serving as a hermeneutic guarantee) interiority. The book imitates the world through the binary logic of the dialectic method. The correlation with the logic of the copy is evident as the root-book, through similarity and internal derivation, represents a metaphysical world where convergence, circularity, and harmony prevail. The root-book is a root-cosmos, in which an unshakable axis works in the object while a dichotomous either-or logic works in the subject: "The pivotal taproot provides no better understanding of multiplicity than the dichotomous root. One operates in the object, the other in the subject" (TP, 5). The root-book presupposes a foundation from which all individual parts emanate in a relation which comes out with no remainder when you divide the whole by the parts. There is an analogous relation between the world and the root-book, and there is an organic relation between each individual element of the root-book and its totality (the One becomes two which become four and so forth).

According to the young Georg Lukács, there seemed to be no discrepancy between life and being or between act and intention in the antique world picture, and everything seemed to inhabit a predetermined place in the whole. If any friction would occur between man and the world, it would never come to an irreversible destabilisation of being, at most only to the termination of a human life: "Even if menacing and incomprehensible forces become felt outside the circle which the stars of ever-present meaning draw round the cosmos to be experienced and formed, they cannot displace the presence of meaning; they can destroy life, but never tamper with being; they can cast dark shadows on the formed world, but even these are assimilated by the forms as contrasts that only bring them more clearly into relief" (Lukács, 33). In this way, the form of Graecism, the monocentric circle, which in return is an expression of the articulation in myth of the eternal return of the same, absorbs any attempt to embrace the madness of becoming, since destiny or the divine order keeps every element in its allotted place in the cosmic space of eternity. Here there is no trace of any transcendental homelessness, and the homeless wanderer's journey across the landscape is only an act of migration from one point to another within an organic closure, in which the basic structure is constituted only by the reciprocity between the whole and its individual parts. Consequently, movement does not entail any qualitative leaps.

Homer's *Odyssey* may serve as an example of both Lukács's and Deleuze's points. When Odysseus returns to his beloved Ithaca, having fought in Troy for ten years and then roamed the oceans for another ten, a surprise lies in wait for him, his home having been invaded by suitors who aim for his throne and lust for Penelope, his chastely waiting wife. The suitors represent simulacra, the false pretenders and the "menacing and incomprehensible forces" that strive to destabilise the ruling order in the absence of the transcendental fix point and guarantor of this order, the king Odysseus. So a collapse of the existing hierarchy is in the offing where the monocentric circle is derailed and a new and different order is installed with one of the suitors as the new, but unlawful ("false") king. However, Odysseus defeats all of the suitors, aided by his son Telemachos (who is symptomatic of the logic of the eternal return and the "true" continuation of the family line). And the attempts at causing friction must now bow to the circular rhythm of the eternal return of the same, the suitors "cannot displace the presence of meaning", order is re-established and cosmos prevails.

In the novel *Ignorance* (2000), Milan Kundera offers an interesting reflection on the themes of nostalgia and adventure in connection with Odysseus' return:

> Rather than ardent exploration of the unknown (adventure), he chose the apotheosis of the known (return). Rather than the infinite (for adventure never intends to finish), he chose the finite (for the return is a reconciliation with the finitude of life). (...) Without waking him, the Phaeacian seamen laid Odysseus, still wrapped in his bedding, near an olive tree on Ithaca's shore, and then departed. Such was his journey's end. He slept on, exhausted. When he awoke, he could not tell where he

was. Then Athena wiped the mist from his eyes and it was rapture; the rapture of the Great Return; the ecstasy of the known; the music that sets the air vibrating between earth and heaven: he saw the harbor he had known since childhood, the mountain overlooking it, and he fondled the old olive tree to confirm that it was still the same as it had been twenty years earlier (Kundera, 2002, 8-9).

Odysseus' immediate confusion is replaced with clarity through divine intervention, a clarity where the familiar makes itself known by its self-identity. And so the great epos ends; by necessity one is almost tempted to say.

We also find a representation of the monocentric form in ancient tragedy. The tragedy is "tragic" precisely because the friction that occurs between the individual and the world has to give way to the superimposed circularity of the myth and its consequent logic of eternity: the hero is always led back to monocentric passivity through destiny. Everything has its predestined place in the cosmic world picture, and it is certain that anyone who tries to break out of this mythical structure will be put back in his or her right place. The tragic hero whom we sympathise with does not get what he deserves, he is struck by injustice, hence the tragedy. The comic hero, on the contrary, gets what he deserves, hence the comedy.

If we turn our gaze from the general ontological assertions of the tragedies to their stylistic techniques, we may find assistance in some of the Aristotelian key concepts from *The Poetics*, such as necessity, the unity of action, beginning, middle, and end. In Antiquity the concept of necessity is determined on the basis of a pre-existing cosmic order, whereas necessity in Deleuze's philosophy is determined by and arises from accidence: "It is the accident of the encounter that guarantees the necessity of what is thought" (PS, 16). In this way encounters in the modern age contain the potential of new thinking or the materialisation of new formal constructions, whereas encounters in the Antique world picture can only serve as confirmations of things that already exist.

Likewise the unity of action in tragedy may be ascribed to a superjacent cosmos, insofar as it operates with the idea that any macrocosm (the law, logos) may be represented through its microcosms (the tightly constructed, unilateral thread of action), just as the concepts of beginning, middle, and end reflect an activity that invariably moves from balance to imbalance and back to balance, causing the universe to close in on itself once again. This is the case, for instance, in Sophocles' *Oedipus Tyrannos*, in which the imbalance that occurs in cosmos, due to Oedipus' patricide and incest, materialises as sickness among the Thebans, but at the end of the tragedy, when the reader or the audience have been taken through the superbly organised intrigue, all the missteps are solved. It may be argued that Oedipus' act of blinding himself is an action that escapes the will of the gods, that Oedipus acts as a completely free individual in this terrible scene, but his action does not result in any profound becoming in the universe. On the contrary, it causes a reciprocal conversion, as Oedipus is transformed from a sighted blind person to a blind seer. Oedipus' insight is just an insight into the same cosmic order which was before outside his reach; his newly gained self-knowledge confirms logos. So, with this we are still within the period in world history in which the "principle of corruption" (Hegel, 279), which Hegel associates with Euripides, has not yet come about.

    In the radicle-book the world has become chaotic, but the subject does not cease to institute order in chaos. The principal root has aborted, but new supplementing roots graft onto the unsuccessful root and retain the principal root as a guiding perspective, either as a future hope of unity or as a past longing for unity. The world has lost its axis of rotation and the subject keeps hold of the institution of a new kind of order which, rather than the unity of the binary logic, constitutes a unity of ambiguity, always taking the shape of the supplementary dimension of the object: "unity is consistently thwarted and obstructed in the object, while a new type of unity triumphs in the subject (...). The world has become chaos, but the book remains the image of the world: radicle-chaosmos rather than root-cosmos" (TP, 6). To Deleuze and Guattari ambivalence is not a positive attribute, because it is incapable of catalysing any distinct becoming. Ambivalence is illustrated by the supplementary roots that are grafted onto the aborted root, which, in itself, operates centripetally and keeps the new roots in a kind of vibration, but a vibration going nowhere. Multiplicity is still founded on the one, and it is the author's nostalgia for the order of the old world that seems to be the source of the radicle-book. A representational logic is upheld as the world as chaos is reflected in the immediate chaos of the work, the book imitating the world as an "Œuvre totale": "At any rate, what a vapid idea, the book as the image of the world" (TP, 6). Here Deleuze and Guattari adduce a direct and unequivocal critique of mimesis, implying that mimesis is understood as imitation or copy (*mimesis* versus *creatio*). If the work of art is representative or mimetic, then from where is the new supposed to come – the new as the very raison d'être of art as it is held by Pound, Kundera, Rushdie, Kjærstad, and others? May art in this case serve as anything but a confirmation of doxa?

The most ambivalent work according to Umberto Eco, as defined in "The Poetics of the Open Work," is Joyce's *Finnegans Wake* (1939), and we may use this novel as an example of how Deleuze and Guattari differ from Eco (I will return to the relation between Deleuze and Eco later). Eco writes the following about Joyce's last novel: "The principal tool for this all-pervading ambiguity is the pun, the *calembour*, by which two, three, or even ten different etymological roots are combined in such a way that a single word can set up a knot of different submeanings, each of which in turn coincides and interrelates with other local allusions, which are themselves 'open' to new configurations and probabilities of interpretation" (Eco, 10). What Eco sees as the openness of the work par excellence is exactly what Deleuze and Guattari criticise: the ambiguity of a pun has as its pivotal point all these linguistic roots that create knots of meaning. To Deleuze and Guattari, the pun is merely a technique which makes it possible to add an infinity of supplementary dimensions without this necessarily leading to innovation, metamorphosis, and becoming; its roots symbolise the underlying authority of order, the author, or the signifier, which assures the a priori totality of the work and its unitary foundation.

In the case of *Ulysses* (1922), one finds an underlying mythical structure deriving from *The Odyssey* which is used as a meaning-making explanatory framework and a model in the projection of the chaotic world. Accordingly, Ulysses represents the world as chaosmosis.[9] In the same

9   It calls for an explanation why the concept of chaosmosis is associated with the radical here, since I have insisted on the relevance of the concept in Deleuze's ontology earlier on. When chaosmosis is applied in connection with the radicle-book it suggests a closure of becoming. The suffix in chaos-mosis must be seen here as a conclusive element in a final movement from object (chaos) to subject (cosmos). As

way one may sense a desire for continuity in T.S. Eliot's *The Waste Land* published the same year behind the surface of its fragmentary appearance. Both works are written with the experience of the First World War as a base of resonance, which obviously explains the incessant return to a past well of wisdom and order as an attempt to cope with the period's breakdown of values. However, it would be a misreading simply to focus on Eliot and Joyce's uses of myth in their works as pure seriousness. On the contrary it is important to underline how they work with the demise of the downright authoritative role of myth. Nevertheless, one significant difference between Eliot and Joyce's radicle-books and the rhizome, to anticipate this concept, manifests itself in the use of myth which, in respect to the former type of work, is still brought into play with a degree of nostalgia, whereas the latter type of work makes use of myth for more parodic and ironic purposes, underscoring the rhizome as a concept that embraces transcendental homelessness as a basic human condition. Apparently, we are in a grey zone when it comes to the radicle and the rhizome books, as their relation seems to be one of gradual distinction. The use of myth in modern and postmodern novels respectively may be one of the places where the distinction between the two emerges, and it does so, it seems, according to the degree of nostalgia, parody, or irony in the novel's employment of myth.

If the logic of the root-book may be illustrated with the following pattern: $1 \Leftrightarrow 2 \Leftrightarrow 4 \Leftrightarrow 8$ and so forth, understood as a reversible process, and the logic of the radicle-book may be characterised, correspondingly, as a multiplicity derived from the one, or to which the one attaches itself, that is: $1+n$ or $n+1$, then the logic of the rhizome is completely different: "The multiple must be made, not by always adding a higher dimension, but rather in the simplest of ways, by dint of sobriety, with the number of dimensions one already has available – always $n-1$ (the only way the one belongs to the multiple: always subtracted). Subtract the unique from the multiplicity to be constituted; write at $n-1$ dimensions. A system of this kind could be called a rhizome" (TP, 6). The book as rhizome

opposed to this, the way I have employed the concept earlier suggests a continuous imbalance between chaos and form in both object and subject; in other words: the dynamic of becoming form.

is anti-genealogical, without any primary source, it is anti-hierarchical and transversal rather than vertical-hierarchical. In the architecture of the rhizome as a subterranean stem, connections are made where any random point may join with any other random point. As a result there are several possible entryways into the rhizome. Hence, the rhizome cannot be traced to any pre-existing structural or generative model supporting the rhizome like a foundation. In the Middle Ages, for instance, Dante's *Divine Comedy* would be read on exactly four levels: literally, allegorically, morally, and anagogically. The meaning of the work was limited to these four entryways owing to the fact that a Christian world picture was superimposed on any reading or understanding of the work. As opposed to this, there is no logos incarcerating the semantics of the rhizome within a limited number of readings.

A deep structure based on a genetic axis does not correspond to the geography of the rhizome which is characterised by its lack of beginning and end. The rhizome is always middle, *intermezzo*. The absence of a centre or any established origin in the rhizome makes it a multiplicity in constant movement and therefore it is actually impossible to speak about points in the rhizome: "Unlike a structure, which is defined by a set of points and positions, with binary relations between the points and biunivocal relationships between the positions, the rhizome is made only of lines: lines of segmentarity and stratification as its dimensions, and the line of flight or deterritorialization as the maximum dimension after which the multiplicity undergoes metamorphosis, changes in nature" (TP, 21). So, according to Deleuze and Guattari, a rhizome consists of lines rather than points. Yet, it would be wrong to perceive the rhizome as pure chaos or pure dissolution as its lines assume two different qualities: firstly, the rhizome is characterised by lines which take flight towards strata and segmentary formations (a becoming-point), and secondly, it is characterised by lines that decompose or dissolve tendencies to point formations (a becoming-dissolved). A traditional structural analysis is insufficient when dealing with a rhizomatic work because an analysis like that only seeks to capture the lines and vectors of the rhizome within stable points and positions. The rhizome is not an assemblage of constituent parts, but of dimensions, or rather directions in movement. Deleuze and Guattari turn their gaze to the instances in the text where ruptures occur and mobility manifests itself, which, in other words, are the metamorphic tendencies that the work of art may contain. The rhizome cannot be sealed in the closure of reciprocity, but requires an acceptance of dividuality (n-1), hence the differentiality of the work. The rhizome is an open Totality of becoming.

Deleuze and Guattari do not dismiss that literature as rhizome contains tendencies to become points, as the rhizome stretches between territorialisation, deterritorialisation, and reterritorialisation. Once again imbalance shows itself as the force of dynamism and movement. The question is not whether there is movement, but what form the movement takes. Is it a movement that sets free or is it a movement of encasement? In this way one may identify arborescent tendencies in the rhizome and rhizomatic tendencies in the root. Nevertheless, it is important that we retain a decisive distinction between rhizome and root in parallel with the distinction, mentioned earlier, between a reading of the world that takes difference as its point of departure (map, rhizome, creatio), and a reading that takes identity as a point of departure (copy, root, mimesis). One may then be tempted to ask whether the pair root-rhizome is not yet another binary construction? According to Deleuze and Guattari the answer is no:

> The important point is that the root-tree and canal-rhizome are not two opposed models: the first operates as a transcendent model and tracing, even if it engenders its own escapes; the second operates as an immanent process that overturns the model and outlines a map, even if it constitutes its own hierarchies, even if it gives rise to a despotic channel. (...) It is a question of a model that is perpetually in construction or collapsing, and of a process that is perpetually prolonging itself, breaking off and starting up again (TP, 20).

The rhizome makes any stable model impossible, as was the case with the simulacrum: "we employ a dualism of models only in order to arrive at a process that challenges all models" (TP, 20). The model and the copy progress through reproduction whereas the map produces. A map must be constructed, but not on the basis of a pre-existing model or original. Hence, with the map the world may be said continually to start all over again: the construction of maps (cartography) creates the new, the world expands, and new modes of existence are constituted. But how exactly is one to understand the concept of the map? A map is not literally a map of the world as we know it from geography. A map may also be a novel whose language creates a mental and a sensuous indication of the world in a way that makes the reader revise his or her former perception of society, love, art, or death; to create a cartography means that one understands the world symbolically rather than literally. The copy presupposes a metaphysical space of eternity striving for resemblance, whereas the map accepts that nothing escapes being only a provisional suggestion of the world and is never elevated above contradictions.

Deleuze and Guattari clearly advocate a pragmatic and functionalist strategy of reading which focuses on mapping the lines in a work: "This is why the question of schizoanalysis or pragmatics, micro-politics itself, never consists in interpreting, but merely in asking what are your lines, individual or group, and what are the dangers on each?" (D, 143). The rejection of interpretation as the main purpose of literary analysis carries an implicit criticism of hermeneutics. The motive of Deleuze and Guattari's suspicion against interpretation is that, in many cases, it does not result in anything new or productive. On the contrary, it is caught within the attempt to "uncover things," seeking only to re-present or re-produce the original (but the literary forms of the novel, of drama, or of poetry do not lend themselves to transitions into other forms). However, in Deleuze's *Proust and Signs* interpretation is actually a key concept. His point is that Marcel's process of interpretation in Marcel Proust's *In Search of Lost Time* is prompted by the violent encounter with a sign (the Outside), an encounter which in a way suspends subjectivity (the body with organs) because violence and contingency place man within the immanence of becoming where subjectivity is produced as an effect: "Involuntary sensibility, involuntary memory, involuntary thought that are, each time, like the intense totalising reactions of the organless body to signs of one nature or another" (PS, 182).

As far as I can see, Deleuze and Guattari expand the typology that Eco delineates in "The Poetics of the Open Work": the root-book corresponds to "the closed work," whereas the radicle-book corresponds to "the work in movement." What is characteristic about Eco is that he presents "the open work" as an Einsteinean universe, in which the work is constituted by poly-perspectivism and a fundamental indefiniteness: "relativity means the infinite variability of experience as well as the infinite multiplication of possible ways of measuring things and viewing their position. But the objective side of the whole system can be found in the invariance of the simple formal descriptions (of the differential equations) which establish once and for all the relativity of empirical measurement" (Eco, 18). It is always possible to objectify relativity, since Einsteinian metaphysics, according to Eco, reflects a basic confidence in the totality of the universe: "The God in Spinoza, who is made into an untestable hypothesis by Einsteinian metaphysics, becomes a cogent reality for thework of art and matches the organizing impulse of its creator" (Eco, 19). As I have already suggested, T.S. Eliot may serve as an example of how chaos in the world of objects (relativity) is fixed as cosmos through the author (God).

At the same time, Eco sets up the artist and the reader as the mainstay of his methodology, but such concepts are, as will be shown later, extremely problematic factors and should be considered, rather, as linguistic functions in the invitation of a text to dialogic communication.[10] In coupling Einstein's universe with the universe of the text, Eco simultaneously employs Bohr's quantum physics as an analogy of the reader's role, insofar as different readings project complementary pictures of the work which, according to Eco, are mutually exclusive. But if the radicle-book or the open work corresponds to the theory of relativity (the matter of perspective being subordinated to a pre-existing principle of order), it

10 In order to accommodate the possible misunderstandings that interpretation might lead to in the time succeeding the allegorical frameworks of the Middle Age, Schleiermacher suggested, among other things, that interpretation must find support in the author's psyche or biography. Correspondingly, Eco speaks of the writer's intentions as a condition and frame of the work's meaning and circumstances of interpretation. This is an exceptionally complicated problems, but I am not sure that Deleuze would appreciate readings based on the author's intentions. In Rushdie's case the question of intention is particularly interesting, given the fact that he has become a "victim" of the polysemantic nature of language in connection with *The Satanic Verses* and, as a consequence, he has had to contribute with a reading of his own novel in order to clarify his intentions and, with that, apply the brakes to the novel's infinite semantic machine.

is my conviction that the rhizome goes one step further, unfolding Bohr's universe not only in the reading of the text, but in the text itself. Through its textual body per se, the rhizome can include complementary universes which carry no reference to any a priori harmony or totality. Rushdie's novels may not only be read in many ways, they themselves read and construct the world in many ways.

As in Einstein's universe, the unity of the open work takes the form of an original, rational, and schematisable world picture, whereas unity in the rhizome only occurs when a reading activates the transversal lines of connection, causing elements to affect each other reciprocally and create new group formations. Deleuze defines transversality in the following way: "It is transversality that permits us, in the train, not to unify the viewpoints of a landscape, but to bring them into communication according to the landscape's own dimension, in its own dimension, whereas they remain noncommunicating according to their own dimension" (PS, 168). Accordingly, the unity of a work is never given beforehand, but is tied to the form that emerges in the tracks of readings that pursue the lines of connection (transversals), prioritised internally by the work's textual body. Unity is a product, not a cause or something predetermined.

In *Proust and Signs* Deleuze draws on Eco in his argumentation and there is a remarkable affinity between the two, but I still think that Deleuze's project deviates a bit from Eco's. In Eco's "The Poetics of the Open Work," and in hermeneutics in general, the work is perceived as an organic totality where the individual parts must be understood in relation to the work as a whole, and the work as a whole must be understood in relation to the individual parts.[11] Deleuze rejects the work as a predeter-

---

11   Poul Lübcke says about hermeneutics in general: "We only understand a text if we want it to tell us something, that is if we agree that the text may say something true. But a text can only be true if it comprises a 'perfect unity,' in a way that prevents any discrepancy between the individual parts of the text and its entirety. The demand of the text to say something true about its theme (its 'cause') involves the condition that there be no disagreement within the text itself, i.e. there be no conflict between the text as a whole and the individual parts of the text" (Lübcke, 168-69). *The Satanic Verses* orchestrates a play between its individual parts and its entirety which renders synthesis impossible, the novel's heterogeneous elements sticking out in every direction. As will be shown, the novel definitely plays host to disagreement.

mined, collective totality: "We have given up seeking a unity that would unify the parts, a whole that would totalise the fragments. For it is the character and nature of the parts or fragments to exclude the Logos both as logical unity and as organic totality" (PS, 163). Hence, Proust's idea of unity does not appear as a principle to Deleuze, but as an effect, as an effect of multiplicity. Frederik Tygstrup makes the same observation in an article about Deleuze's understanding of form in which he also alludes to Deleuze's reading of Proust:

> Here Deleuze argues (...) against the (at the time) prevalent idea that the unity in *À la recherche* manifests itself in a complete and rounded as well as self-supporting form, the consummate objectification and hermeneutic integration of the subject matter. Oppositely, he claims that the work is basically fragmented (we would say a multitude of elements that stick out in every direction), and that unity, as a result, does not consist in the idea that every element is in its right place in a superior, stable form, but rather in the idea that heterogeneous elements, that we habitually try to bind up in independent groups, "planes" or "threads" in the work, are linked in a transversal dimension. Within this new dimension the elements enter into different, functional connections which enunciate them in a specific way in relation to this alternative context (Tygstrup, 1995, 190-91).

Accordingly, Deleuze and Guattari's concept of rhizome involves a more radical understanding of a work's objectivity, seeing that the material and compositional aspects of the work are in focus rather than its deep semantics and invitations to subjective interpretation.

In Eco the reader turns up with a personal horizon of experience which is projected onto the work, whereas in Deleuze there is an attempt to ignore this horizon as much as possible, centring on the local grammar of the work. Tygstrup again: "For this reason, when we ask how a novel coheres, we ought to refrain from using any conviction of how to construct an imaginary universe on the basis of certain types as a point of departure, which is in actual fact the same as anticipating that the novel thinks a thought that we already know. We can never know how a novel coheres. But we can always analyse it, coherence is quite literally always in the technical-formal dimension" (*ibid.*, 193). What Tygstrup indirectly takes shots at is the hermeneutic idea of a pre-understanding of the text as decisive for the total meaning of the text. Any pre-understanding locks the novel's thought within existing frames and blocks newness.

Maybe Deleuze cannot disclaim a hermeneutic method of his own because interpretation is an inevitable method in our dealings with otherness. However, it is characteristic of Deleuze that he tries to go round the notion of a pre-existing structure (meaning) by focusing on the becoming of form, whereby the traditional idea of subjectivity (the body with organs) is played down. "Form is not a 'natural' property of an object, but a property that is attached to it through a process of understanding and interpretation" (*ibid.*, 186), writes Tygstrup. The process of interpretation is prompted in the encounter with the violent and contingent sign or materiality of a work which determines the result of the reading and the interpretation through a logic of immanence. Immanence, or we could say the body without organs (BwO), arises because the reader's subjectivity, understood as a stable and rooted organism, dissolves in front of the work of art. Through the compositional strategies of the rhizome, the reader is forced into new perceptive situations which he or she is not caused to undergo in everyday life. In everyday life the situational restraint of one's subjectivity is intact, the subject is defined by natural perception which is a perception that requires unity in the phenomenal space: the coherent milieu (the horizon) of the perceiver and the perceived. But the unity of the phenomenal space and the rootedness of the subject are annulled in the rhizome, in which enunciation may assume a paradoxical status, bonding otherwise incompossible elements. Tygstrup concludes:

> A reading forms a transition from the encounter with the work as an assemblage of incompossibilia, each of which implicates its own characteristic, conventional and contextual universe, making the work appear as a discontinuous assemblage of "examples of language," to a charging of the discontinuous which turns it into compossible elements in a universe through the zones of the composition, crystals and transversals – albeit at the cost that language no longer obeys the set of rules which, outside the work, gave it its conventional and contextual wealth of meaning. Form transforms language through the machinery of com-

position, transforms it (...) into "a kind of foreign tongue" in the heart of the familiar (*ibid.*, 191).

Whereas hermeneutics focuses on the possibilities of interpretation and meaning, Deleuze focuses on the possibilities of understanding and sense. Interpretation and meaning involves concepts like recognition, a priori truths, and subjectivity, whereas understanding and sense involves concepts like violence, sensuous experience, and materiality: "sense is never a principle or an origin, (...) it is produced. It is not something to discover, to restore, and to re-employ; it is something to produce by new machinery" (LS, 72).

According to Deleuze and Guattari English and American writers in particular have managed to write rhizomatically:

> American literature, and already English literature, manifest this rhizomatic direction (...); they know how to move between things, establish a logic of the AND, overthrow ontology, do away with foundations, nullify endings and beginnings. They know how to practice pragmatics. The middle is by no means an average; on the contrary, it is where things pick up speed. *Between* things does not designate a localizable relation going from one thing to the other and back again, but a perpendicular direction, a transversal movement that sweeps one *and* the other away, a stream without beginning or end that undermines its banks and picks up speed in the middle (TP, 25).

Newness seems to emerge in the intermezzo-position, that is, between the banks of the stream, which are to be understood as two lines rather than two fixed positions. For that reason, the rhizome operates through the inclusive conjunctive logic ET (and) rather than the attributive verbal logic EST (is). In a conjunction (e.g. Saleem and India), two elements are joined in a transversal connection; the elements do not synthesise, but preserve their distinctiveness. Rather than synthesis, a zone of proximity arises between the elements, which still causes a transformation of each of them. So, the transversality that occurs between the two elements forms a launching pad for intensity and metamorphosis, triggering the production of the new as well. Conjunction becomes a way of describing and shaping the processuality of the world, where any element (organic or material) is constantly situated within these zones of proximity in which they are transformed and, accordingly, turned into lines instead of points. Through attribution one annuls the process, as attribution turns elements into points (e.g. Saleem is a snotnose) rather than capturing its movement and becoming (e.g. Saleem is both a snotnose and a sniffer and...).

Deleuze and Guattari also describe literature as a machine consisting of many fluxes where writing can never be an end in itself, as it always has to be linked to an Outside. To Deleuze and Guattari pragmatics is always superior to linguistics: "To write has no other function: to be a flux which combines with other fluxes – all the minority-becomings of the world. A flux is something intensive, instantaneous and mutant – between a creation and a destruction. (...) There is no assemblage which functions on a single flux. This is not a matter of imitation, but of conjunction" (D, 50, 44). Hence, mono-flux does not exist according to Deleuze and Guattari because each element constantly collides with other elements. The field of tension between the element of literature and the element of world is dynamic. They are mutually dependent or influence each other which makes a discussion of the reality of literature ridiculous; literature has a direct influence on the world, it deterritorialises the world which in turn produces a reterritorialisation of literature.

Furthermore, transversality brings about an anti-genealogy and an aparallel evolution:

> Transversal communications between different lines scramble the genealogical trees. Always look for the molecular, or even submolecular, particle with which we are allied. We evolve and die more from our polymorphous and rhizomatic flus than from hereditary diseases, or diseases that have their own line of descent. The rhizome is an anti-genealogy.
> The same applies to the book and the world: contrary to a deeply rooted belief, the book is not an image of the world. It forms a rhizome with the world, there is an aparallel evolution of the book and the world; the book assures the deterritorialization of the world, but the world effects a reterritorialization of the book, which in turn deterritorializes itself in the world (if it is capable, if it can) (TP, 11).

The book forms a rhizome with the world in an aparallel evolution. In regard to evolution, this means that it no longer advances from a traditional root structure but from crossings and collisions. Parallelism secures a kind of purity of lineage or offspring, whereas aparallelism points towards a bastardisation. In a way, this implies that the novel and the world are the same thing (becoming), not to be understood in the sense that the novel is a mimetic copy of the world, but in the sense that the novel and the world are entangled entities, both articulating a kind of constructivism and vitalism that causes them to ceaselessly reinvent each other in a cartographic process.

We may now ask what implications the rhizome as a root system has for identity? May subjectification, that is, the process of becoming a subject, be ascribed to the processes of aparallel evolution and cross-pollination?

*

We have already touched upon the edges of a theory of subjectification in the above, for example in the concept of the event, in the idea of the violent sign or encounter, and in the discrepancy between concepts like cause and effect. To Deleuze the subject is an effect rather than a cause. The course of becoming-subject relates to a sensuous stream of heterogeneous and differential impressions, resulting in a ceaseless process of becoming-human. Even so, the subject is characterised at the same time by habits and a representational logic with which it tries to protect itself against the submerged stream of flowing perceptions that dissolves the solid core of identity. Malene Busk says about the subject of habit that:

> The principles of association – cause, proximity, and equality – speak of a sad becoming-subject, a subject that lives by its habits, safeguarding itself against losing its footing by clinging to illegitimate, but comfortable convictions, doxa. Cut off from the becoming of its sensibility, the subject superimposes sensibility with habits: by reducing awareness to things and states of affairs, by generalising and practicing the habit of saying "I" as the starting point for the safety of conscious perception, as "Ur-doxa" (Busk, 146).

In this way Deleuze works with two levels of subjectivity. He operates with a plane of immanence where the subject is in a process of becoming and is designated as a body without organs. Defined as a body without organs, man is located in a kind of perfect virtuality, severed from the coordinates that usually define him. The other level is the plane of transcendence, and here man is perceived as an organism which is established, as Busk points out, by habits and ideas of similitude.

The plane of immanence is a state of pre-individuality and a-consciousness, expressed as singular events or haecceities; individuations, to be more specific, where phenomena and people are transformed. As a solid organism, the subject's thought is filled up with good intentions, for instance in its search for truth, but a conscious, intentional search can only confirm doxa, as it is subject to a structure of equivalence between, on the one hand, a meaningful, categorical and stable world and, on the other, a primary and a priori defined subject reflecting this world. But the becoming of sensuality undermines the solid subject through its status as violent signs because it pushes the categories of reason into a state of disharmony:

> In the thought as a form of "forced movement," our mental faculties are no longer concerned only with sensing present states of being, recalling past states of being or thinking intelligible states of being. They are directed towards transcendental questions about sensing the sensuous being itself, recollecting the pure past of recollection and comprehending the unthought of conceptual thought. They transgress, transcend, their arbitrary representational function: the transcendent objects of thought pull our mental faculties apart in opposite directions, where none of the others can follow, so that, rather than confirming the cohesion of the self by capturing "the same object" in cognitive harmony, the self is diffused. The violence or the element of force means that our mental faculties in each their way are saddled with and "suffer a passion," or discover each their passion. Every faculty is driven towards its privileged object, towards the becoming of a certain way of "thinking" (sensing, recollecting, comprehending, and so on), towards its "faculty" understood as a particular and irreducible force (*ibid.*, 158).

So, the disharmonious state of our mental faculties, which makes a cognitive harmony between a subject filled with good intention and a world filled with common sense impossible, results in a diffusion of the self. The diffusion of the self is a basic human condition and we may only sporadically and illusorily put the pieces together to a wholeness. Therefore, man is to be perceived as a network of roots rather than a deep-seated taproot, which, from a centre in motion, spreads in a horizontal dimension. Among other things, there is a reminder in this of the sociality of the subject, and a criticism of the, at times, one-sided focus of psychoanalysis on the familial triangle, where desire understood as an immanent force is blocked in a representational theatre in which something always stands for something else. In Deleuze and Guattari the subject does not desire a thing because it is in need of something; it is desire itself that is in need of a stable subject.

The dualism between the organism and the body without organs comprises the same basic structure we have encountered before in connection with the dualism between copy and simulacrum and between root and rhizome. On the one hand, the organism constructs a model which, on the other hand, is constantly destroyed via the process prompted by the pre-individual intensities and differences distributed by the body without organs. With their understanding of man as a body without organs, Deleuze and Guattari attempt to liberate man from the determinant lines and coordinates of stratification which are constantly established by, for instance, the school, the family, the church, and the media. Inspired by Spinoza the point is to ask: what is a human capable of becoming, what is it capable of feeling and what is it capable of sensing? "They – we – are capable of being much more than we seem" (GB, 297), is Rushdie's answer.

It is time to look at Rushdie's universe again, and, hopefully, my presentation of Deleuze's ideas of literature have set out some frameworks which may help us to a better understanding of certain aspects of Rushdie's novels, such as their strategies of composition, techniques of enunciation, problematisations of identity, as well as their general stylistics and uses of language.

RUSHDIE'S CARTOGRAPHY

RUSHDIE'S CARTOGRAPHY: 1981-1988

> "But in art there is no such thing as an originator, a precursor (at any rate in the scientific sense of the words): everything being comprised in the individual, every man takes up the continuous attempt of art or of literature on his own account, and for him the works of his predecessors are not, as they are for the scientists, a fund of truth which those who come after may profit by. A present-day writer of genius has it all in his hands. He is not much further forward than Homer."
> – Marcel Proust: "The Method of Sainte-Beuve"

In this chapter I will make an in-depth analysis of *Midnight's Children*, *Shame*, and *The Satanic Verses*, the first and latter arguably being the two best and most important novels by Rushdie. After a thematic summary of each novel, I will move on to examine Rushdie's distinctive strategies of composition and, in extension of this, his techniques of enunciation. In doing so we may already at this early stage get an indication of the possible rhizomatic character of the novels. However, an analysis of Rushdie's view on human identity is unavoidable when it comes to an understanding of the general aesthetics of the novels. After the sub-chapter on human identity, I will try to pin down two central artistic ploys, namely a metaphorical and a metonymical writing style. Subsequently I will take a look at the use of language in the novels and their political status. This is followed by a longer sub-chapter on historiographic metafiction, in which I will discuss the Rushdie Affair. Finally, I will discuss the ways in which Rushdie has shaped the endings of his novels.

Midnight's Children

Midnight's Children is centred on Saleem Sinai, the novel's main character and narrator. Saleem is born the very instant India is born as an independent nation. The novel, which is a fabulistic, picaresque family novel in line with *Tom Jones, Tristram Shandy*, and *David Copperfield*, opens in the following hesitant manner: "I was born in the city of Bombay... once upon a time. No, that won't do, there's no getting away from the date: I was born in Doctor Narlikar's Nursing Home on August 15th, 1947. And the time? The time matters, too. Well then: at night. No, it's important to be more... On the stroke of midnight, as a matter of fact. Clock-hands joined palms in respectful greeting as I came" (MC, 9). The opening points to a combination of fairy tale and realism, and through Saleem's birth Rushdie implicitly thematises the difficulties of initiating a narrative. Accordingly, the style is faltering and tentative, but also playful, and in the ensuing course of the story the narrator unexpectedly makes a loop back in time to begin the novel once again, this time in 1915 focusing on his grandfather.

The amalgamation of story and history, that is, Saleem's personal story and the national history of India, forms an overall structural skeleton of the novel. Through the two simultaneous births, Saleem's and India's, Rushdie sets up a mirror between events in Saleem's family and events in India's tumultuous history from 1915 to 1978, a period that includes the following major incidents and eras: 1) The colonial era; 2) World War One; 3) World War Two; 4) Independence from England; 5) Pakistan's secession from India; 6) The war between India and Pakistan; 7) The war between Pakistan's Eastern and Western wings; 8) The secession of Bangladesh (the Western wing) from Pakistan; 9) Indira Gandhi's State of Emergency; 10) The Lifting of the State of Emergency.

Within this macrocosmic game, we follow Saleem's family which also experiences ups and downs until most of them die in 1965 during the Indo-Pakistani war. Throughout the novel Saleem tries to make sense of the chaotic manifestations of history and his own life, and far into the narrative he maintains the illusion that he plays a central and important role in India's history. Yet, he eventually realises his fate as a peripheral person, just as he realises that he is not even the child of Ahmed and Amina Sinai. At midnight on 15 August 1947 yet another boy child is born apart from Saleem and in an attempt to exercise her own social justice, the nurse Mary Pereira swaps the two boys. Saleem turns out to be the biological son of the poor Vanita and the Englishman William Methwold.

The other child, Shiva, whose real parents are then Ahmed and Amina, is deprived of the opportunity to grow up in a wealthy family and turns into Saleem's ferociously violent alter ego instead. In addition to that, and as a result of subtle coincidences, Shiva winds up as the father of Saleem's foster-son.

In the first part of the novel Saleem unfolds the entire family album, with his grandfather Aadam Aziz as a point of departure, without the reader knowing about the true genealogical connections. In 1915 Aadam Aziz returns to his home in Kashmir having studied in Heidelberg for five years to become a doctor. He is soon confronted by the boatman Tai, whom he loved to sail with as a young boy while Tai was telling him stories. Tai despises the preference in the West of science and the belief in progress, he represents a mythical and an unchangeable universe. Like this, the novel consists of antagonistic worldviews which it often allows to stand as autonomous entities in dialogue or in confrontation with one another.

As a returned doctor, Aadam is called to the home of a landowner to attend to his daughter, Naseem. Naseem is concealed behind a white sheet with a hole at the centre through which Aadam must examine her for the good of decency. Aadam and Naseem fall in love despite all the precautions, and the landowner eventually yelds his consent to their marriage, but all this happens bit by bit. Later on we will see how this fragmentary perspectivism, symbolised in the perforated sheet, forms both a narratological and an epistemological point in Rushdie's works. Aadam and Naseem settle down in Agra where they have two sons and three daughters. The family is whirled around by a number of macro-cosmic events and problems, including the massacre in Amritsar, the flourishing of the nationalist movement, and the problematic question of religion. After her first unsuccessful and unperformed marriage, the middle daughter Mumtaz marries Ahmed Sinai and is given the new name Amina. Ahmed and Amina move to Bombay where Ahmed embarks on several dubious business adventures, generating fortunes for the family but also threatening it with ruin. The family buys a great villa owned by William Methwold in an affluent part of Bombay. The takeover takes place exactly as India gains its independence and Saleem is born. Hence, the main character does not enter the world until at the end of the first part of the novel. The second part is about Saleem's happy childhood in Bombay and it contains biographical features from Rushdie's own life. The reader is presented with an exceptionally affectionate and empathetic portrait of the city, and a hatful of humorous incidents are brought out with Saleem at the centre and later also his sister, The Brass Monkey.

The 1001 children who are born in the novel's India in the midnight hour when the country gains its independence all grow up with magic skills. They are brought together by Saleem whose magic skill is the ability to move about in other people's minds. He founds the Midnight's Conference Club, the purpose of which it is to contribute to the development of India in a positive direction. However, Saleem soon has to give up the good intentions as the dream of harmony and collectivity is undermined by the pluralist complexity of the club. This movement from hope to resignation also turns out to become a movement that characterises the development of both Saleem and India. The novel's initial tone of optimism grows increasingly rough and pessimistic and the illusions of childhood burst when Saleem enters puberty and adulthood. At least this is how things appear if we allow Saleem to be the centre of our judgement: Saleem loses his entire family in a bomb attack; he is struck by amnesia in the same decisive incident; later on he is enlisted in the Pakistani army as a tracking-dog; and, finally, he is tortured and vasectomised.

One may argue, however, that the pessimism at the personal level is counterbalanced by the form of the novel which signals optimism and an alternative spectrum of possibilities with its welter of self-generating stories, its pluralism, and lack of closure. Actually, Rushdie has suggested this idea himself as a comment to the Indian criticism of the novel's pessimism:

> What I tried to do was to set up a tension in the text, a paradoxical opposition between the form and content of the narrative. The story of Saleem does indeed lead him to despair. But the story is told in a manner designed to echo, as closely as my abilities allowed, the Indian talent for non-stop self-regeneration. This is why the narrative constantly throws up new stories, why it "teems." The form – multitudinous, hinting at the infinite possibilities of the country – is the optimistic counterweight to

Saleem's personal tragedy. I do not think that a book written in such a manner can really be called a despairing work (IH, 16).

Regardless of what feeling one is left with after reading the novel, it remains a fact that the development of India in the years after the publication of the novel proved to kill any of the positive hopes the novel may contain. On the occasion of the fortieth anniversary of India's independence, Rushdie visited the country to make a documentary on the real midnight children. In the subsequent essay, "The Riddle of Midnight: India, August 1987," Rushdie reflects on development of the country and the ending of his novel:

> I remember that when *Midnight's Children* was first published in 1981, the most common Indian criticism of it was that it was too pessimistic about the future. It's a sad truth that nobody finds the novel's ending pessimistic any more, because what has happened in India since 1981 is so much darker than I had imagined. If anything, the book's last pages, with their suggestion of a new, more pragmatic generation rising up to take over from the midnight children, now seem absurdly, romantically optimistic (IH, 33).

Thus it was a sad Rushdie who took stock of his visit. Yet he finishes the essay indicating an uninterrupted belief in the continued existence of India as a nation.

The novel has rightly been viewed as one of the best novels of the second part of the twentieth century. First of all it is highly equilibristic in terms of style, and Rushdie's narrative drive and energy is not surpassed in any of his successive novels. But secondly, and perhaps more importantly, the novel, in terms of literary history, has come to epitomise something new on account of its hybridity and internationalism, betokening a showdown with the traditional concept of national literatures. In Franco Moretti's words, the novel may be characterised as "a perfect compromise formation" between the oriental and the occidental. "For the first time in modern history, the centre of gravity of formal creation leaves Europe, and a truly worldwide literary system – the *Weltliteratur* dreamed of by the aged Goethe – replaces the narrower European circuit"

(Moretti, 1996, 249, 233), says Moretti. This development was initiated by Gabriel García Marquez's *One Hundred Years of Solitude* (1968), but Moretti also adds *Midnight's Children* to the process.

Shame

With *Shame* Rushdie's focus centres on Pakistan. As the previous novel, *Shame* is a family novel, its narrative spanning three to four generations. In *Shame*, however, we follow not one but three families' mutual relations. In the first part of the novel we are introduced to the peripheral hero Omar Khayyam Shakil who is born in his grandfather's death-bed by three mothers, Chhunni, Munnee, and Bunny, whose lives are so concurrent that the narrator cannot tell which one is Omar's real mother. The only thing we know about Omar's father is that he is English and that Omar's conception takes place during a grandiose party thrown by the three sisters shortly upon their father's death when they realise that the family fortune is nonexistent. Omar grows up as a "spoiled and vulpine brat" (S, 31), isolated in the labyrinthine house Nishapur (the city of night): "Omar Khayyam Shakil was afflicted, from his earliest days, by a sense of inversion, of a world turned upside-down. And by something worse: the fear that he was living at the edge of the world, so close that he might fall off at any moment" (S, 21). Omar spends his time reading in his grandfather's library and (unsuccessfully) mapping the internal architecture of the house with its innumerable rooms and corridors during his nocturnal strays. As a child he also develops the voyeuristic tendencies that, for the rest of his life, will characterise him as "a creature of the edge: a peripheral man" (S, 24) determined by other people's actions.

On his twelve-year birthday, Omar is allowed for the first time to leave the claustrophobic atmosphere of Nishapur as he is to start at school. It is Omar's wish to get out of Nishapur and this wish has divided the mothers for the first time: "He was not free. His roving freedom-of-the-house was only the pseudo-liberty of a zoo animal; and his mothers were his loving, caring keepers" (S, 35). In school Omar, being a fat oddball with a highly suspicious origin and upbringing, is bullied, beaten, and considered an utter imp, all of which only advances and consolidates his escape into the marginal life of voyeurism. But Omar is extremely intelligent and carries a voluminous intellectual baggage from the hours spent in his grandfather's library where he taught himself Classical Persian, Greek, Latin, German, and French. In addition, his self-education comprises the art of hypnosis which he exploits in the seduction of his schoolmate Farah Zoroaster with whom he is in love. Farah gets pregnant, but Omar escapes any suspicion as their common teacher, Rodrigues, assumes the shame, marries her, and leaves the city. After a desperate phase of drinking and other debauchery, Omar is granted a scholarship for medicine in Karachi and we leave him on the train out of Q.

In the second part of the novel the focus turns to the two families Hyder and Harappa who will later come to represent the supreme power of Pakistan. Alternately, we follow Bilquìs and Raza Hyder, their two daughters Sufiya Zinobia (Shame) and Naveed (Good News), in addition to Rani and Iskander Harappa and their daughter Arjumand (Virgin Ironpants). Rani is Raza's cousin and later Omar marries Sufiya, whereby our peripheral hero re-enters the story. Raza Hyder is a military man and an immigrant from Delhi, where he met Bilquìs under extreme circumstances. Raza becomes a national hero after his conquest of the Aansu valley, but is later sidelined and demoted to the position of commander of the Military Training Academy. Raza does not regain his powerful position until Iskander's election victory. Between the two of them Isky is the profane man-about-town, the epicurean, whereas Raza is the puritan leader who fanatically keeps to the sacred road of virtuousness as instructed by the Koran. Through the stories of the Hyder and Harappa families, the novel provides the reader with a thorough picture of the unfolding of power in Pakistan, and by reducing the story line to two families, Rushdie also emphasises the monopolistic tendencies of power formations in dictatorial, tyrannical, or theocratic states.[12]

---

12   Rushdie has defined the novel as follows: "it's a book about the private life of the master race" (Haffenden, 50). This one-sided view on the elite is criticized by Aijaz Ahmad in his book *In Theory*. Initially Ahmad admits that the technique in the novel has a point in regard to its subject matter: "This plot device of turning all the antagonists into relatives is a wonderful technical resolution for reflecting the monopolistic structure of dictatorial power and the very narrow social spectrum within which this power in Pakistan circulates" (Ahmad, 140). But in Ahmad's emancipatory, Marxist optics it is despairing that Rushdie (according to Ahmad) does not open

Sufiya, the miracle that went wrong, the daughter who should have been a son, turns into an abstract personification of the shame that the surrounding world is too shameless to feel. The characters of the novel are all placed on an axis between shame and shamelessness, which are the two extreme positions from which violence erupts according to the narrator: "Between shame and shamelessness lies the axis upon which we turn; meteorological conditions at both these poles are of the most extreme, ferocious type. Shamelessness, shame: the roots of violence" (S, 115-16). Sufiya, as a mentally retarded character, in this way turns into a tabula rasa, the epitome of innocence, on which the world's stock of unfelt shame inscribes itself, and gradually this innocence turns into a killing machine as shame and humility reach their utmost limits and change into violence. Omar is Sufiya's contrast, the shameless, fattish sensualist and lecher, who in his prime toured the brothels and bars of the city with Isky and exploited his hypnotic skills for sexual purposes, wealthy Western women gladly allowing themselves to be enticed by Omar's exoticism. But shame and shamelessness meet as patient and doctor, and Omar's status as a world famous immunologist dedicated to science forces him to take care of the hopeless case of Sufiya, and little by little he develops a tender care for this partially innocent child in an adult body.

Having shown us the reversals of power, the rigging of elections, corruption, political murders, the suppressed position of women, and the military coups in Pakistan – where Isky becomes the country's first elected president, but is later removed by Raza in a coup – the novel ends with Raza, Bilquìs, and Omar's escape to Nishapur where they seek refuge, Raza having been ousted from power too. However, they also seek protection against Sufiya who has fled from sedation and incarceration in the attic of the Hyders' and now roams Pakistan like a ferocious animal. In this way, Omar returns to his mothers' home for the first time in forty years. But what awaits Omar and Raza are three vengeful women. Omar has lost his position as their favourite son as his younger brother, whom he has never met, has suffered a martyr's death as a guerrilla. Death was

---

up for the potential power of the masses, minorities or women. I do not agree with Ahmad on this point, which I will return to later.

brought upon Babar precisely through Raza Hyder, the chief commander of military operations in Q. at the time. The novel ends like the previous two novels in an apocalyptic explosion. Bilquìs dies from malaria, Raza is killed by the sisters, and Omar is caught up by Sufiya who, like the narrator in *Midnight's Children*, explodes in a nuclear fission.

In *Shame* the themes of migration and exile are developed to encompass new and wider perspectives. This happens both through ideas explicitly put forward by the narrator in essayist, meta-reflective key passages, but, as will be shown, the themes of migration and exile are also expressed more implicitly through the gallery of characters in the fictive universe where a character like Bilquìs, for example, invites an analysis of identity with the concepts of migration and exile as a pivotal point.

The Satanic Verses

The Satanic Verses is – with or without the Rushdie Affair – Rushdie's most complex novel. The Affair has merely contributed to this complexity, though, as it no longer seems possible to read the novel innocently, detached from the enormous amount of commentary which often wanders off into metaphysical abstractions about the freedom of speech, blasphemy, otherness, and fundamentalism. Knowing that an innocent reading is impossible, I will still make an attempt to approach the novel in a rather craftsman-like fashion and make an effort to carry out a literary analysis of the novel's complexity that prioritises the novel itself. I will postpone a more detailed account of the course of the Rushdie Affair and its ramifications to the end of the book.

The novel's two protagonists are the Muslim Indians Gibreel Farishta and Saladin Chamcha. They both grow up in Bombay, Gibreel in poverty and Saladin in an affluent home. Like his father, Gibreel is hired by a company that delivers lunch-pails to offices in Bombay, and when his mother and father die, he is invited to live in the home of his superior whereby he gets into contact with the expanding Indian film industry. For four years he has to settle for minor comic parts before he breaks through with several star roles as avatars of Hindu deities. Gibreel Farishta becomes India's most famous film star. Saladin Chamcha is sent to a boarding school in England at an early age and, whereas Gibreel develops an early hostility to English influence, Saladin embraces Englishness and deserts his Indian background, encouraged not least by the problematic relationship he has with his father, the businessman Changez Chamchawalla. Like Gibreel, Saladin ends up in the entertainment industry, as an actor and imitator of voices.

The novel opens *in medias res* with the two main characters falling from an exploded aeroplane, which they survive miraculously. The scene immediately establishes the required contract with the reader who is led to understand that this novel is based on imagination and a tone of playfulness. Gibreel and Saladin land on the English coast where they stay with the ageing Rosa Diamond for a brief while. For both of them, the after-effects of the fall turn out to be severe. Saladin slowly transforms into a goat, complete with devil's horns, a thick covering of hair, a sulphurous breath, and hooves, whereas Gibreel assumes angelic features, noticeable primarily by the luminous halo above his head. Saladin is arrested by the police, with Gibreel as a passive onlooker, and is subjected to terrible abuse which does not tally with his immaculate idea of England and its law enforcement. After his release, he turns to his English wife Pamela who, expecting her husband to be dead, has started an affair with Saladin's old study mate, the thumb-sucking Jumpy Joshi. Saladin is allowed to live in the attic of the Shaandaar Café which he has been escorted to by his repentant friend, Jumpy, and here he undergoes another metamorphosis before finally regaining his human features.

Gibreel has crossed the oceans with the purpose of locating Alleluia Cone, the female conqueror of Mount Everest, with whom he has had a brief, but electric relationship in Bombay after losing his belief in God. Like Saladin, Gibreel goes through a number of metamorphoses during his stay in London, and as his relationship with Allie develops, he becomes pathologically jealous, which grows into paranoid schizophrenia and eventually leads him to kill Allie and his agent, the stuttering S.S. Sisodia. Saladin, on the other hand, recovers and appears to have accepted a compromise between his English and Indian roots.

As his mental health deteriorates, Gibreel is haunted by two episodic dreams, charting parallel universes alongside the contemporary story about Gibreel and Saladin. One of the dream tracks is about the history of the creation of the Koran and about Mohammad's revelations. It is predominantly passages from this track in the novel's narrative that have enraged Muslims all over the world. Gibreel dreams about himself as the archangel Gabriel and when Gibreel loses faith in God in the course of a serious disease, the dreams turn into a drama about faith and doubt, about originality, authenticity, and blasphemy. The other dream track is about the inhabitants of the village of Titlipur in present day India where a girl of humble birth, Ayesha, is suddenly transformed into a butterfly girl upon receiving a revelation from the archangel Gabriel. The revelation orders the villagers to complete a pilgrimage to Mecca on foot. Ayesha succeeds in convincing the villagers of the truth of the revelation and the only one who opposes the project is the local zamindar, Mirza Saeed Akhtar. Thus the contrasts of faith and science and of miracles and rational explanations are played out in this track of the narrative.

Above all, the novel is an examination of human identity. "When a man is unsure of his essence, how may he know if he be good or bad?" (SV, 192). Human identity is examined for all its diversity in *The Satanic Verses* and by introducing themes like history, religion, the past, family, nationality, and doubt, Rushdie weaves a canvas of humanity in which several historical ages coexist.

In terms of narrative technique, the novel also orchestrates an indecisive game between the satanic and the divine as the narrator of the novel, who mainly keeps a distance to the fictive universe, is of an evanescent and elusive quality and asserts himself/herself as satanic-angelic. In this way the key themes of the novel about faith and doubt and the satanic and the divine are not only played out on the level of story, they are also produced by the actual enunciation, that is to say the way in which the story is told.

COMPOSITION AND ENUNCIATION

> "A story has no beginning or end: arbitrarily one chooses that moment of experience from which to look back or from which to look ahead."
> – Graham Greene: *The End of the Affair*

Any analysis of the compositions of Rushdie's novels will have to answer the following questions: What significance does beginning, middle, and end have? Are the compositions of the novels linear or digressive? Is there a connection between composition and content? In analysing the novel's enunciation, on the other hand, the following questions will have to be answered, which are for the most part mutually dependent: What do we see? From where do we see it? Who is speaking? In what way is he or she speaking? The answers to these questions establish the first important step in our examination of the novels' rhizomatic character as they provide us with a fairly precise idea of the novels' formal designs.

Midnight's Children

Midnight's Children is a tightly composed novel in three parts. It comprises two storylines (the first being the story of Saleem's life, the second being the story about the writing of the book) and a level of narration (meta-reflective commentaries). The outer form of the novel makes up a 1-2-1 composition where the part in the middle is double the length of the first and the last part. The first book consists of eight chapters of 112 pages in all, the second book consists of fifteen chapters of 224 pages and the third book consists of seven chapters of 118 pages. The length of the chapters varies from ten to twenty-two pages, but most chapters are about fifteen pages long. Accordingly, the composition bears the stamp of symmetry (the length of the three parts corresponds to a 1-2-1 ratio, and the number of chapters is also characterised by the fact that the part in the middle equals the sum of the first and the last part), a steady rhythm (the length of the chapters is more or less even) and, finally, a conspicuous propensity to create designs. Hence, the outer form seems like a carefully devised piece of structural engineering, holding together the novel's multitude of interlaced stories.[13]

The narrated time of the novel spans sixty-three years from the early spring of 1915 to August 1978. One of the climaxes in the story is Saleem's birth which takes place in 1947, thirty-two years before the beginning of the narrated time and thirty-one years before the end of it. This level of the novel is also characterised by symmetry. The novel is chronologically constructed on the level of the first storyline as the first book deals with the years from 1915 to 1947, the second book is about the years from 1947 to 1965 and the third book is about the years from 1965 to 1978. Yet, the novel contains ellipses of time, in the sense that the years 1919-42, 1965-70 and 1973 are not narrated. Once again we may identify a symmetrical pattern spreading out across the eighteen narrated years in the second part of the novel insofar as nine years are narrated in the first part and eight years are narrated in the third part. Clearly the frame and the outer form of *Midnight's Children* have been carefully conceived and are remarkably well-composed, and may be characterised as a 1-2-1 composition on several levels.

---

13   The concept of story is to be understood as the causal storyline of literature, characterised by a basic chronology. The concept is related to *fabula* in Russian Formalism and Genette's *histoire*. When the story is aesthetically motivated, that is to say when it is no longer represented in the form of an immediate logic of causality, I will use the concept of plot or discourse, which is related to the Formalists' idea of *sjuzet* and Genette's *récit/discours*. I will refer to the actual act of enunciation as the act of narration, in line with Genette, or, in short, narration. Another distinction that I will make is between history (high story, Hi-story) and story (low story or his story). Story has been described above, whereas history is to be understood as the macrocosmic forces that have influence on or are influenced by the microcosmic stories. One example of this is the distinction between Saleem's story and India's history.

Part of the Novel	Book One	Book Two	Book Three
Composition	1	2	1
Chapters	8	15	7
Pages	112	224	118
Narrated Periods	1915-19 + 1942-47	1947-65	1970-73 + 1974-78
Narrated Time	9	18	8

The outer form of *Midnight's Children*.

To sum up, the symmetrical 1-2-1 composition is repeated in the number of chapters in each part of the novel (8-15-7), in the length of each part (112-224-118) and in the length of the narrated time (9-18-8). Moreover, Saleem's birth occupies the centre of the narrated time.

On the other hand, if we include the level of the second storyline and the level of narration in our analysis, the symmetry, the steady rhythm and the immediate order begin to take a completely different shape and, at times, it even splinters. The time of Saleem's enunciation (his act of narration), that is, the time of writing down his auto-biography, constitutes the weeks leading up to his thirty-first birthday on 15 August 1978. The framing story of the novel, the level of the second storyline, takes place in a pickles factory where Saleem is the creative chef of the production of pickles and chutney in the day time, while in the night time he writes his autobiography with Padma as a listener.

The storytelling of the novel is characterised by Saleem's digressions and establishment of connections, constantly breaking the linear progression of the main story. As a consequence, the steady rhythm in the length of the chapters that we have identified in the outer form of the novel is replaced by a rhythm which persistently varies between main stories and sub-stories. Figuratively speaking, millions of stories have been inscribed in and on Saleem's body, which are all waiting to be told, which also explains why Saleem does not always manage to hold them back or tell them at the right moment in regard to the chronology of the general story. The narrator's slips of tongue provide the reader with premonitions of future events and often it is told explicitly what will happen, but not when and how it will happen. In addition to the many anticipations of events (prolepsis), Rushdie also uses the reverse technique, analepsis or resumé, where the foregoing events are summarised, assisting the reader in keeping stock of the confusion of stories that the novel contains. The meta-fictive passages that are incessantly inserted by Saleem in-between the stories he tells also infuse more nuance into the rhythm. In this way the novel shifts between past and present, between the narrated events on the two levels of story and the reflective passages on the level of narration, the latter dealing with the pragmatic conditions of the novel, that is, with the question of how a novel functions.

The rhythm of the plot in *Midnight's Children* turns out to be more complicated than the outer form indicates at first sight on account of the length of the chapters. As Nancy Batty points out, the rhythm of the entire novel is determined by the tension between the listener Padma's "what-happened-nextism" and the narrator Saleem's play with concealment and disclosure: "Saleem's narrative, for all it stutters, stumbles and digresses – *because* it stutters, stumbles and digresses – strikes a carefully poised balance between concealment and disclosure" (Batty, 56). *Midnight's Children* thus assumes the quality of an erotic machine of seduction where the narrator and the listener enter into a dialogical partnership as each other's complementary factors. As far as Padma is concerned, she cannot be viewed as the chorus of a Greek tragedy, the way Uma Parameswaran does (Parameswaran, 1988, 8), which is constantly present on stage without prompting any action. It is true that Padma is Saleem's necessary ear (a passive listener), but at the same time she is an active co-creator of the narrative performed by the narrator Saleem (in the construction of an auto-biography).

Saleem's use of prolepsis and analepsis resembles the technique we know from film-trailers and resumés of TV-series. The thirty chapters of the novel (of almost equal length) draw on an episodic structure: "the chapter by chapter progression of the novel resembles the structure of an episodic film, or serial, in which synopses of previous events provide a rhythmical counterpoint to the tantalizing teasers which anticipate events to come" (Batty, 57). The rhythm is characterised by a shifting between a summarising synopsis and an anticipatory sensationalism, and both techniques represent the narrator's invitation and accommodating gesture towards the reader who is incorporated into the communicative act of the enunciative situation.

One of the great structuring trailers in the novel is Shri Ramram Seth's prophecy of the child that Amina is carrying in her womb. With its enigmatic, metaphorical language the prophecy contains the most important chords to Saleem's life story, but the mysticism of the prophecy leaves the reader (and Amina) puzzled as to the literal content of Ramram Seth's prophecy. As the first storyline of the novel gradually unfolds, the narrator is made aware of the truth and significance of the prophecy. Both prolepsis and analepsis contribute to the creation of order – in small clusters – in the otherwise chaotic texture of the novel. As we have already seen in connection with *Grimus*, Rushdie's compositional principle seems to be of a rather complex nature. *Midnight's Children* confirms this complexity inasmuch as its composition is both 1) a chaotic confusion, irrational, open with a myriad of loose ends and 2) stringently structured and more or less geometrically composed. James Harrison rightly says: "Rushdie delights in 'frayed edges,' 'loose ends,' and 'lives juxtaposed by accident rather than some grand [allegorical] design.' Yet through all his work, cheek-by-jowl with, creating the need for, and counterbalancing this tendency to chaos, there is a constant fascination with pattern, with design, with linking chains of repeated images, motifs, names, and so forth" (Harrison, 40).

The most recurrent principle of composition in *Midnight's Children* is the narrator's insistence on the existence of an analogy between Saleem and India, between story and history, between microcosm and macrocosm. The analogy does not have a natural foundation, however. It represents the narrator's subjective and intellectual endeavour to establish order in chaos. Hence events in India's history are persistently connected with events in Saleem's story, through which public and private space are brought into interaction. Saleem enumerates four "modes of connection" between family and nation: "actively-literally, passively-metaphorically, actively-metaphorically and passively-literally, I was inextricably entwined with my world" (MC, 238). The active-literal mode represents Saleem's direct influence on history (e.g. when he collides with a group of demonstrators on his bicycle and, as a result, causes a subsequent outbreak of riots). The passive-metaphorical mode represents the influence of larger socio-political movements on Saleem's life (e.g. Saleem sees a connection between how India grows much too fast into "adulthood" and his own too fast growth). The active-metaphorical mode represents incidents in Saleem's life which are indirectly connected with events in history (e.g. the mutilation of Saleem's body is seen as a metaphor of India's condition). Finally, the passive-literal mode is the direct influence of history on Saleem's story (e.g. how the freezing of Ahmed's financial means by the state and the blasting of a water reservoir have immediate significance for Saleem's family). Actually, it is only the latter mode that we may consider to be reliable, as the first modes are undermined in the course of the novel as Saleem realises that he has never had a central role in history after all. As has been shown, the two metaphorical modes represent a subjective, intellectual effort of establishing a sense of meaning in a chaotic reality. Saleem tries to harmonise trans-individual forces and the life of the individual through the transversal connections he constructs through history and story or through the state and the individual.

The most important *leitmotif* in the novel is the perforated sheet, which recurs in all three generations of Saleem's family. It becomes a metaphor on several levels of the novel. The first time we meet it is in connection with Aadam Aziz's sick call to his wife-to-be, Naseem, whose father will not allow the young doctor to see his daughter in full body. Instead he has to get to know her fragment by fragment through the "eye" of the sheet. Later on in the novel, Amina teaches herself to love her husband through a persistent sharpening of focus on one part of his body at a time: "she fell under the spell of the perforated sheet of her own parents, because she resolved to fall in love with her husband bit by bit" (MC, 68). In the third generation of the family, it is Saleem's sister, The Brass Monkey or Jamila Singer, who conceals herself behind a sheet-like cloth, covering almost all of her face. Thus, the perforated sheet represents a concrete image of the narrative tension between concealment and disclosure. Apart from representing a concentrate of Saleem's narrative technique, the perforated sheet also points to the existential condition of man who is destined to perceive and realise the world in fragments. And with this we are moving on to the novel's point of view and narrative condition.

*

Enunciation and, with that, the novel's point of view and narrative condition, is not stable in *Midnight's Children*. The narrator Saleem writes down his story in 1978 which provides him with a distance in terms of time to his material and his previous self. For this reason Saleem also shifts between "I" and "he," when he speaks of the main character Saleem. The narrator is both present and absent in the narrated events; he shifts between empathy and distance in relation to his past self. In addition, he is dramatised, meaning that he actively participates and has actively participated in the events of the story; he is present on the level of both story (in the auto-biography and in the framing story) and discourse (the level of narration). It is through Saleem that the story is served to us, the readers, and in this way the consciousness of the narrator becomes the central communicator of the novel's universe.

The narrator moves "plastically" between several different positions: at times he knows more than, at other times he knows as much as, and finally sometimes he knows less than what the situation on the level of events and characters logically allows. When Saleem is confronted with his mother's "black mango" during his stay in the laundry basket and is afterwards transformed into a telepathic communication centre, the main character, hence the narrator, is given access to information that human characters in novels do not usually have. But in this case the narrator's position is not necessarily elevated above the situation of events since the miraculous situation in itself provides the main character with unusual insights. Therefore the narrator only knows as much as the internal logic of the novel's universe allows, a logic determined by the main character's ability to roam through other people's minds.

Obviously, the narrated time before Saleem's birth is problematic with respect to the authority of the narrator. When Saleem tells his grandfather's story, he is placed outside the natural reach of his own perception: "I've been sniffing out the atmosphere in my grandfather's house in those days after the death of India's humming hope" (MC, 52). Saleem explains this knowledge with his olfactory super-skills, but the explanation only succeeds in convincing us in a metaphorical sense. The narrative position in this case contains more information than is logically possible for Saleem to know. Often the point of view is simultaneous with the events before the birth of the narrator, and at times we are given perspectives from within the characters of the novel, as in this case where the observations are about his grandfather's concerns, feelings and physical state in the minutes leading up to the massacre in Amritsar: "He is, I know, feeling very scared, because his nose is itching worse than it ever has" (MC, 35). A very important point may be deduced from passages like this one: the narrator Saleem does not only function as a passive observer and active agent in the novel, he also functions as a creator of the novel's universe and the story that is being told.

A "knowing-more" may also be at issue when it comes to the time distance between the main character Saleem and the narrator Saleem. The narrator's retrospection equips him with a natural omniscience and intellectual surplus in the processing of his material. With his retrospective knowledge, the narrator may withdraw from the storyline and comment on events from an elevated position. The narrator's knowing-more obtained through a distance in time is tied to the level of events and hence there is nothing unnatural about the position.

The same may be argued in cases when the time distance results in a limited point of view and causes a shortage of information. In such cases the narrator does not have access to certain parts of the story's world of experience: "but the curtain descends again, so I cannot be sure" (MC, 87), Saleem admits at one point when memory fails him. The narrator's most important instrument in the creation of his auto-biography is of course his memory, but often this instrument proves to be unreliable: "the past failed to reappear" (MC, 452). The limited point of view is not necessarily a product of the whims of memory, however. Even if memory works well, jumping across the distance of time, the main character, and the narrator Saleem, may find himself excluded from the surrounding world or the people around him: "I must leave the question-marks hanging, unanswered" (MC, 428).

Saleem's dependency on other people's evidence may be seen as another technique of establishing a point of view, which is apparent in comments like these: "he was heard to remark" (MC, 225), and "I am obliged, perforce, to reply on the account of others" (MC, 410). Here the narrator is subjected to the categories of time and space in the novel's universe, which limits his narrative position; our access to parts of the universe depends on the formation of secondary narrators.

As has already been noted, memory is the narrator's most important instrument in the reconstruction of his life story. But memory is a porous foundation which, apart from being capricious, is useless in the reconstruction of the periods that lie outside Saleem's lived life, both in terms of time (before 1947) and in terms of space. Secondary narrators may remedy this problem, but Rushdie's primary solution is to grant the narrator a creative and innovative role in reconstructing the family story, which the following quote may illustrate: "already there are fadings, and gaps; it will be necessary to improvise on occasion" (MC, 384).

In addition to being a reflective and dramatised narrator, Saleem is also a self-conscious narrator. He interrupts the scenic (mimetic) and panoramic (diegetic) levels of enunciation, pertaining to the narrated story, with meta-reflective passages, pertaining to the act of narration and the actual construction of the auto-biography: "'I told you the truth,' I say yet again, 'Memory's truth, because memory has its own special kind. It selects, eliminates, alters, exaggerates, minimizes, glorifies, and vilifies also; but in the end it creates its own reality, its heterogeneous but usually coherent version of events; and no sane human being ever trusts someone else's version more than his own'" (MC, 211). First of all this passage is about Saleem's reflection on his own working method insofar as memory is explicitly considered as a tool in the creative process; secondly, it is a reflection on the ontology of memory which is described as having its own logic of truth.

Saleem's enunciatory freedom, that is, his use of imagination, memory, and secondary narrators, makes him an unreliable narrator. However, as the meta-reflective level of narration may be said to superimpose the two storylines, in such a way that the narrator Saleem is fully aware of and open about his own unreliability, Rushdie's technique of enunciation is different from that of, for instance, Henry James. The narrator in James is unreliable, but this unreliability is not discussed explicitly, whereas the unreliability of Rushdie's narrator is acknowledged and discussed by the narrator himself: "Because I am rushing ahead at breakneck speed; errors are possible, and overstatements, and jarring alterations in tone; I'm racing the cracks, but I remain conscious that errors have already been made, and that, as my decay accelerates (my writing speed is having trouble keeping up), the risk of unreliability grows" (MC, 270).

Both writers seem to recognise unreliability as the condition of subjectivity in perceiving the world, though. Here is Rushdie: "History is always ambiguous. Facts are hard to establish, and capable of being given many meanings. Reality is built on our prejudices, misconceptions and ignorance as well as on our perceptiveness and knowledge. The reading of Saleem's unreliable narration might be, I believed, a useful analogy for the way in which we all, every day, attempt to 'read' the world" (IH, 25). Yet, in James there is an attempt to keep up a mimetic-realistic illusion which is completely ripped open in Rushdie: "I must interrupt myself. I wasn't going to today, because Padma has started getting irritated whenever my narration becomes self-conscious, whenever, like an incompetent puppeteer, I reveal the hands holding the strings" (MC, 65). In *Poetics of Postmodernism* Linda Hutcheon comments on the narrator's role in the postmodern novel and correctly characterises Saleem's point of view as provisional and limited, and she elaborates on this point by drawing special attention to the narrator's repudiation of his own authority: "The perceiving subject is no longer assumed to a coherent, meaning-generating entity. Narrators in fiction become either disconcertingly multiple and hard to locate (as in D.M. Thomas's *The White Hotel*) or resolutely provisional and limited - often undermining their own seeming omniscience (as in Salman Rushdie's *Midnight's Children*)" (Hutcheon, 11). It is beyond doubt that Saleem is the generator of meaning in the novel, but, as we have seen and will see later, his position is not coherent.

The narrator's conscious unreliability - one may be tempted to call it his reliable unreliability - and the fact that the narrator is dramatised, and, as a result, does not have the same distance to his material as a non-dramatised narrator's "objective eye" would have had (e.g. the narrator in Flaubert's *Madame Bovary*), contribute to the enhancement of the novel's fictional nature because it is explicitly acknowledged on the level of narration that the storylines, particularly the first one, are marked by being unreliable and constructed.

Returning to the general compositional aspects of the novel, it might already at this stage be interesting to examine the extent to which the novel corresponds to a rhizomatic construction. The novel consists of thirty chapters, the order of which is determined by a relatively strong subjacent storyline following a causal principle of chronology; but the dominant architecture of the novel is not constituted by a one-stringed storyline. On the contrary, it is characterised by a hotchpotch of stories interlaced with each other and, added to that, the logic of chronology is disrupted by the digressive technique of the narrator who does not only initiate other stories but also inserts reflections and meta-fictive passages, providing the narration with a leaping character.[14] The anti-linear mode of narration relativises and cancels out the traditional structure of beginning, middle, end. The rhizome is precisely characterised as an intermezzo, that is, as something which is persistently situated in the middle. Accordingly, *Midnight's Children* may be said to be an intermezzo-novel in regard to its composition, among other things because it is distinguished by its multiple points of entry: there is no internal necessity in the fact that the novel takes its beginning in 1915 with Saleem's grandfather is not determined by any internal necessity. The narrator might just as well have started his story at any other point in time and space (Aadam is, as you will remember, not even Saleem's grandfather). The novel's ending, with the narrator's vision of his imminent fission, is equally contingent. It might just as well have ended otherwise. Saleem explicitly indicates the contingency of his choice by pointing to the fact that other endings are indeed squeezing for space: "An infinity of new endings clusters around my head" (MC, 444).[15] Accordingly, it only seems to be the requirement

14   Rushdie sees the technique of digression as more important than linear progression, which he has affirmed in an interview with Jean Pierre Durix, among others, in Gothenburg, 1982: "the digressions are almost the point of the book, in which the idea of multitude is a central notion. When I started writing, I just tried to explain one life, and it struck me more and more that, in order to explain this life, you had to explain a vast amount of material which surrounded it, both in space and time. In a country like India you are basically never alone. The idea of solitude is a luxury which only the rich people enjoy" (Durix, 2000, 13).

15   Likewise Linda Hutcheon pays attention to *Midnight's Children*'s "resolutely arbitrary closure" (Hutcheon, 59). This is also what Lukács means when he speaks of the lack in the novel of a "true-born organic relationship": "The consequence of this, from the compositional point of view, is that, although the characters and their actions possess the infinity of authentic epic literature, their structure is essentially different from that of the epic. The structural difference in which this fundamentally

of symmetry in the outer form that motivates the choice of a beginning and an end. Moreover, the novel reflects the basic view we have come across in Grimus that any ending contains the seed of a new beginning. This is shown on the level of composition in *Midnight's Children* through the multiplicity of stories that incessantly generate each other.

The novel reflects a processual worldview in which beginnings and endings are contingent, illusory points and in which also the chronological, straight line is replaced by discontinuity and autonomous time-images. In addition, the hierarchy between the main plot and the sub-plots seems to be an untenable abstraction as the stories are mutually dependent. The cartography of the novel is charted as a tapestry of interwoven and anti-hierarchical stories rather than a hierarchically determined division of plot and subplot. We still remember that the narrator Saleem and his life story are complex entities: "To understand just one life, you have to swallow the world. I told you that" (MC, 109).

Accordingly, the composition of the novel seems to correspond to a rhizomatic construction. *Midnight's Children* deconstructs the traditional hierarchy between main story and sub-stories and establishes a "flat" cartography where the stories are interlaced with one another as in a network of grass-roots. The stories become almost self-generating and, as such, they are just waiting to be told. The symmetrical outer form of the novel turns out to be contingent, but at the same time the form is an outcome of the necessary cutting of material that the narrator has to undertake in a world where everything leaks into everything else: "'Things – even people – have a way of leaking into each other,' I explain, 'like fla-

conceptual pseudo-organic nature of the material of the novel finds expression is the difference between something that is homogeneously organic and stable and something that is heterogeneously contingent and discrete. Because of this contingent nature, the relatively independent parts are more independent, more self-contained than those of the epic and must therefore, if they are not to destroy the whole, be inserted into it by means which transcend their presence. In contrast to the epic, they must have a strict compositional and architectural significance" (Lukács, 76). What Lukács says, among other things, is that the composition of a novel does no longer naturally shape itself according to an existing material as in the epic. On the contrary, composition has now become the designing principle itself, the task of which it is to "master" an unmanageable chaotic material, cognisant of the fact that it will always remain a contingent frame.

vours when you cook'" (MC, 38). The contingent but absolutely necessary choices the narrator – and the writer – has to make in regard to beginning and end indicate the status of the novel as an incision into chaos (Deleuze) or as a strip of the canvas of the universe (Kundera). Hence the thirty chapters of the novel and the stories they tell may, to a certain extent, be said to be replaceable and thus interchangeable. The episodic structure of pro- and analepsis causes the novel to remain an open structure with several different entryways where the element of contingency produces proliferating connections between the stories rather than a pre-existing hierarchy.[16]

Yet, on the face of things, the narrator seems to make up the central source of the flood of stories in *Midnight's Children*. But on the other hand, the narrator's unreliability leads to a continuous self-correction which undermines any claim to an immovable centre. Nevertheless, in order to consolidate the novel's character as rhizomatic, it is necessary to carry out a careful analysis of identity in *Midnight's Children*. But before I do that, we will examine composition and enunciation in *Shame* and *The Satanic Verses*.

Shame

We do not find the same forced mania for formal design in *Shame* as was the case in the outer form of *Midnight's Children*. The novel consists of five parts and, if anything, the five parts allude to the form of the tragedy consisting of five acts. In terms of content the novel is also a tragedy in many ways, although the satirical tone results in an intermixture of the comic and the tragic, which is something Rushdie himself has commented upon: "Although the relationship between Raza and Iskander is basically tragic, the actual figures are clowns – gangsters, hoodlums – and not people who deserve Shakespearian tragedy. So you have to bring comedy into it – you have to write black comedy, because they are

---

[16] Rushdie says to Durix: "The logical extension of the phrase 'to understand one life you have to swallow a world' is that the book never finishes. So you have to find a convention for limiting it" (Durix, 2000, 13).

black-comedy figures – and I rewrote the entire book, changing the tone, making it lighter" (Haffenden, 39).

The structure of the novel is circular: it begins by describing Omar's childhood in Nishapur from his birth to the bibliofilia of his puberty years, and the end of the novel takes the reader back to Nishapur where Omar fights for his life in exactly the same bed of death and birth, only to be finally consumed by Sufiya's mesmerising eyes and her subsequent explosion. The story line winds away from Nishapur like a spiral and returns to Nishapur – together with the remaining main characters Omar, Bilquìs, Raza, and Sufiya – by way of the spiral, too.

Shame is composed by two levels, the fictive universe of the story, which constitutes the story line itself, and of a meta-level which comments, evaluates and reflects on the events in the fictive universe in a self-conscious manner. The narrative voice in *Shame* also differs from that of *Midnight's Children* as it is contained on the level of narration and is never dramatised on the level of the fictive events. In other words, the narrator does not participate and has never participated on the level of the story the way Saleem does; accordingly, Rushdie moves from a first person narrator to a third person narrator. Still, one may point to the fact that many of the narrative techniques used in *Midnight's Children* are also employed in *Shame*, with a few variations of course.

The narrator in *Shame* carries numerous biographical resemblances with Rushdie himself, which has caused many critics to draw a problematic link between narrator and author. Admittedly, the narrator's discourse in Shame is in many ways more monologically and politically unambiguous than in Rushdie's other novels. In contrast to the writer's position vis à vis his material in *Midnight's Children*, the writer's distance to his material in *Shame* does not depend on the whims of memory only. Rushdie writes about a Pakistan where he has never really been and for that reason it is necessary for him to dress the novel's narrator with a certain kind of authority, who would otherwise face great difficulty in maintaining a bond of credibility with the reader. This explains the biographical material in which the narrator is wrapped. It serves the purpose of endowing the novel's enunciation with reliability. However, this does not mean that the narrator lays a claim to an unambiguous objectivity in regard to his material, rather, as in *Midnight's Children*, the narrator continuously points to an unavoidable perspectivism in his point of view: "I think what I'm confessing is that, however I choose to write about over-there, I am forced to reflect that world in fragments of broken mirrors, the way Farah Zoroaster saw her face at the bollarded frontier. I must reconcile myself to the inevitability of the missing bits" (S, 69); in addition, he concedes that his material and stories are products of selective choice: "every story one chooses to tell is a kind of censorship, it prevents the telling of other tales" (S, 71); in extension of this, he continues: "All stories are haunted by the ghosts of the stories they might have been" (S, 116).[17]

Biographical similarities between the narrator and the writer include, for instance, the narrator's confession that he resides in London: "I, too, know something of this immigrant business. I am an emigrant from one country (India) and a newcomer in two (England, where I live, and Pakistan, to which my family moved against my will)" (S, 85). As the narrator, Rushdie and his family moved to Karachi in Pakistan. Moreover the narrator mentions his relation to his youngest sister, whom he has only seen a few times with years inbetween, and, finally, one of the three events that constitute the character of Sufiya may be said to contain biographical elements; the episode of the girl being assaulted on the Underground train in London is an exposure of an incident experienced by Rushdie's oldest sister, Sameen. There are other events on the novel's meta-level that carry traits of biographical material, for example the narrator's night with Pakistani friends at the theatre and the episode in Pakistan where the narrator visits a fellow-writer later to be arrested. As

17   Likewise the historian and philosopher Hayden White notes the inevitability of the selective choice that historians deal with despite their intentions of objectivity: "For in fact every narrative, however seemingly 'full,' is constructed on the basis of a set of events which might have been included but were left out; and this is as true of imaginary as it is of realistic narratives" (White, 10). Selectivity results in an inescapable coupling together of narrativity and morality, says White, and we may draw a parallel to Plato's moral distinction between the good and the bad pretenders. Similarly, there is a claim to the good or true story in traditional historiography, whereas in Rushdie one finds an attempt to carry out an archaeological excavation in Foucauldian terms, which primarily emerges through the combination of lenses (points of view) Rushdie applies by turning his gaze to, for example, the women's discourse in *Shame*.

said, this discourse is necessary for Rushdie in order for him to forestall expected criticism of his status as an outsider without authority, a criticism that the narrator also explicitly anticipates in the novel:

> *Outsider! Trespasser! You have no right to this subject!...* I know: nobody ever arrested me. Nor are they ever likely to. *Poacher! Pirate! We reject your authority. We know you, with your foreign language wrapped around you like a flag: speaking about us in your forked tongue, what can you tell but lies?* I reply with more questions: is history to be considered the property of the participants solely? In what courts are such claims staked, what boundary commissions map out the territories? (S, 28).

The narrator insists on his right to chart his subjective territories and indirectly points out the advantages of distance in the cartographic process initiated by the artist: "It is the true desire of every artist to impose his or her vision on the world" (S, 87).

However, the requisite claim to authority via the plane of events on the meta-level is interlaced with a concurrent recognition of the limitation of the perspective in the fictive universe that comprises the actual storyline in *Shame*. The narrator emphasises the conditionality of his point of view several times: he depends on rumours and family legend: "there are rumours" (S, 13), "I am quoting from the family legend again" (S, 90); he points out the uncertainty of events in the fictive universe: "What is almost certainly true is" (S, 13); he admits his own incapacity: "I am unable to clear away the improbabilities" (S, 16); in short, "I can't be expected to know everything" (S, 238), he concludes. Thus the narrator is characterised by a double role: first, an authoritarian role, but at the same time also a role of alignment on par with the characters and the reader.[18]

---

18 In an interview with David Brooks in 1984, Rushdie says: "to present the author in the work at the same level as the fictional material, instead of saying here I am above the story telling you what to think about this thing that you already think strong things about. To put yourself into the story, or myself into the story, was a way of saying that I was only a part of the thing that I was discussing, and to explain where it was that I was coming from, where it was that my point of view emerged from, and to make myself part of the dispute, part of the debate. Because then, it seemed to me, it was legitimate to use that material in the way that everybody else

Authority does not only emanate from the credibility-building biographical material that the narrator dresses himself in. Authority emerges through assertions like this too: "it is my unshakeable opinion" (S, 20) where the narrator clearly claims to be familiar with the status of the fictive universe. As readers we do not have any reason to suspect him either, as the narrator, by his own admitting, is not a neutral observer of events, but aware of his partisan role, which he constantly points out to the reader. As in *Midnight's Children*, he stands forth as a self-conscious creator of the fictive universe, through which, of course, he is automatically bestowed with a considerable amount of authority. For example, the narrator's control of his own material is expressed in the following exclamation: "I command this death scene back into the wings at once: shazam!" (S, 23).

The narrator adds yet another layer to the novel's problematic of authority as he claims that the country he is talking about may only be partially perceived as Pakistan: "The country in this story is not Pakistan, or not quite. There are two countries, real and fictional, occupying the same space, or almost the same space. My story, my fictional country exists, like myself, at a slight angle to reality. I have found this off-centring to be necessary; but its value is, of course, open to debate. My view is that I am not writing only about Pakistan" (S, 29). Here, the mimetic accuracy of the novel's universe is relativised and the narrator elevates his discourse to a higher level of abstraction, whereby he also precludes the potential scepticism of the novel's authenticity mentioned before. The narrator pretends to write about shame, abuse of power, tyranny, and religion in general.

---

would in a discussion" (Brooks, 60). To Haffenden Rushdie underlines exactly this double role of the narrator as the novel's writer and reader: "In *Shame* the author sometimes knows less than a character, and he's obliged to say that there are things he doesn't know. Normally an author is omniscient or not, and to try to make an authorial voice which would shift between the two positions was technically one of the things I enjoyed in the book – sometimes the author is the writer of the story, sometimes he's the reader of the story, and I thought that was quite valuable in providing shading" (Haffenden, 44).

The Satanic Verses

Milan Kundera has characterised the composition of *The Satanic Verses* as a musical rondo (Kundera, 1996, 24). As I have already mentioned, the novel consists of three story lines: A) The story of two contemporary Indians living in Bombay and London. B) The story of Mahound (Muhammad) and the creation of the Koran. C) The story of Ayesha and the villagers' pilgrimage to Mecca. As Kundera notes, the nine parts of the novel are dispensed in the following way: A-B-A-C-A-B-A-C-A. The distinctive characteristic of a rondo is a returning main theme interspersed with a number of sub-themes. Quantitatively, the A-line takes up five-sevenths of the novel's space, whereas the B- and C-lines comprise one-seventh each. The lengths of the chapters are meted out in the following way: A(85)-B(36)-A(74)-C(36)-A(114)-B(36)-A(73)-C(35)-A(37).

As in *Midnight's Children*, *The Satanic Verses* has an equally tight composition, in which it is noteworthy that the B- and C-lines are both of the same length. In this way the outer form plays a part in furnishing this otherwise effervescent novel with a rhythmic precision on the macro-compositional level. So, the novel's centre of gravity is comprised by the A-line about Gibreel and Saladin's contemporary lives, but, as Kundera makes clear, it is within the B- and C-lines – in spite of their subordinate quantitative status – that the *"aesthetic wager"* of the novel is concentrated

> for it is these B and C parts that enable Rushdie to get at the fundamental problem of all novels (that of an individual's, a character's, identity) in a new way that goes beyond the conventions of the psychological novel: Chamcha's and Farishta's personalities cannot be apprehended through a detailed description of their states of mind; their mystery lies in the cohabitation in their psyches of two civilizations, the Indian and the European; it lies in their roots, from which they have been torn but which, nevertheless, remain alive to them (*ibid.*, 22)

Kundera rightly insists on the importance of the composition in relation to the thematic level. He thus supports the definition of Rushdie's novels as political and collective, as subjective identity is inseparably connected with macro-political forces or machines like history, nation, and religion.

The human psyche is not an isolated island in the ocean of the world. In an interview Rushdie tells John Clement Ball about the idea behind the composition: "And I suppose I used in my mind an idea of construction which was mosaic rather than linear, so that I would take a number of stories which were fitted together in a mosaic pattern rather than a straightforward linear pattern. Although each story in itself has obviously – at least I hope so – a strong linear narrative drive. But they fit together at tangents to each other, and that job of making them fit was what was difficult" (Ball, 102). The quote reflects how important composition is to Rushdie: the formation of a mosaic through an amalgamation of heterogeneous elements has more significance than the linear drive of the individual lines. Accordingly, the transitions and the spaces between elements become interesting as this is where metamorphosis takes place: "And I thought that, well, if you're going to write a novel about transformation, then the novel itself should also be metamorphic in form, so it should constantly change" (*ibid.*, 102).

In many ways the mode of narration in *The Satanic Verses* is far more traditional than in Rushdie's previous novels while at the same time it may also be said to be more complex. Narration is predominantly restricted to third person descriptions and the meta-fictional breaches of illusion, which are abundant in *Midnight's Children* and *Shame*, have been toned down. Likewise, the superior, self-conscious handling of the plot through pro- and analepsis that characterised *Midnight's Children* is almost absent. In contrast, we are now presented with an elusive narrator who refuses to identify himself unequivocally; the narrator reveals himself a few times in the course of the novel, but his identity remains obscure. The first time we come across a meta-fictive, self-conscious passage, the narrator poses the following question: "Who am I? Who else is there?" (SV, 4).

Typically, the narrator asks a number of questions when he pops out from the story, which cannot be answered directly. The answers are to be found in the novel's stories, and even here it seems impossible to arrive at any firm conclusions. The following tirade of questions results from the novel's fabulous, breakneck opening when the reader meets Gibreel and Saladin frantically plummeting from 29.002 feet, their jumbo jet having just exploded, the former singing, at times curled up like a ball, at other times doing breaststrokes or crawling through the air, and the latter wearing a suit and English bowler hat, diving head down and arms stiffly straightened along the sides of his body:

> How does newness come into the world? How is it born?
> Of what fusions, translations, conjoinings is it made?
> How does it survive, extreme and dangerous as it is? What compromises, what deals, what betrayals of its secret nature must it make to stave off the wrecking crew, the exterminating angel, the guillotine?
> Is birth always a fall?
> Do angels have wings? Can men fly? (SV, 8).

Here the engaged narrator rolls out a condensed catalogue of the novel's themes: newness, birth and death, compromise and inflexibility in addition to the states of falling and flying. Yet, as said, the questions remain suspended in midair, to some extent at least. But then again, the narrator does make a concession that gives us a clue of his position and character:

> I know the truth, obviously. I watched the whole thing. As to omnipresence and -potence, I'm making no claims at present, but I can manage this much, I hope. Chamcha willed it and Farishta did what was willed.
> Which was the miracle worker?
> Of what type – angelic, satanic – was Farishta's song?
> Who am I?
> Let's put it this way: who has the best tunes? (SV, 10).

Is the narrator satanic, angelic, or simply human? In connection with the opening scene, the narrator claims to know the answer to the questions asked, and, in regard to the ambiguity of his status as satanic or angelic, the last question in the passage indicates that we are dealing with a satanic narrator, insofar as the Devil is said to have the best tunes.

In one of his dreams, in which Gibreel is haunted by agonising doubt, he suddenly sees a man sitting on his bed: "He saw, sitting on the bed, a man of about the same age as himself, of medium height, fairly heavily built, with salt-and-pepper beard cropped close to the line of jaw. What struck him most was that the apparition was balding, seemed to suffer from dandruff and wore glasses. This was not the Almighty he had expected" (SV, 318). The description clearly draws on the traditional icon of God, in view of the heavy body and the beard, but at the same time it is a parody of this archetype, who is suffering from dandruff, a receding hairline and wearing glasses. Is this Ooparvala, the man from "upstairs," or Neechayvala, the man from "downstairs"? Or is this Rushdie himself? Still the text does not provide us with any clear-cut answers, on the contrary, the man on the bed throws a tantrum in response to Gibreel's doubt, refusing to explain his status: "'We are not obliged to explain Our nature to you,' the dressing-down continued. 'Whether We be multiform, plural, representing the union-by-hybridization of such opposites as *Oopar* and *Neechay*, or whether We be pure, stark, extreme, will not be resolved here'" (SV, 319). The appearance of this figure intensifies the complexity of the novel's enunciation as the figure is evidently not the actual narrator. Within the passage there is a cue through which the actual narrator reveals himself as someone else than the figure on the bed ("the dressing-down continued" is not stated by the man on the bed). Yet this figure clearly believes himself to be the novel's narrator, which the following quote plainly illustrates:

> I'm saying nothing. Don't ask me to clear things up one way or the other; the time of revelations is long gone. The rules of Creation are pretty clear: you set things up, you make them thus and so, and then you let them roll. Where's the pleasure if you're always intervening to give hints, change the rules, fix the fights? Well, I've been pretty self-controlled up to this point and I don't plan to spoil things now. Don't think I haven't wanted to butt in; I have, plenty of times. And once, it's true, I did. I sat on Alleluia Cone's bed and spoke to the superstar, Gibreel. *Ooparvala or Neechayvala*, he wanted to know, and I didn't enlighten him (SV, 408-09).

In my view we are dealing with an inconsistency between the two passages above: the first passage unequivocally contains a narrator who is not identical with the figure on the bed and the other passage indicates that the man on the bed is the narrator of the novel. The critics I have read all fail to see this inconsistency, their readings simply identifying the figure on the bed as the novel's narrator. But is it important to make this distinction? Perhaps it just supports the idea of the schizoid narrator who hides behind numerous masks. Besides, Rushdie may not have been conscious about creating the inconsistency.

If the question of the best tunes is an indication of the narrator as satanic and the figure on the bed once again casts doubt on whether the narrator is satanic or angelic, then the following passage presents us with a new indication of the satanic element. The narrator ponders over the fall of the two main characters and the ensuing metamorphoses:

> One man's breath was sweetened, while another's, by an equal and opposite mystery, was soured. What did they expect? Falling like that out of the sky: did they imagine there would be no side-effects? Higher Powers had taken an interest, it should have been obvious to them both, and such Powers (I am, of course, speaking of myself) have a mischievous, almost a wanton attitude to tumbling flies. And another thing, let's be clear: great falls change people. You think *they* fell a long way? In the matter of tumbles, I yield pride of place to no personage, whether mortal or im-. From clouds to ashes, down the chimney you might say, from heavenlight to hellfire... under the stress of a long plunge, I was saying, mutations are to be expected, not all of them random. Unnatural selections (SV, 133).

The narrator proudly claims his fall from heavenlight to hellfire to be an ultimate, matchless fall. Satan? Or Santa Claus? "From the beginning men used God to justify the unjustifiable. He moves in mysterious ways: men say. Small wonder, then, that women have turned to me" (SV, 95). Here the idea of the narrator as God seems unmistakably refutable, but whether it is Satan that women put their trust in is still uncertain. James Harrison challenges any univocal reading in that regard: "there is no case to be made for Satan as the consistent narrator throughout the novel" (Harrison, 114).

The point is that the narrator remains elusive and it is not a static opposition between belief and unbelief that defines Rushdie's universe: "Question: What is the opposite of faith? Not disbelief. Too final, certain, closed. Itself a kind of belief. Doubt" (SV, 92). The logic of exclusion (faith or disbelief) is replaced by a logic of inclusion, in which the narrator may be said to assume a status as being both angelic and satanic – or perhaps rather a human status, as an implicit allegory of the role of the writer. Thus, the pivotal point of the novel's enunciation is doubt, human doubt, which endows the narrator and the novel's universe in general with a schizophrenic nature, explicitly accentuated through the following *leitmotif* that recurs several times throughout the novel: "Once upon a time – *it was and it was not so*, as the old stories used to say, *it happened and it never did* – maybe, then, or maybe not" (SV, 35). In a universe like this, notions like true and false lose their significance as the story carries its own form of truth, that is to say a truth of possibilities.

So far, my examination of the narrator's status has determined him as both satanic and angelic, or perhaps simply human. What do I mean by this? Can we not reach a more precise characterisation? We have to think beyond the traditional connotations about God and Satan as conveyed to us by the Bible and the Koran. It is necessary to anthropomorphise the divine and the satanic, which Deleuze may be said to have done already with his idea of simulacrum.

The narrator in *The Satanic Verses* is a simulacrum. A simulacrum contains both something satanic and something divine. In modernity man ceases to resemble God without ceasing to be an image of God. In an optics like that man is furnished with a grain of divinity, which is expressed precisely in the unique perspective that characterises man as a monad. On the other hand, man as a monad may also be characterised as man as a nomad whose unique perspective is a differential one, and thus he becomes a producer of difference, and it is precisely the satanic part of man, a part that will always preclude any unifying perspective, which will allow diversity to disrupt closed systems of classification.

It is in light of this that I think it is possible to identify the narrator as both satanic and angelic: there is a flicker of (romantic) divinity in the work of art as a unique creation (an incision into chaos, a strip of the canvas of the universe, the monadic perspective), but the angelic element never gets to represent anything pre-existing, such as a divine hierarchy or system, because of the simultaneous presence of the demonic, differential perspective.

The Satanic Verses opens with an epigraph from Daniel Defoe's *The History of the Devil* and Martine Hennard Dutheil calls attention to the alteration Rushdie projects in relation to the "original": in Defoe Satan is portrayed as a migrant, whereas in Rushdie the migrant is portrayed as satanic. Accordingly, and as mentioned above, we need a redefinition or replacement of concepts like the satanic and the divine. Perhaps we should characterise the narrator as a migrant rather than in terms of the satanic and the angelic. In Rushdie's terminology the migrant is a metaphor of humanity, corresponding to Deleuze's nomad and schizoid. Rushdie himself acknowledges the idea of the narrator as a migrant: "If *The Satanic Verses* is anything, it is a migrant's-eye view of the world. It is written from the very experience of uprooting, disjuncture and metamorphosis (slow or rapid, painful or pleasurable) that is the migrant condition, and from which, I believe, can be derived a metaphor for all humanity" (IH, 394).

*

When the narrator appears implicitly in the novel, more or less anonymously and indirectly that is, Rushdie employs various methods in order to chart the universe of the novel. For example, as is also the case in *Midnight's Children* in particular, *The Satanic Verses* is inspired by the narrative techniques in films which function as a contrast to the narrator's discourse exemplified above. As we have seen so far, the narrator's discourse shows commitment and is a questioning discourse, but the novel also makes use of a more neutrally observing camera-eye in its enunciation. Nicholas Rombes has analysed the novel's facets of filmic narration and he also points out the dichotomy in the novel between a committed narrative voice and a disinterested camera description. In addition, Rombes notes how the novel is inspired by film in terms of both language use, point of view, and narrative technique.

Several characters are introduced in a brief, laconic, and pertinent manner as if we were dealing with the stage directions in a screenplay. Mahound is presented as follows: "The businessman: looks as he should, high forehead, eaglenose, broad in the shoulders, narrow in the hip. Average height, brooding, dressed in two pieces of plain cloth, each four ells in length, one draped around his body, the other over his shoulder. Large eyes; long lashes like a girl's" (SV, 93). The filmic vocabulary is also used for sending off characters, as for instance when Miss Pimple Billimoria leaves a (movie)scene with Gibreel: "Exit Pimple, weeping, censored, a scrap on a cutting-room floor" (SV, 13). The novel contains numerous mise-en-abyme scenarios like these, in which representations are enfolded within other representations. In the case of the description of a film shooting, a vocabulary is moved from one area of enunciation, namely the film, to another, namely the novel. Pimple is not only literally censured out of the movie, but also figuratively out of the novel. In relation to the movie, she is literally to be perceived as a useless strip of film tossed on the table in the cutting room, but in a figurative sense she may be understood the same way in relation to the novel. By transferring a filmic use of language to the discourse of the novel like this, Rushdie establishes a close connection between the film and the novel. The novel sponges on the movie, which is not to be understood in a condescending way. What we are witnessing is what Arjun Appadurai calls "the transformation of everyday discourse" (Appadurai, 3), and, along with that, a transformation of the sensibility and epistemological apparatus of the subject; the senses of the reader are sharpened, too, by the de-automatising effect of Rushdie's language use.

Additionally, the filmic strategy is employed by Rushdie to create unusual perspectives on the novel's universes, as for instance in Gibreel's dreams where we come across several reflections on possible angles, as will be shown in the following quote where the novel is once again conveyed as if it were itself a film being shot:

> Gibreel: the dreamer, whose point of view is sometimes that of the camera and at other moments, spectator. When he's a camera the pee oh vee is always on the move, he hates static shots, so he's floating up on a high crane looking down at the foreshortened figures of the actors, or he's swooping down to stand invisibly between them, turning slowly on his heel to achieve a three-hundred-and-sixty-degree pan, or maybe he'll try a dolly shot, tracking along beside Baal and Abu Simbel as they walk, or hand-held with the help of a steadicam he'll probe the secrets of the Grandee's bedchamber (SV, 108).

Perspectives like these cause the universe to be rather flat as the description and the view are subject to a certain two-dimensionality. The eye of the camera is destined to describe surfaces, whereas the discourse of the committed narrator is three-dimensional in its projection of character and universe. In line with this, Nicholas Rombes notes:

> That is, unlike "normal vision," the photographed image is presented on a plane in which the foreground and background tend to gravitate toward each other, reducing three-dimensional images to two-dimensional ones. (...) Yet the image is distorted even further, beyond flatness, as the aerial vantage point tends to reduce parts to whole. If anything, these "high shots" reveal the relativism of perspective – what we're shown from up close becomes something else from an aerial view (Rombes, 49).

Thus, the camera introduces a form of relativism in the creation of the fictive universe. However, according to Rombes, the technique does not only indicate a flatness in the perception of events, this flatness simply becomes one of Rushdie's themes in describing the fictive universe on several levels: the political, the ethical, the artistic. In view of this, the novel is not only postmodern on the level of statement, it is postmodern in its enunciation as well, that is to say the way in which the novel works.

Moreover, the film media affects the novel's narrative techniques, for example in the way Rushdie uses montage or crosscutting. In *Midnight's Children* there is an example of cross-cutting in which four lines are combined: 1) Doctor Aadam Aziz and Tai in the boat on their way to Ghani and Naseem; 2) Aadam conversing with his mother; 3) Ghani at home waiting for Aadam; 4) Saleem in front of his desk in the pickles factory writing the novel. Each line, recurring several times in the course of three pages (pp. 18-21), is introduced with three full stops, "…", indicating that the scene continues from where we left it last time. In addition, the lines are connected in time by the word "while," indicating the simultaneity between some of these lines.[19] Lines one and three occur

---

19   In modernist classics such as John Dos Passos's *Manhattan Transfer* (1925) and Alfred Döblin's *Berlin Alexanderplatz* (1929) simultaneity is also a theme which is

simultaneously, whereas line two takes place before lines one and three; line four may be said to concur with the three others as this line incorporates the act of narration that recounts the three others; yet line four is played out on another ontological level, the meta-fictive level, whereas lines one, two, and three unfold on the fictive level.

The cross-cutting technique underscores the narrator's control over his material and at the same time it also makes the universe more dynamic for the reader. Generally, Saleem may be said to be driven by an inclusive desire to incorporate the entire world, which is why we, as readers, encounter these decelerations of time (often characterised by simultaneity), that is to say a complete slowing down of time, bringing virtuality into play through the opening of new spaces. Simultaneity gives rise to a focusing on the unimaginable number of possibilities in a given space and simply emphasises the "schizophrenic" nature of subjectivity in an eternally displacing and expanding movement.

Another way of establishing shifts in time and space is by slowly fading out the first scene while fading in the next, as in a kind of filmic cross-fading. One example of this is the transition from Gibreel's dream about the Imam to the dream of Ayesha in *The Satanic Verses*, which have been iconographically separated for the reader by the small flower that is used throughout the novel as a symbol of changes of scenes. The textual transition to "the next narrative" sounds like this:

> ... what story is this? Coming right up. To begin at the beginning: On the morning of his fortieth birthday, in a room full of butterflies, Mirza Saeed Akhtar watched his sleeping wife...
>
> *
>
> On the fateful morning of his fortieth birthday, in a room full of butterflies, the zamindar Mirza Saeed Akhtar watched over his sleeping wife, and felt his heart fill up to the bursting-point with love (SV, 216).

While the story of the Imam slowly dissolves, a new story emerges and is eventually replaced by the previous story again; the link between the two

formally articulated through a filmic montage technique. This may be explained by the fact that both novels were written within the first decades of film.

stories is created by the uniformity of the linguistic material, smoothening the abrupt transition in time and place. Apart from that, it is a fine example of how Rushdie plays with repetitions, which are never "mechanical" repetitions as they always contain small variations. Thus, the passage may be seen as a condensate of the comprehensive themes of translation, crossing, displacement, mutation, and renewal, expressed in the novel's idiosyncratic version of the history of the original satanic verses. In this respect, the filmic narrative technique, the montage, is intertwined with a greater game of transfers, passages, and their inevitable character of creativity and becoming. Finally, and with reference to the above, the example shows us the difficulties of any beginning, and at the same time the arbitrariness of the shape that any beginning may take is suggested. It is implied that everything may have been told in another way with small variations.

Accordingly, Rombes is right when he points out that "Rushdie not only uses film language and technique to imbue the novel with the 'feel' of cinema and to shape the novel narratologically, but to raise epistemological questions as well" (Rombes, 50-51). The epistemological problem is present as an implicit, at times as an explicit, reflection of the status and constitution of the point of view. As we have seen, the novel's narrator shows a persistent interest in the storyline and the characters, and the motives behind this interest may be satanic and they may be divine; in any case the narrator's discourse is informed by a singular alertness.

But what about the constitution of the camera-eye? According to Rombes, the camera does not succeed in capturing the situational circumstances and intentions behind the captured facts: "Whereas the narrator is concerned with truth and meaning, the camera can only record facts, which strip away circumstances and intentions" (*ibid.*, 52). Rombes's observation is only partially correct. If we take a look at the scene in which the riots in Brickhall have placed the police and the media on full alert, we encounter a few implicit reflections on the meaning-making and intentional method of the camera:

> Television cameras arrive just in time for the raid on Club Hot Wax.
> This is what a television camera sees: less gifted than the human eye, its night vision is limited to what klieg lights will show. A helicopter

hovers over the nightclub, urinating light in long golden streams; the camera understands this image. The machine of state bearing down upon its enemies. – And now there's a camera in the sky; a news editor somewhere has sanctioned the cost of aerial photography, and from another helicopter a news team is *shooting down*. No attempt is made to chase this helicopter away. The noise of the rotor blades drowns the noise of the crowd. In this respect, again, video recording equipment is less sensitive than, in this case, the human ear.

– Cut. – A man lit by a sun-gun speaks rapidly into a microphone. Behind him there is a disorderment of shadows. But between the reporter and the disordered shadow-lands there stands a wall: men in riot helmets, carrying shields. The reporter speaks gravely; petrolbombs plasticbullets policeinjuries watercannon looting, confining himself, of course, to facts. But the camera sees what he does not say. A camera is a thing easily broken or purloined; its fragility makes it fastidious. A camera requires law, order, the thin blue line. Seeking to preserve itself, it remains behind the shielding wall, observing the shadow-lands from afar, and of course from above: that is, it chooses sides (SV, 454-55).

Rombes seems to think that the novel, via the camera, may realise the Jamesian and Lubbockian ideal of pure showing. But the camera cannot be reduced to a neutrally registering eye only, which the passage above shows: the camera is biased; it is operated by a person; there are financial considerations behind every news-shot. The camera may not be as "skilled" as the human eye and therefore it may often have only a limited point of view, but the opposite may also be true: in certain situations the camera may take in what the human eye does not, causing the two perceptive modes to supplement each other. Moreover, at a later point in the text, the image of the camera is endowed with opinion when it "observes the wax models with distaste" (SV, 455). In this way the intentionality of news images is accentuated; they can never sever themselves from ideological opinions; the frame will always contain an inside and an outside and the frame-setting will inevitably lead to the establishment of its own individual centre of enunciation and ideology. Rushdie critically reflects on the news coverage of the race riots in "Brickhall," where the state machine is colluded with the news machine through financial, social, and ideological power relations. The bashful "of course," inserted in connection with the strictly factual discourse of the news reporter, comprises a micro-political, ironic subversion of the reporter's sincerity and objectivity.

The dichotomy between the committed narrator and the partially neutral filmic description helps the reader maintain a critical stance to the novel's methods of representation as it involves a reflection on the manipulative strategies of discourse. In this respect, Rushdie seems to agree with Appadurai's considerations on the role of the mass media in the development of the modern subject's position between passivity and agency. Appadurai believes that the mass media do not necessarily entail a general dumming down and idleness. Rather, along with mass migration, the mass media may be considered as a factor that ensures the critical sense of the subject: "There is a growing evidence that the consumption of the mass media throughout the world often provokes resistance, irony, selectivity, and, in general, *agency*" (Appadurai, 7). The complex orchestration in Rushdie of a migratory enunciation, in which filmic inspiration plays a major role, may scare off a lot of readers, but those who manage to struggle through one the most important books of the 1980s are without doubt better prepared for global modernity with its hybrid and cross-cultural formations of subjectivity and its unstable and liquid images of the world. The novel "fine-tunes" and updates the reader's epistemological apparatus.

*

Enunciation in *The Satanic Verses* may also be determined as free indirect discourse, which is a form in-between direct speech and indirect speech occurring in passages where the narrator and a character's speech slide into each other. Vološinov defines it as "a combination not of empathy and distancing within the confines of an individual psyche, but of the character's accents (empathy) and the author's accents (distancing) within the confines of one and the same linguistic construction" (Vološinov, 155). Accordingly, free indirect speech is characterised by a double movement and a duality of voice: the empathic movement happens through the character's idiom and accentuated use of language, whereas the distancing movement happens through the idiom and accentuated language use of the narrator. The character's idiom is not presented as direct speech, but often appears as a character's conversation with him-/herself in the form of thoughts shaped by the character's distinctive use of language. In this way the discourse provides the narrator with an opportunity to represent a character's mental and linguistic idiom via an empathic movement, whereby the portrayal of the character acquires greater precision, but at the same time we, as readers, may sense the narrator's own distanced voice which relativises the precise picture of the character and the contents of his/her thoughts and speech. The technique is primarily known from Flaubert and Joyce, and in an interview with W.L. Webb, Rushdie himself shows his awareness of the technique when he says that "if you're writing dialogue, the reader should be able to tell who's speaking without 'he said, she said.' It should be possible without naming the speaker for the speaker to be clear" (Webb, 98).

In his book about Dostoevsky Bakhtin draws a detailed table on the scope for variation in free indirect discourse, extracting three functions: stylisation, parody, and hidden polemic. These functions all determine the use of language as dialogical, "double-voiced," and never neutral. Deleuze and Guattari acknowledge Bakhtin's (and Pasolini's) work on free indirect discourse and they even take it as far as to claim that "all discourse is indirect, and the translative movement proper to language is that of indirect discourse" (TP, 97).

Rushdie does not only employ free indirect speech in *The Satanic Verses*, it is operative in all his works where he allows idioms of narrator and character to taint each other, thereby giving rise to discursive complexity.[20] Accordingly, the motif and the metaphor "rivers of blood" resurfaces in several passages: Jumpy Joshi uses the motif in his poetic

20 Martin Leer ascribes the emergence of newness, the main theme of *The Satanic Verses*, to free indirect discourse: "What is new in the novel, even revolutionary, in spite of its dominance of western literature for almost two hundred years, lies in its inclination to 'free indirect speech,' as the Russian critic Mikhail Bakhtin and his successors have pointed out. The novel opens a lingual space in which author, narrative voices and fictive characters enter into a dialogue which, at its limits, suspends the distinction between fiction and reality, in the sense that 'reality' turns into fiction, and between author and reader, in the sense that the author becomes the reader and the reader becomes a co-author" (Leer, 26).

endeavours, but originally it derives from a racist (and real) slogan by Enoch Powell in the 1960s. Powell used the term as a bogey in his campaigns against immigration, firmly believing that the "flooding" of the country by immigrants would lead to "rivers of blood." Jumpy's theory of language seeks to reclaim terms of abuse, clichés, and insulting images by inverting their meaning and redeploying them in the struggle against the oppressor. In Jumpy's poetry "rivers of blood" thus emerges as a double-voiced motif, covertly and overtly carrying a controversy against the original sense of the term in Powell's rhetoric.

However, the motif is also presented through Hanif Johnson's speech, raising it to the third power of accentuation, in a manner of speaking:

> "Inner voices," Hanif said solemnly. "Upstairs on his desk there's a piece of paper with some verses written on it. And a title: *The River of Blood*."
>
> Jumpy jumped, knocking over his empty cup. "I'll kill you," he shouted at Hanif, who skipped quickly across the room, singing out, "We've got a poet in our midst, Sufyan Sahib. Treat with respect. Handle with care. He says a street is a river and we are the flow; humanity is a river of blood, that's the poet's point. Also the individual human being," he broke off to run around to the far side of an eight-seater table as Jumpy came after him, blushing furiously, flapping his arms. "In our very bodies, does the river of blood not flow?" *Like the Roman*, the ferrety Enoch Powell had said, *I seem to see the river Tiber foaming with much blood*. Reclaim the metaphor, Jumpy Joshi had told himself. Turn it; make it a thing we can use. "This is like a rape," he pleaded with Hanif. "For God's sake, stop" (SV, 186).

The quotation illustrates a mixture of direct, indirect, and free indirect speech. Hanif's direct speech, that is, Hanif as narrator, offers an apparent parody of Jumpy's rather sophisticated deployment of the "rivers of blood" motif, whereas the novel's actual narrator interrupts the scene and presents Powell's primary discourse in italics and proceeds to clarify Jumpy's intentions with the motif. The metaphor Jumpy uses at the end of the quotation (Hanif's interpretation = rape) subtly indicates how the demonstration of force in language is never neutral in free indirect discourse, vibrating between empathy and distance, and at the same time it forms the ironic point that Jumpy's use of the metaphor is in itself a "rape" of Powell's initial intention.

The proliferation of the motif does not end here, though. It is mentioned later on in the novel, this time by the narrator imparting Jumpy's mixed feelings of envy and resentment:

> Hanif was in perfect control of the languages that mattered: sociological, socialistic, black-radical, anti-anti-racist, demagogic, oratorical, sermonic: the vocabularies of power. *But you bastard you rummage in my drawers and laugh at my stupid poems. The real language problem: how to bend it shape it, how to let it be our freedom, how to repossess its poisoned wells, how to master the river of words of time of blood: about all that you haven't got a clue* (SV, 281).

Here is a pure example of free indirect discourse, Jumpy's lingual and mental peculiarity being accentuated through empathy while at the same time we sense the narrator's distance, for example through the italicised passage, apparently mocking Jumpy's anger by means of the incomplete punctuation of the syntax. Jumpy desperately tries to maintain his idiosyncratic intention with the motif and metaphor "rivers of blood," but characteristically he fails to invest his thoughts with sufficient authority as his poems are never published.

Finally the narrator uses the motif to characterise Baal, the satirist and poet in the chapters about Mahound: "'A poet's work,' he answers. 'To name the unnamable, to point at frauds, to take sides, start arguments, shape the world and stop it from going to sleep.' And if rivers of blood flow from the cuts his verses inflict, then they will nourish him. He is the satirist, Baal" (SV, 97). The quotation begins with Baal's direct speech succeeded by the narrator's comment on Baal's verse, from which "rivers of blood" may flow. In this way the repetitive use of the motif in various contexts strikes a chord that causes the heterogeneous lines to resonate without merging. The motif retains its ambiguity and represents the capability of free indirect discourse to produce variations on the same motif.

There is another example of free indirect discourse in the following passage: "He smiled, shook hands, was pleased to meet her" (SV, 428). Here the narrator recounts Saladin's meeting with Alleluia Cone, and the first two parts of the sentence only operate on the descriptive, outer level, whereas the last part of the sentence may be interpreted as Saladin's inner feelings about meeting Allie, or, perhaps, it is just the narrator paraphrasing Saladin's greeting of Allie. Whether or not it is Saladin speaking or merely his unspoken mood, it is certain that the narrator is tainting Saladin's idiom with his own, as "pleased to meet her" refers to a previous description of Saladin as satanic. After Saladin's transformation into a goat, his nightmares about his devilish status begin to come true in the streets of London: "At first these dreams were private matters, but pretty soon they started leaking into the waking hours, as Asian retailers and manufacturers of button-badges sweatshirts posters understood the power of the dream, and then all of a sudden he was everywhere, on the chest of young girls and in the windows protected against bricks by metal grilles, he was a defiance and a warning. Sympathy for the Devil: a new lease of life for an old tune" (SV, 286). "Sympathy for the Devil" is the title of the famous song by The Rolling Stones, in which Mick Jagger, impersonating the devil, sings, "pleased to meet you, hope you guess my name." In the novel the song is played on the radio and is reproduced with Jagger's distorted, nasal voice: "*Pleasechu meechu*, the radios sang, *hopeyu guessma nayym*" (SV, 286). During the meeting between Saladin and Allie the narrator thus cunningly informs the reader that Saladin's motives are satanic: like Jagger (Devil), Saladin is "pleased to meet." Saladin's anger and satanic vindictiveness flare by the sight of Allie and Gibreel as he misinterprets their situation as the antithesis of his own unwarranted fate. The invocation of The Rolling Stones's song, the motif "pleased to meet you," and the puzzle of the name of the speaker ("hope you guess my name"), may also be seen as an additional variation of the narrator's masquerade.

HUMAN IDENTITY

> "Rather than disintegration, I choose to call it branching out. Modern man is not fragmented, but coheres in another way than through a centre."
> – Jan Kjærstad: *Menneskets felt* (*The Human Zone*)

As we have already seen in connection with *Grimus*, the question of human identity is important to Rushdie whose characters are projected from his own experience of the existential condition of nomadism. The majority of Rushdie's characters have been caught in an intermezzo which breeds unstable identities. The foundation of his novels' way of thinking human identity is made up of an anti-genealogical ontology as identity seems to be determined by a rhizomatic a-parallel evolution, which may prompt us to say, along with Deleuze, that identity is created in an interplay with a collective society-machine rather than in an interplay with a closed family triangle, and even less through a traditional logic of origin: "Family: an overrated idea" (MC, 396), Saleem thus concludes late in *Midnight's Children*.

Midnight's Children

Saleem's family tree is meticulously drawn in the first part of *Midnight's Children* and to a great extent genealogy determines what and who Saleem is. Drawing a family tree is the usual way of rooting a person as the tree symbolises the relations of cause and effect in the story of a person's life, and thus it comes to represent an explanatory model in describing the person. However, the genealogical structure is completely subverted when we realise that Saleem is not the son of Amina and Ahmed. Hence, the narrator's choice of beginning his life story in 1915 with Aadam Aziz as his ancestor seems even more contingent; Saleem turns out to be a simulacrum in the genealogies of the Aziz and the Sinai families, just as

Flapping Eagle was in relation to Grimus. This is radically different from, for example, Dickens where the family tree works as a frame of explanation and a stabiliser of the social hierarchies in the novel's universe. Having endured so much misery, Oliver Twist finally discovers his proper and reputable position on the social ladder towards the end of the novel when a lot of entanglements are unravelled and his true identity, and thus his genealogy, is revealed. In Dickens there is often a movement from suffering, injustice, confusion, and chaotic circumstances, caused by the absence of genealogy, to a state of happiness, justice, and order, caused, in contrast, by the legitimising role of genealogy in for instance the case of Oliver. At the beginning of *Midnight's Children*, a fair amount of energy is spent on illusory genealogy, but only to replace it later on with completely different frames of explanation.

When Saleem's ayah, Mary Pereira, confesses to the swapping of the babies, the Sinai and Aziz families acknowledge, after a while, that ties of blood are weaker than past experiences: "when we eventually discovered the crime of Mary Pereira, we all found that it *made no difference*! I was still their son: they remained my parents. In a kind of collective failure of imagination, we learned that we simply could not think our way out of our pasts" (MC, 118). It seems as if love can only exist within a common experience of lived life: "maybe, I say, in spite of all these provocations, my parents loved me" (MC, 301). Accordingly, identity is not created along parallel lines, but in crossfields in which transversal connections function as catalysts of metamorphoses and development. Family as understood by a traditional logic of origin must yield both to a new concept of family and to the macrocosmic forces of history: "In fact, all over the new India, the dream we all shared, children were being born who were only partially the offspring of their parents – the children of midnight were also the children *of the time*: fathered, you understand, by history" (MC, 118). Saleem represents Rushdie's attempt to wrench identity away from a narrow family framework as he is open to lines of connection with the history and politics of the Indian subcontinent, but also with a collective sphere of friends and midnight children. As Martine Hennard Dutheil remarks, "the vertical, linear, genealogical familial logic gives way to a wide, intricate and changing network of multiple relationships which open up the familial unit to the outside and the other: the old family tree is felled and transformed into the leaves upon which the transformative action of writing can take place" (Dutheil, 2-3).

As mentioned earlier, the novel opens with an episode in 1915 when Saleem's grandfather Aadam, who of course turns out not to be his grandfather anyway, has just returned from his medical studies in Heidelberg in Germany. But if Aadam is not Saleem's grandfather, why is the episode so important to Saleem? If Rushdie with the illusory genealogy problematises blood as the determinant of identity, does the scene of Aadam's return then contain any elements that are of significance to Saleem's identity? Yes, because both Saleem and Aadam are characterised by an inner void as a result of their realisation that religion is no longer a satisfactory and sufficient frame of explanation in their interpretations of life. The void, or their doubt, becomes a metaphor of the desire that at all times joins man with an Outside and, in consequence, catalyses the continual flux of identity. On his return from Heidelberg, Aadam finds himself positioned between Muslim faith and Western science: "But it was no good, he was caught in a strange middle ground, trapped between belief and disbelief, (...) knocked forever into that middle place, unable to worship a God in whose existence he could not wholly disbelieve. Permanent alteration: a hole" (MC, 12). Aadam is not a disintegrated person; rather he represents an identity that branches out. He has not been forced into an excluding logic of either-or; rather he is gifted with an inclusive logic of both-and: on the one hand he cannot worship God, on the other, he cannot stop believing in the existence of God. Aadam remains a "half-and-halfer" throughout his life and this is the characteristic that Saleem "inherits" from him. They are both caught in-between faith and disbelief and, as such, they are both doubters, and it is their doubt that functions as a catalyst of continuous transformations and metonymic slippages.

Identity is also a fictive construction in the sense that Saleem invents several fictive parents: "giving birth to parents has been one of my stranger talents – a form of reverse fertility beyond the control of contraception" (MC, 243). Throughout his life Saleem has longed for "fictional ancestors" (MC, 110), and in this way he accumulates a long list of mothers, including his biological mother Vanita, his foster mother Amina, his nanny Mary Pereira, and his aunt Pia Aziz. Along with that, he revives these seven fathers: his biological father William Methwold, Vanita's real husband Wee Willie Winkie, his foster father Ahmed Sinai, Amina's first husband Nadir Khan, the snake expert Dr Schaapsteker, his uncle Zulfikar, and, finally, the magician Picture Singh. This accentuates Saleem's hybrid identity as it may be said that he, through this line of more or less fictive ancestors, plants his roots in a network that branches out into several countries, namely England, France, India, Pakistan, but also into several religions, namely Christianity, Hinduism, and Islam.[21]

*

The transformations Saleem undergoes until 1965 do not deprive him of a relatively coherent identity. He is changed, but through his consciousness and memory he remains a fairly continuous individual. Nonetheless, the accident in 1965 when Saleem is hit on the head by a spittoon results in a severe fit of amnesia which completely breaks down Saleem's identity: "I am stripped of past present memory time shame and love (...) all the Saleems go pouring out of me" (MC, 343). Rushdie exploits this tabula rasa to project an entirely new identity with a new name. The narrator Saleem starts referring to the main character in the third person: Saleem "had been pulled up by his roots to be flung unceremoniously across the years, fated to plunge memoryless into an adulthood whose every aspect grew daily more grotesque" (MC, 345). The distance between narrator and main character is never as great as in this part of the novel. The distance is not only determined by time, but is even more so an expression of the difference of identity at its maximum: "But I insist: not I. He. He, the Buddha" (MC, 360). The Buddha is deployed as a tracking-dog in the special units of the Pakistani army CUTIA (bitch), and the war scenes and the chapter as a whole, taking place in the jungle of Sundarban, is some

---

21   The theme of the polyglot character of genealogy also applies to Rushdie himself: "it is perhaps one of the more pleasant freedoms of the literary migrant to be able to choose his parents. My own – selected half consciously, half not – include Gogol, Cervantes, Kafka, Melville, Machado de Assis; a polyglot family tree, against which I measure myself, and to which I would be honoured to belong" (IH, 20-21). In the interview with Haffenden, nationality is in the firing line: "I don't define myself by nationality – my passport doesn't tell me who I am. I define myself by friends, political affinity, groupings I feel home in… and of course writing. I enjoy having access to three different countries, and I don't see that I need to choose" (Haffenden, 56).

of the most powerful writing Rushdie has achieved. Severed from his (human) past, Saleem's identity becomes all the more rhizomatic.

Through Saleem, Rushdie projects a range of exceptional conditions where the human body and mind are forced into the extreme. In the jungle of Sundarban we experience some of the purest examples of Rushdie's cross-pollination technique where everything seeps into everything else and the borders between subject and object are liquefied: "In the turbid, miasmic state of mind which the jungle induced, they prepared their first meal, a combination of nipa-fruits and mashed earthworms, which inflicted on them all a diarrhoea so violent that they forced themselves to examine the excrement in case their intestines had fallen out in the mess" (MC, 362). In this way metamorphosis is set off through molecular miasmas, collisions, and fusions, caused by the irrational logic of space and time in the jungle in the oscillating expansion between man and world.

Through intensive linguistic constructions Rushdie creates radical human intensities. Saleem's identity assumes a schizophrenic nature: he goes through a becoming-dog, a becoming-transparent, a becoming-jungle, in addition to other monstrous metamorphoses. The transparent condition represents the ultimate form of interaction between subject and object, a condition in which the body is completely open to the world's inscription. A becoming-world in the words of Deleuze and Guattari: "We are not in the world, we become with the world; we become by contemplating it. Everything is vision, becoming. We become universes. Becoming animal, plant, molecular, becoming zero" (WP, 169).[22] In the terminology of Deleuze and Guattari Saleem may be described as a "body without organs" (BwO) which denotes a type of recoding of the subject in which the subject is as open to new possibilities as possible.[23] In other

22   Rushdie sees art the same way in the following quote where he speaks of the erasure of the line between the artist and the world: "Literature is made at the frontier between the self and the world, and in the act of creation that frontier softens, becomes permeable, allows the world to flow into the artist and the artist to flow into the world" (IH, 427).
23   "Bodies are not defined by their genus or species, by their organs and functions, but by what they can do, by the affects of which they are capable – in passion as well as in action" (D, 60), Deleuze and Parnet write. In his discussion of Deleuze's

words, Saleem is in a state of sheer virtuality. Man conceived as a BwO is an almost utopian state of being, but at the same time it is a genuine attempt to open up the possibilities of man and the human body towards new intensities. Therefore M.K. Naik is not quite right in arguing that "Identity is, in turn, shown as a sham, as mistaken and confused, fractured and fragmented, merged and super-imposed, subjected to oblivion and dwarfed and reduced to animal level, totally lost, and as barren and sterile" (Naik, 63). This argument has a far too negative sound to it, and Naik's notion of barrenness and sterility is not in tune with *Midnight's Children*. Above all, the novel seems to celebrate the fragmentation of life as a creative force rather than viewing fragmentation as a sterile dead-end. As mentioned before, Saleem, in his intensive metamorphic condition, launches a number of subtle and radical human possibilities.

Another episode which triggers something new is the episode in the laundry basket where Saleem hides from the demand of the surrounding world that he assume the role of a central figure in history. The episode may be interpreted as a castration scene inasmuch as Saleem is heavily shocked by the sight of his mother's "black mango." His desire is not blocked in an oedipal triangle, however. It is channelled into a veritable communication-machine, giving rise to the Midnight's Children Conference. At a first glance, the notion of sterility also seems to correspond to Saleem's literal impotence caused by the realisation that he is in love with his sister, Jamila Singer. Yet this impotence, along with his bodily decline, becomes the actual catalyst for Saleem's writing activity, and in that way "want" is sublimated into the production-machine which eventually brings about the existence of *Midnight's Children*.[24] It

---

idea of the subject and the body, Pearson notes: "going 'beyond' the human condition does not entail leaving the 'human' behind, but rather aims to broaden the horizon of its experience" (Pearson, 1999, 20), and he continues: "there are conditions of life that are peculiar to embryonic life, conditions of possibility which exceed the limits of species, genus, order, or class" (*ibid.*, 94).

24   As may be recalled, desire is not determined in Deleuze by want, which Pearson also makes clear in a Bergsonian passage: "Life proceeds neither via lack nor the power of the negative but through internal self-differentiation along lines of divergence" (Pearson, 1999, 25).

is true that Saleem's "other pencil" does not work, but his real "pencil" does indeed: "'so now that the writery is done, let's see if we can make your other pencil work!'; despite everything she tries, I cannot hit her spittoon" (MC, 39). Accordingly, the family sphere once again turns out be superimposed by a more comprehensive politics, connecting Saleem with machines of a more collective nature.

When Saleem is bitten by a large snake during his stay in the jungle of Sundarban, he is "rejoined to the past, jolted into unity by snake-poison, and it began to pour out through the buddha's lips" (MC, 364). Just as religion is the glue that keeps Pakistan together as one country, memory and consciousness keep human identity together. Reunited with his past, Saleem is enabled to tell his life story which pours out through the buddha's lips to the great puzzlement of the listening soldiers. Now it is only Saleem's own name that is lacking before he may once again feel like a relatively coherent individual, and Saleem gets his name back from one of the almost forgotten midnight children, his most faithful companion from the past, Parvati-the-witch, who recognises him during the liberation of what is later to be known as Bangladesh.

On the self-conscious level of narration, the narrator calls attention to his complex identity and hence the complex identity of all the main characters:

> Who what am I? My answer: I am the sum total of everything that went before me, of all I have been seen done, of everything done-to-me. I am everyone everything whose being-in-the-world affected was affected by mine. I am anything that happens after I've gone which would not have happened if I had not come. Nor am I particularly exceptional in this matter; each "I," every one of the now-six-hundred-million-plus of us, contains a similar multitude. I repeat for the last time: to understand me, you'll have to swallow a world (MC, 383).

The individual is a world, and, in view of that, it is endowed with a certain degree of infinitude as well as it is inevitably placed as an active/passive entity in the running of the world. Infinity and processuality are slowed down through the writer's incision into chaos, that is, through the unavoidable contingency of the work of art, but, for that reason, also through the requisite outer form, beginning and end. The narrator establishes order in chaos through the transversal connections that he creates between the stories, motifs, images, and characters.

The narrator in *Midnight's Children* is a modern monad. Philosophically Leibniz conceives the concept of the monad as a being without doors or windows, giving rise to a problem of communication. The closed Leibnizian monads all have the same stock at their disposal, all developing and expressing the same world; each monad holds its own position of enunciation, bringing about different perspectives on the same world, which God enables them to unfold. In this way Leibniz re-establishes a pre-existing entity and totality in the form of a God who inserts the same world into each monad and creates a correspondence between their individual loneliness. However, to Rushdie every perspectivist position of enunciation unfolds a world without any pre-existing entity or order. In his novels there may be just as many different worlds as there are views on the world:

> Reality is a question of perspective; the further you get from the past, the more concrete and plausible it seems – but as you approach the present, it inevitably seems more and more incredible. Suppose yourself in a large cinema, sitting at first in the back row, and gradually moving up, row by row, until your nose is almost pressed against the screen. Gradually the stars' faces dissolve into dancing grain; tiny details assume grotesque proportions; the illusion dissolves – or rather, it becomes clear that the illusion itself *is* reality... (MC, 165-66).

The quote says: reality *is* a simulacrum and vice versa. Accordingly, Rushdie's characters, for the most part, assume a monadic and nomadic disposition: perspectivism is inseparably tied to mobility. We find a specific example of this at the beginning of the novel when Aadam Aziz returns to Kashmir from his stay in Heidelberg and the valley no longer feels familiar: "Now, returning, he saw through travelled eyes" (MC, 11). At the same time, the quote indicates the problem of viewpoint that criss-crosses Rushdie's novels, resulting in what we may term Rushdie's stereoscopic, microscopic, and telescopic lenses, respectively.

The stereoscopic view is determined by Rushdie's position as both insider and outsider, which he regards as crucial himself: "Indian writers in these islands, like others who have migrated into the north from the south, are capable of writing from a kind of double perspective: because they, we, are at one and the same time insiders and outsiders in this society. This stereoscopic vision is perhaps what we can offer in place of 'whole sight'" (IH, 19). Apart from that, Saleem is destined to shift from the telescopic lens to the microscopic lens the closer he gets to the time of his enunciation as a unifying all-inclusive perspective is impossible: "The movement towards the cinema screen is a metaphor for the narrative's movement through time towards the present, and the book itself, as it nears contemporary events, quite deliberately loses deep perspective, becomes more 'partial'" (IH, 13).

As long as there is desire, Saleem is joined with the world and writes his auto-biography, but as soon as desire ceases, the narrative stops: "Once, when I was more energetic, I would have wanted to tell his life-story; the hour, and his possession of an umbrella, would have been all the connections I needed to begin the process of weaving into my life, and I have no doubt that I'd have finished by proving his indispensability to anyone who wishes to understand my life and benighted times; but now I'm disconnected, unplugged, with only epitaphs left to write" (MC, 457). Throughout the novel, Saleem has spent his energy on fusions, collisions, and cross-pollination in order to establish some kind of meaning of himself and for himself. As he concludes on the last page of the novel he has run through a number of nomadic conditions: "I have been so-many too-many persons, life unlike syntax allows one more than three, and at last somewhere the striking of a clock, twelve chimes, release" (MC, 463). Now time has come to dissolve and release himself, fusion is replaced with fission, blowing up Saleem into thousands of tiny molecular fragments.

The idea of the novel's overall rhizomatic architecture is supported by the fact that identity is understood as a network of roots rather than one deeply anchored tap root. In the analysis of the composition we saw that the novel does not display any vertical hierarchy between the stories and, in addition, the reader is left with many loose ends as several of the stories are not finished (e.g. Commander Sabarmati's trial, Uncle Puff's seven daughters, and Cyrus' transformation into Lord Khusro

Khusrovand).[25] Consequently, the trimmings made by the narrator and the writer often have a contingent shape, indicating a subjacent processual ontology in which things are always situated in the middle on their way to new places. With the status of identity as flux through a-parallel (r)evolutions, a clearer picture of the aesthetics in *Midnight's Children* emerges: the novel is a rhizome, an a-centred system in which the "centre" (Saleem) is in constant movement and equipped with a complicated and pluralistic genealogy. The system is open and has several possible entryways as the novel's structure, with pro- and analepsis, digressions and meta-reflective passages, superimposes the connecting thread of the chronological storyline. Likewise the novel reflects an intermezzo-aesthetics, which is expressed by an inclusive both-and logic (and ethics) rather than by an exclusive logic of either-or. The novel displaces characters, such as Aadam Aziz, in intermezzo-positions, but on the plane of narrative technique the novel may also be said to hover in a position between the Western and the Eastern paradigms of oral and written traditions.

Shame

The problem of identity in *Shame* is of a slightly different character than in *Midnight's Children* as focus is preserved unilaterally on the narrator in the latter. In *Shame* the gallery of characters is more even in the sense that there is not one main character but many; hence Rushdie presents a more varied spectrum of possible identities. As usual he explores the characters in relation to the poles of rootlessness and rootedness.

The anti-hero Omar Khayyam, is, as we have seen, constantly situated in the borderland between existence and non-existence. Omar is born into a world which to him is turned upside down and in which he

---

[25] Rushdie has said to John Haffenden: "But one of the deliberate efforts in the book was to leave loose ends; I was very interested in the idea of implying a multitude of stories in one's structure, through which one picked one narrative path. There are stories you just happen to bump into and that you never see again, or stories that are just fragments of themselves and not completed. It was structured to contain that kind of waste material in it, because that was part of what I was trying to say" (Haffenden, 37).

plays a passive role: "'You see before you,' he confided, 'a fellow who is not even the hero of his own life; a man born and raised in the condition of being out of things. Heredity counts, dontyouthinkso?,'" he asks Isky. "'That is an oppressive notion,' Iskander Harappa replied" (S, 24). The tension between predetermination and the ability of man to renew himself is present as a central theme in the entire novel, as in all of Rushdie's writings. In one passage, however, Omar is granted a role which resembles Saleem's in *Midnight's Children*: "it was the fate of Omar Khayyam Shakil to affect, from his position on the periphery, the great events whose central figures were other people but which collectively made up his own life" (S, 108). Like Saleem, Omar is mainly determined by a peripheral, passive role with but limited influence on the world around him. Omar and the narrator are quick to realise this, whereas Saleem sets out with the claim that he plays a central role in the History of India.

Omar is named after the Persian poet Omar Khayyam, but, contrary to the original Omar, our anti-hero never manages to wring a single word from his pencil in spite of the maternal expectations of a brilliant writing career. In this way Omar turns out to be a degradation of the original, a simulacrum, who has to settle for a place in the margin. Still, Omar manages to make a glorious career as a scientist from this marginal existence and in this respect he may be said to give shape to something positive through the mode of inversion he has been born into.[26]

It is interesting that Omar, when he realises that he has lost his status as the favourite son at the end of the novel, is told that his father was in collusion with the devil, whereas Babar's father was an archangel. It seems to be a characteristic in Rushdie that the demonic is often bequeathed with more favourable survival terms and productive capacities than the angelic ones; in *The Satanic Verses* it is Saladin and not Gibreel who survives and escapes the blind alley of death; in *Shame* Omar may not survive, but he plays a far greater role in the novel than Babar. Babar spends his childhood years in the shadow of Omar's memory and winds up burning all the memories his mothers have collected of Omar in his

---

26   Harrison points to Rushdie's use of names with geographical or mythico-historical origin as "satirically indicative of a sad decline from the originals" (Harrison, 77).

absence. Subsequently, he flees into the jungle and dies a martyr's death. In addition to his unflattering characteristics, Omar is attributed with a number of positive values, particularly through the way he looks after Sufiya. The interesting thing is that we may refer the characterology in Rushdie's novels to Deleuze's concept of simulacrum at a more general level. As said, simulacrum is characterised as being pure difference, a singularity and a subversive force which guarantees the production of the new by inserting difference into hierarchies. Likewise, Rushdie's characters bear the mark of being false pretenders as they often turn out as disparaged and distorted versions of the original models. As we have seen, the demonic streak is exactly an expression of the peculiarity of the simulacrum as the demonic creeps into the metaphysics of similitude as an inevitable force of difference. Accordingly, diversity is animated in Rushdie when the status of the characters as degraded versions of the original models is not necessarily to be understood as a negative feature. That is the existential condition of (late) modernity.

Omar is also characterised by a nebulous origin, as is the case of most of Rushdie's characters. Born by three mothers and an unknown father and raised by a Parsian ayah, Omar's roots are of a dubious nature. Moreover, his rootlessness is indicated by the dizzy spells that he suffers from when he feels too close to geographical, psychological, and physical borderlands. Naturally, Omar seeks a fixed place and periodically he experiences stable conditions as, for instance, in the company of Mr. Rodrigues: "Unable to locate a father, the boy selected one for himself out of available personnel, bestowing the accolade without any reservations upon Mr Eduardo Rodrigues the schoolmaster, who was himself a recent arrival in Q." (S, 46). It is, however, inconsistency that distinguishes Omar as a character, which causes the narrator to discharge the following volley against his "hero": "How is one to account for such a character? Is consistency too much to ask? I accuse this so-called hero of giving me the most Godawful headache" (S, 142).

Metamorphosis is a human condition in Rushdie's writings. Death and rebirth are motifs that we encounter incessantly in connection with the characters. After being inseparable and practically identical for many years, a fissure occurs within the trinity of Chhunni-Munnee-Bunny when they are confronted with Omar's wish of either being let out of

Nishapur or told his father's name. The division results in the individual rebirth of each sister: "In the chaos of their regeneration the wrong heads had ended up on the wrong bodies; they became psychological centaurs, fish-women, hybrids" (S, 40). Hybridity is thus another condition for the human being in Rushdie's novels and it is this inbetweenness that actually causes metamorphoses (into new hybrids) when the heterogeneous forces or positions defining the hybrid space clash. In the case of Chhunni-Munnee-Bunny, hybridity materialises when their state of isolated unity is suddenly confronted with an Outside, that is, Omar's wishes, through which the processual transformation is provided with a breeding ground. The passages of metamorphosis correspond to what Deleuze calls "lines of flight." The transformative elements, which primarily occur in meetings or confrontations (that is, hybrid spaces), effect the deterritorialisation of fixed territories. Through Omar's stated wish, the indivisible unity and stable territory of the motherly trinity is deterritorialised.

Bilquìs, another of the novel's protagonists, emigrates from India to Pakistan after the partition. She is raised by her father, who, because her mother has died, has to assume the role of both father and mother, which is why he is called "Woman." Things being turned upside down, she forms a repetition of the theme of inversion. The narrator hesitates between several possible descriptions of Bilquìs: "I am wondering how best to describe Bilquìs. As a woman who was unclothed by change, but who wrapped herself in certainties; or as a girl who became a queen, but lost the ability possessed by every beggar-woman, that is, the power of bearing sons; or as that lady whose father was a Woman and whose son turned out to be a girl as well" (S, 67-68). Ambivalence recurs in all three possible descriptions. Change literally tears the clothes off Bilquìs when her father's eclectic cinema, showing both Hindu and Muslim movies, is blown up by unidentified perpetrators, leaving Bilquìs naked and orphaned in the crowds of Delhi; but at the same time Bilquìs is dressed in the sense that she wraps her rootless self in certainties like the faith in her predetermined life as a queen, which is reinforced when she meets Raza Hyder who gradually re-clothes her with the dresses he takes from bodies in the river. The second description departs from Bilquìs's status as a queen, but at the same time her inability to give birth to sons is pointed out and undermines her status. The last description encompasses the oxymoronic character structure Bilquìs suffers from as her origin and offspring, her father and her son, both turn out to be female. Her contradictory nature makes it impossible for her ever to be in agreement with herself, and she turns out to be one of the most helpless characters in Rushdie's novels in terms of dealing with changes. She becomes manically obsessed with the attempt to sustain a state of stasis around her: "She developed a horror of movement, and placed an embargo on the relocation of even the most trivial of household items. Chairs, ashtrays, flowerpots took root, rendered immobile by the force of her fearful will. (...) the disease of fixity was hers" (S, 68). Yet, in the end she is the one who provides the black cloths that Raza, Omar and she herself escape in, which shows that her paranoia and neurosis have not brought her to a total dead-end.

Another interesting character in the novel is Iskander Harappa who finds the concept of heredity oppressive. Isky is also the novel's opportunist. At the beginning, in the company of Omar Khayyam, he is a bonvivant and a womaniser, but later on he manages to recreate and rebuild his own personality from scratch: "He stifled for ever the high-pitched giggle of his unreliable playboy self and substituted a rich, full-throated, statesmanlike guffaw" (S, 125). Part of the credit for Isky's metamorphosis goes to his daughter Arjumand, or Virgin Ironpants, who despises her own gender and thinks the female body does not bring anything but "babies, pinches and shame" (S, 107). Virgin Ironpants idolises her father and assumes the responsibility of getting him on the right track through a force of will meant to suppress her own femininity. We find parallels to Grimus and Flapping Eagle in the relationship between Iskander and Raza. Just as Flapping Eagle turns out to be the bad pretender and the distorted offspring in relation to Grimus, Raza becomes a kind of simulacrum whose force subverts the established hierarchy: "*From darkness into light, from nothingness into somethingness. I made him, I was his father, he is my seed. And now I am less than he. They accuse Haroun of killing his father because that is what Hyder is doing to me. (...) The father should be the superior and the son, inferior. But now I am low and he, high.* An inversion: the parent become the child. *He is turning me into his son*" (S, 230). Here the inversion that is so characteristic of the structure in *Shame* is emphasised once again. However, things are not only turned upside down in simple inversions of hierarchies, a displacement of the centre takes place at the same time so that the old order is replaced by a fundamentally new one. As it is, the continued development of the Isky-Raza relation results in Isky's execution, which removes him from the scene and reduces his continuation to the scene of the Virgin's orchestration of him as a myth and icon. Again Rushdie underlines processuality in the case of Raza as he suffers the fate of Iskander and is dethroned: "even a giant can be pygmified" (S, 271), Bilquìs concludes in a rare moment of clarity at the end of the novel. The carnivalistic trait of Rushdie's basic view entails the idea that the higher you fly, the deeper you are deemed to fall.

As mentioned, the mentally retarded Sufiya Zinobia personifies the abstract concept of shame. Sufiya epitomises the complexity of identity as her personality reflects the interdependence of shame, innocence and violence. The narrator designates her as both the Beauty and the Beast: "The beast inside the beauty. Opposing elements of a fairy-tale combined in a single character..." (S, 139). In *Shame* the characters tend towards one-dimensionality, which is a prerequisite for Rushdie's principally satirical project. Accordingly, the characterisations often appear cartoon-like, but this is not an irrefutable argument. One never finds pure evil or pure goodness in Rushdie, at least not for long: Sufiya who is portrayed as pure innocence at the beginning of the novel transforms into pure violence at the end;[27] in spite of his ugliness and unscrupulousness, Omar is attributed with sympathetic features such as compassion, concern, and scientific competence; Raza is portrayed as a ruthless, fanatic, and religious tyrant, but he also demonstrates a heart-felt care for his daughter, Sufiya, who is utterly rejected by her mother Bilquìs; Isky is heralded as the most capable statesman Pakistan has ever had, but he will stop at nothing on his way to the top. At one point Isky is described as Danton whereas Raza is characterised as Robespierre, but the narrator corrects himself: "We are Robeston and Danpierre. The inconsistency doesn't

---

27   At the beginning Sufiya Zinobia is the beautiful Miss Hyder and later she turns into the monster Mrs Shakil. Obviously, Rushdie alludes to Stevenson's Dr Jekyll and Mr Hyde, but in Sufiya's case the Hyde-side is the good side whereas the Jekyll-side is the evil one.

matter; I myself manage to hold large numbers of wholly irreconcilable views simultaneously, without the least difficulty. I do not think others are less versatile" (S, 241-42). Hence, everything contains its own contradiction, according to Rushdie.

*

If we return to Bilquìs, we find a number of interesting observations of identity in the course of her stay with Raza's grandmother Bariamma who functions as the great matriarch of the forty women living under her roof. Bilquìs is installed in this *zenana* of women together with Raza's big family after she has emigrated from Delhi with Raza. In Delhi she stood naked in the midst of change, pulled out of continuity, and with burnt-off eyebrows. The narrator reflects on the condition of the migrant, implicitly referring to Bilquìs's situation: "All migrants leave their pasts behind, although some try to pack it into bundles and boxes – but on the journey something seeps out of the treasured mementoes and old photographs, until even their owners fail to recognize them, because it is the fate of migrants to be stripped of history, to stand naked amidst the scorn of strangers upon whom they see the rich clothing, the broaches of continuity and the eyebrows of belonging" (S, 63-64). For this reason, it is difficult for Bilquìs to settle down among the clique of rooted and self-satisfied women in Raza's family who, according to Bilquis's norms, lead a primitive and unenlightened life: "that house in which it was believed that the mere fact of being married did not absolve a woman of the shame and dishonour that results from the knowledge that she sleeps regularly with a man" (S, 74). The shame of sexuality is subdued through the strange arrangement in Bariamma's house where the husbands steal into their wives' beds at night like Ali Baba's forty thieves. After a short while, a rhythmic squeaking sound is produced which is, after all, drowned in the name of decency by Bariamma's rising snores.[28] On top of it all, it is indicated that the men might often find the wrong bed.

28 Rushdie has commented on the thematic function of shame in the novel: "When the book starts, the shame is private and sexual – to do with being pregnant when you don't know who the father is – and the book develops by building variations on that theme, showing how shame is part of the architecture of the society the novel describes, and perhaps not only that society" (Haffenden, 40).

Bilquìs has difficulties achieving acceptance and she is an outsider due to her posh manners and queenly aspirations. She does win a bit of respect, though, through Raza's military victories and growing position and all of the women consider Raza as a good man: "the women admitted that he was a good man who did not beat his wife. This definition of goodness alarmed Bilquìs, to whom it had never occurred that she might be beaten" (S, 76). Another way of winning respect turns out to be through storytelling which becomes a determinant of identity. Through her peculiar and astonishing life story, Bilquìs is adopted into the family's genealogical delineation which is inscribed on the last pages of the Koran: "Lost in the forest of new relatives, wandering in the blood-jungle of the matriarchal home, Bilquìs consulted the family Quran in search of these family trees, and found them there, in their traditional place, monkey-puzzle groves of genealogy inscribed in the back of the holy book" (S, 74).[29] The narrator goes on: "In that generation many women, ordinary decent respectable ladies of the type to whom nothing ever happens, to whom nothing is supposed to happen except marriage children death, had this sort of strange story to tell. It was a rich time for stories, if you lived to tell your tale" (S, 65).

In the company of the women a lot of time is spent on recounting and retelling the family legends which reflect a rich diversity of ups and downs, tragedies, and fatal events. The stories provide the women with safety and security despite their distinct focus on catastrophes and negativity; storytelling becomes a form of survival for the women: "stories, such stories, were the glue that held the clan together, binding the generations in webs of whispered secrets. Her story altered, at first, in the retellings, but finally it settled down, and after that, nobody, neither teller or listener, would tolerate any deviation from the hallowed, sacred text" (S, 76). In the case of Bilquìs, her stories fascinate the women in the zenana who are particularly attracted by the curious circumstances surrounding the meeting between Bilquìs and Raza. As the narrator points

---

29 Rushdie's emphasis on the theme of genealogy is reinforced by the fact that he has delineated the family trees of the Shakils, Hyders, and Harappas at the beginning of the novel. These family trees tend towards the grotesque by including categories like "11 legitimate sons", "(many illegitimate offspring)", "(the 'three mothers')" and "32 boys."

out, it takes a while before her story subsides, but when that happens no alterations are tolerated. The sanctification of the story is an attempt to create a stable identity based on "initiation, kinship, blood" (S, 77).

Rushdie embarks on an interesting undertaking with his focalisation on the female voices of the novel. The narrator reflects on the turn *Shame* makes from masculine power-history to female family-saga:

> Once upon a time there were two families, their destinies inseparable even by death. I had thought, before I began, that what I had on my hands was an almost excessively masculine tale, a saga of sexual rivalry, ambition, power, patronage, betrayal, death, revenge. But the women seem to have taken over; they marched in from the peripheries of the story to demand the inclusion of their own tragedies, histories and comedies, obliging me to couch my narrative in all manner of sinuous complexities, to see my "male" plot refracted, so to speak, through the prisms of its reverse and "female" side. It occurs to me that the women knew precisely what they were up to – that their stories explain, and even subsume, the men's (S, 173).

Accordingly, the novel stages a polyphony of voices in which each voice fights for superiority, and Rushdie manages in this way, through his combination of different lenses, to bring in the female discourse, through which the masculine is undermined with the result that the official image of Pakistan cracks. So, Rushdie problematises the traditional relation between centre and periphery and, through a female discourse, he projects a new texture which is often neglected in conventional and official historiographies.

The subversive quality of the female discourse in the novel's fictive universe is limited, however. Most of the female voices remain isolated in the private sphere, of which Bilquìs is perhaps the best example. The same may be said about the tales that circulate in Bariamma's matriarchal house which never leave the family's Koran to influence the official, masculine power-discourse. The most positive example of a female voice is that of the shawl broidered by Rani which turns into allegories of the atrocities committed by her husband and the shamelessness of Pakistan and survives long after the fall of the characters: "a completed shawl as delicately worked as anything made by the craftswomen of Aansu, a masterpiece amidst whose minuscule arabesques a thousand and one stories had been portrayed, so artfully that it seemed as though horsemen were galloping along her collarbone, while tiny birds flew along the soft meridian of her spine" (S, 111). Rani packs her suitcases with eighteen completed shawls and long after Isky's death she sends them to their daughter Arjumand: "An epitaph of wool. The eighteen shawls of memory. Every artist has the right to name her creation, and Rani would put a piece of paper inside the trunk before she sent it off to her newly powerful daughter. On this piece of paper she would write her chosen title: 'The Shamelessness of Iskander the Great.' And she would add a surprising signature: *Rani Humayun*. Her own name, retrieved from the mothballs of the past" (S, 191). However, Virgin Ironpants refuses to accept Rani's version of History: "People engaged in building new myths have no time for embroidered criticism" (S, 277), she comments laconically.

In view of this, it may be seen as a justifiable point of criticism when Inderpal Grewal claims that Rushdie does not succeed in giving voice to femaleness: "There is a disjunction between the mode of inclusion in which the narrative is written and the authoritative stance of the writer suggested in the novel, a stance that breaks down a coalition between the writer and women" (Grewal, 124-25). According to Grewal, Rushdie does not manage to meet the intention of inclusion, expressed explicitly by the narrator, as the voice through which the women are refracted has an authoritarian, masculine status. The case of Rani also underlines the isolation of the discourse, given the fact that her eighteen shawls do not reach beyond the private sphere. However, I agree with Margareta Petersson when she counters Grewal's position and grants Rushdie's project a great deal of success: "Grewal's (...) criticism of the novel has the weakness of lifting out the portraits of the women as isolated and too meagrely analysed structures. They disregard the functions these structures have in the entirety, that is, genre, character, and theme" (Petersson, 175).

Grewal is right in observing that the female discourse rarely challenges the masculine, but she is not right in perceiving the entire female discourse as refracted through the narrative voice as the female voices often speak directly through a mimetic configuration in the novel. Hence, the reader does not only encounter the novel's female voices through the diegesis of the narrator (sheer narration or free indirect discourse). If we move a step further along the scale of enunciation, we obviously end with the writer himself giving voice to his characters, but Rushdie is indeed capable of creating convincing female voices in spite of being male. Claiming the opposite would be an extremely unfruitful perception of art as incapable of creating a diversity of plausible voices and, with that, possible beings. What we are left with in *Shame*, in my opinion, is a credible image of female discourse which may not succeed in undermining the official power discourse on the level of story, but achieves its force and autonomy in the narrative performance and on the overall plane of aesthetics in art. One may say that the fact that female discourse is cowed in Pakistan is convincingly manifested in the novel on the level of the story (the fictive level), but through the frames Rushdie sets up in the novel the subjugated discourse of women is granted autonomy, extroversion, and, not least, a central role in the novel's overall picture (the pragmatic level).

Grewal's criticism implies that Rushdie legitimises passivity and the lack of female identity by describing it, but the narrator seems to pre-empt such analysis through the following passage:

> I hope that it goes without saying that not all women are crushed by any system, no matter how oppressive. It is commonly, and I believe, accurately said of Pakistan that her women are much more impressive than her men... their chains, nevertheless, are no fictions. They exist. And they are getting heavier.
> *If you hold down one thing you hold down the adjoining.*
> In the end, though, it all blows up in your face (S, 173).

What is oppressed may explode precisely by providing it with a voice, as outlined in *Shame* on the pragmatic level. Rani's shawls are not useless just because they are not seen by the fictive characters in the novel. On the contrary, the shawls represent images that are consistent with the overall code of the novel, and, apart from the narrator, Rani is the richest character in terms of insight. Similarly, it may be said that Bilquìs, despite her passivity and psychological instability, is aware of Raza's ruthless brutality, and so is the reader through her. The fictive level, or the level of the story, provides us with a multiplicity of voices, of which the female voices in particular remain peripheral and ineffective, but on the pragmatic level, or on the overall plane of aesthetics, the voices are orchestrated as a polyphony in which the peripheral voices are assigned with strength and potency. The pragmatic level and the configuration of frames only exist within the sphere of art, and so it is only through art that dominated and peripheral discourses may achieve equality and autonomy in relation to the official power discourse; herein lies the distinctive potential of the genre of the novel.

As we have already noted, the narrative voice in *Shame* adopts a more monological and authoritarian character than in Rushdie's other novels. But at the same time we have seen that the narrator admits the failure and limitations of his perspective several times. If we maintain the authoritarian profile of the narrative voice and relate it to the female discourse, we may conclude that the authoritarian discourse does in actual fact contribute to a reinforcement of the strength and autonomy of the female discourse, as for instance in the passage cited above.

Just as the narrator tries to establish a relation between his own status and the status of women, he identifies a common characteristic between the condition of the international migrant and his own and women's situation:

> I, too, know something of this immigrant business. I am an emigrant from one country (India) and a newcomer in two (England, where I live, and Pakistan, to which my family moved against my will). And I have a theory that the resentment we *mohajirs* engender have something to do with our conquest of the force of gravity. We have performed the act of which all men anciently dream, the thing for which they envy the birds; that is to say, we have flown.
>
> I am comparing gravity with belonging. Both phenomena observably exist: my feet stay on the ground, and I have never been angrier than I was on the day my father told me he had sold my childhood home in Bombay. But neither is understood. We know the force of gravity, but not its origins; and to explain why we become attached to our birthplaces we

> pretend that we are trees and speak of roots. Look under your feet. You will not find gnarled growths sprouting through the soles. Roots, I sometimes think, are a conservative myth, designed to keep us in our places.
> The anti-myths of gravity and of belonging bear the same name: flight. *Migration, n., moving, for instance in flight, from one place to another.* To fly and to flee: both are ways of seeking freedom (S, 85-86).

Thus the narrator traces the overall tension between roots and rootlessness, between gravity and flying, between belonging and fleeing. The migrant enjoys an advantage in having conquered gravity in a metaphorical sense as he/she has been pulled up by the roots and has flown across land. As the quote implies, there is a lot of positives attached to this condition, whereas rootedness is perceived as a conservative and restrictive myth which is used only to control the movement of people, such as flight and exit ways out of fixed territories, in both a geographical, cultural, psychological, and physical sense. In an interview Rushdie points out that, to him, the consequences of migration are a matter of excess rather than absence: "I don't think that migration, the process of being uprooted, necessarily leads to rootlessness. What it can lead to is a kind of multiple rooting. It's not the traditional identity crisis of not knowing where you come from. The problem is that you come from too many places. The problems are of excess rather than of absence. That's certainly the feeling I have" (Reder, ix).[30]

Lines of flight are significant in Rushdie's fiction, especially because he welcomes migration, nomadism, and root-networks, regarding them as prolific intermezzo-positions and indisputable human conditions. The greatest benefit of the migrant condition is hope and the worst thing is the empty luggage. As the narrator goes on:

> What is the best thing about migrant peoples and seceded nations? I think it is their hopefulness. Look into the eyes of such folk in old photographs. Hope blazes undimmed through the fading sepia tints. And what's the worst thing? It is the emptiness of one's luggage. I'm speak-

---

30 Michael R. Reder quotes an interview from *The New York Times Book Review*, November 13, 1983, made by Michael Kaufmann, "Author From 3 Countries".

ing of invisible suitcases, not the physical, perhaps cardboard, variety containing a few meaning-drained mementoes: we have come unstuck from more than land. We have floated upwards from history, from memory, from Time (S, 86-87).

Accordingly, the narrator, and Rushdie, do not support complete rootlessness unreservedly, but clearly point to the ambivalence of the migrant situation; with no firm ground beneath his or her feet, worlds of opportunity may uncover themselves to the migrant, resulting in optimistic hopefulness, but at the same time the migrant, due to his or her conquest of gravity, has become severed from history, time, and memory.

The cartographic performance occupies a central place in the migrant condition as the migrant's situation prompts the migrant to fill out the holes of the past and the present:

> As for me: I, too, like all migrants, am a fantasist. I build imaginary countries and try to impose them on the ones that exist. I, too, face the problem of history: what to retain, what to dump, how to hold on to what memory insists on relinquishing, how to deal with change. And to come back to the 'roots' idea, I should say that I haven't managed to shake myself free of it completely. Sometimes I do see myself as a tree, even, rather grandly, as the ash Yggdrasil, the mythical world-tree of Norse legend (S, 88).

The mapping of imaginary homelands is a compensation for the disconnectedness of one's past and, as noted previously, Rushdie does not regret this situation. Partially belonging to several countries equips him with a double vision with which he is enabled to project newness:

> Our identity is at once plural and partial. Sometimes we feel that we straddle two cultures; at other times, that we fall between two stools. But however ambiguous and shifting this ground may be, it is not an infertile territory for a writer to occupy. If literature is in part the business of finding new angles at which to enter reality, then once again our distance, our long geographical perspective, may provide us with such angles. (...) A full migrant suffers, traditionally, a triple disruption: he loses his place,

he enters into an alien language, and he finds himself surrounded by beings whose social behaviour and codes are very unlike, and sometimes even offensive to, his own. And this is what makes migrants such important figures: because roots, language and social norms have been three of the most important parts of the definition of what it is to be a human being. The migrant, denied all three, is obliged to find new ways of describing himself, new ways of being human. (...) This is what the triple disruption of reality teaches migrants: that reality is an artefact, that it does not exist until it is made, and that, like any other artefact, it can be made well or badly, and that it can also, of course, be unmade (IH, 15, 278, 280).

Just as the rhizome in Deleuze and Guattari's theory cannot be conceived without a tree (remember that the rhizome and the tree never appear as pure forms; rather, as Deleuze and Guattari underline, the rhizome arborises or the tree rhizomatises), migration is never conceived by Rushdie without a longing for roots. However, the fundamental ontology in both Rushdie and in Deleuze and Guattari is processual whereby any rootedness only occurs locally and provisionally: "In our deepest natures, we are frontier-crossing beings" (SA, 350), says Rushdie. Within recent years, Rushdie has in fact expressed an awareness of a possible shift in his writings in that he now unequivocally prefers not to belong: "There was always a tug-of-war in me between 'there' and 'here,' the pull of roots and of the road. In that struggle of insiders and outsiders, I used to feel simultaneously on both sides. Now I've come down on the side of those who by preference, nature, or circumstance simply do not belong. This unbelonging – I think of it as *disorientation*, loss of the East – is my artistic country now" (SA, 266).

As with *Midnight's Children*, *Shame* may be characterised as a rhizome, although the lines in *Shame*, with the tendency to monological discourse in its narrative voice, appear to arborise to a greater extent than in *Midnight's Children*. Certainly, the composition of *Shame* is primarily informed by a logic of inversion which, at times, fixes diversity in binary oppositions. Yet, the predominant compositional principle is a logic of conjunction which coordinates diversity in an aesthetics of variety rather than in an aesthetics of binaries. This causes the novel's architecture to be flat rather than hierarchical. It is also in *Shame* that Rushdie unfolds the theme of migration in earnest. The novel comprises a conceptual framework with notions like inbetweenness, flight, and excess, which may all be said to concur with Deleuzean concepts like intermezzo, deterritorialisation, and intensity.

The Satanic Verses

The Satanic Verses is noticeably centred on the question of human identity. The novel marks the culmination of the themes of roots and rootlessness, stillness and flux, continuity and discontinuity, and identity and difference, which we have examined so far in Rushdie's earlier novels. In *The Satanic Verses* Rushdie reaches the limit of the project that he launched in *Grimus* and continued in *Midnight's Children* and *Shame*: to invent the ground beneath his feet. While the characters in *The Satanic Verses* in many ways appear as unambiguous extremities on a Rushdian scale, the novel also contains a cautious tribute to the idea of having at least one foot planted on the ground, illustrated with Saladin's fate. Rushdie thus says to W.J. Webb: "I do think that what happens in the novel, one way of saying what happens in the novel, is that the fantasticated character, the kind of grotesque mythological character, comes to a bad end. And the one who is more rooted, or becomes to be more rooted, in some kind of more real version of the world, if you like, survives" (Webb, 91). However, it is important to emphasise that Rushdie does not see the question as one of being either rooted or rootless, to him it is a matter of planting the self in several places.

In *The Satanic Verses* several characters have been given the same name, something which produces variations of a given theme and causes echoes to resound across the heterogeneous lines of the novel's universe. This is the case of Hind, for instance, which is both the name of Muhammad Sufyan's wife, the owner of the Shaandaar Café, and of Abu Simbel's wife in the dream track about Mahound. Hind and Muhammad Sufyan have emigrated from Bangladesh where Muhammad worked as a teacher and a left wing activist. Muhammad is forced to emigrate because of his political activism and Hind, who had identified herself with the role of the submissive blushing bride back in Bangladesh, staying in the shadow of her husband and ruling the kitchen where she practised an eclecticism parallel to her husband's intellectual pluralism, has a hard time coping with the changes of migration: "Everything she valued had been upset by the change; had in this process of translation, been lost" (SV, 249). Exiled from her language, her customs, and her geographical home country, "she had sunk into the anonymity, the characterless plurality, of being merely one-of-the-women-like-her. This was history's lesson: nothing for women-like-her to do but suffer, remember, and die" (SV, 250). Hind is a paradoxical character because her problems of acclimatising to her new surroundings go together with the fact that she is the one who controls the business of the Shaandaar Café: it is her culinary skills that attract a wide range of customers, and it is her sense of business that enables the family to expand the establishment to include letting as well. In short, Hind becomes the master of the house, but the apparent triumph over her husband is regarded as a defeat by Hind as she used to be pleased with her role in the shadow in Bangladesh. Now she sees their inverted roles, that is Hind as the cook and Muhammad as the waiter, as a defeat of the set of values she was raised with.

In contrast Muhammad thrives with his non-committal role as a chatting waiter and appears to consume a fair share of the modern temptations of the West, such as for instance videos *en masse*: "Mr Muhammad Sufyan, prop. Shaandaar Café and landlord of the rooming-house above, mentor to the variegated, transient and particoloured inhabitants of both, seen-it-all type, least doctrinaire of hajis and most unashamed of VCR addicts, ex-schoolteacher, self-taught in classical texts of many cultures, dismissed from post in Dhaka owing to cultural differences with certain generals in the old days" (SV, 243). Throughout the novel, Sufyan is portrayed in a positive light and it is also Sufyan who, in spite of Hind's persistent protests and fear for the innocence of her daughters, allows the frightening, goatlike Saladin to live in his attic. The Sufyans' two girls, the beautiful Mishal and Anahita, have adopted the English way of life and reject Bangladeshi culture out of hand, including both food, language, clothes, and religion. The antagonistic lines between Hind and her daughters are solidly drawn and result in a number of confrontations throughout the novel.

Like Hind Sufyan, Hind Simbel is a strong female figure who winds up exceeding her husband's level of aspirations. In the chapters about Jahilia, she is Mahound's worst enemy, unbending and unchanged for many years. "Only Hind was the same as ever" (SV, 360), the narrator notes about her when Mahound returns to Jahilia after his exile in Yathrib to finally institute his monotheistic religion Submission and consequently abolish the 360 existing god(desse)s spearheaded by Al-Lat.[31] Through the Hind figure, one of the novel's main themes is introduced, the theme of compromise versus intransigence. The butterfly girl Ayesha and the hijacker Tavleen are two other figures who refuse to compromise their ideals and principles.

The novel introduces other axes or models of explanation in connection with the problem of human identity. To start with, Muhammad Sufyan brings in Apuleius at the sight of the transformed Saladin and later on he outlines the quintessence of metamorphosis in Ovid and Lucretius. According to Ovid, the subject is characterised by a consistent essence that remains the same continuously, illustrated by a ball of wax which may take various shapes, but never ceases to be wax. To Lucretius, on the other hand, we are dealing with a complete metamorphosis of the self where the old self has to die in order for the new to be born. The first sentence in *The Satanic Verses*, which serves as one of the novel's *leitmotifs*, echoes precisely this idea: "'To be born again,' sang Gibreel Farishta tumbling from the heavens, 'first you have to die'" (SV, 3). Saleem, it is remembered, was for a brief spell completely free of his old self. Sufyan backs Ovid, whereas Saladin, at this point of time, considers Lucretius's theory as the most plausible (and advantageous).

Through Gibreel and Saladin, two contradictory, yet mutually dependent cartographies of human identity are plotted out. As we have seen, identity in Rushdie's novels is always created through a connection with nationality, religion, history, and politics. Rushdie has said that Gibreel is primarily to be understood through the division that occurs within him when he loses his faith in God during a severe illness; Saladin,

---

31   Jahilia is the Muslim concept of the historic age preceding the holy revelations and means ignorance in Arabic; accordingly, Rushdie's term for pre-Islamic Mecca is ignorance. Yathrib is the pre-Islamic name for Medina. Finally, Islam means submission in Arabic.

on the other hand, is to be understood through his sense of being divided between India and England.[32] I agree with this interpretation.

In Gibreel's case, metamorphosis takes place the moment he realises that he no longer needs Allah: "On that day of metamorphosis the illness changed and his recovery began. And to prove to himself the non-existence of God, he now stood in the dining-hall of the city's most famous hotel, with pigs falling out of his face" (SV, 30). In defiance and to prove to himself that God does not exist, Gibreel throws himself at the buffet, stacking his plate "with the gammon steaks of his unbelief and the pig's trotters of secularism" (SV, 29).[33] The scene contains yet another key factor for the rest of Gibreel's life as he, with a mouth full of pig, catches the sight of "Alleluia Cone, climber of mountains, vanquisher of Everest, blonde yahudan, ice queen" (SV, 31); Gibreel loses Allah, but wins Allie.

The religious doubt in Gibreel's mind becomes a catalyst that controls the dream tracks about Mahound, the Imam, and Ayesha. Furthermore, these dream tracks are "fed" by Gibreel's experiences from the film industry, and by the self-understanding his mother has helped under way by calling him *farishta* (angel in Urdu) during his childhood

---

32   Rushdie says in "In Good Faith", for example: "*The Satanic Verses* is the story of two painfully divided selves. In the case of one, Saladin Chamcha, the division is secular and societal: he is torn, to put it plainly, between Bombay and London, between East and West. For the other, Gibreel Farishta, the division is spiritual, a rift in the soul. He has lost his faith and is strung out between his immense need to believe and his new inability to do so. The novel is 'about' their quest for wholeness" (IH, 397). It is necessary to keep Rushdie's motives at the back of one's mind when one uses this essay to support one's analysis as it has been written with the clear-cut purpose of defending the novel against the harshest allegations of blasphemy. Generally I think that Rushdie's reading of his own novel is well argued and plausible, but at the same time he excludes other possible interpretations. In a way he takes the novel into a space of closure in which it does not belong, but the necessity of this tactic is understandable.

33   This episode derives from Rushdie's own life: "God, Satan, Paradise and Hell all vanished one day in my fifteenth year, when I quite abruptly lost my faith. I recall it vividly. I was at school in England by then. The moment of awakening happened, in fact, during a Latin lesson, and afterwards, to prove my new-found atheism, I bought myself a rather tasteless ham sandwich, and so partook for the first time of the forbidden flesh of the swine. No thunderbolt arrived to strike me down" (IH, 377).

and by naming him Ismail Najmuddin, "Ismail after the child involved in the sacrifice of Ibrahim, and Najmuddin, *star of the faith*" (SV, 17). Added to this, we know that Gibreel piled into books in frustration of his unsuccessfulness with the female sex during the first years of his acting career:

> To get his mind off the subject of love and desire, he studied, becoming an omnivorous autodidact, devouring the metamorphic myths of Greece and Rome, the avatars of Jupiter, the boy who became a flower, the spider-woman, Circe, everything; and the theosophy of Annie Besant, and unified field theory, and the incident of the Satanic Verses in the early career of the Prophet, and the politics of Muhammad's harem after his return to Mecca in triumph; and the surrealism of the newspapers, in which butterflies could fly into young girl's mouths (SV, 23-24).

In this passage we hear about the episodes of the satanic verses and the butterfly girl for the first time, which develop into the two dream tracks that, at a later point, make up a significant part of Gibreel's schizophrenic character.

In Saladin's case the division occurs the day he finds a wallet with English bank notes on the pavement and his father, the patriarchal Changez, takes it away from him: "After that the son became convinced that his father would smother all his hopes unless he got away, and from that moment he became desperate to leave, to escape, to place oceans, between the great man and himself" (SV, 36-37). Whereas Gibreel's metamorphosis appears to arise from an accidental situation, which Gibreel tries to defeat to no avail, Saladin's metamorphosis is more willed. The divide between Indianness and Englishness represents a conscious determination on Saladin's behalf to escape his roots and become more English than the English: "his determination to become the thing his father was-not-could-never-be, that is, a goodandproper Englishman" (SV, 43).

When Saladin is sent to the boarding school in England, he overcomes a trying period with bullying and isolation, but "these exclusions only increased his determination, and that was when he began to act, to find masks that these fellows would recognize, paleface masks, clown-masks, until he fooled them into thinking he was *okay*, he was *people-like-us*" (SV, 43). Saladin invents various identities which he alternates between throughout the discontinuous leaps he makes, indeed he is "the Man of a Thousand Voices and a Voice" (SV, 60), whereas Gibreel's identities coexist and seem more continuous. At this point in the novel Saladin seems to form an image of Lucretius's theory on metamorphosis, while Gibreel corresponds much more to Ovid's theory.

Reflecting on Saladin's project, the narrator says:

> A man who sets out to make himself up is taking on the Creator's role, according to one way of seeing things; he's unnatural, a blasphemer, an abomination of abominations. From another angle, you could see pathos in him, heroism in his struggle, in his willingness to risk: not all mutants survive. Or, consider him socio-politically: most migrants learn, and can become disguises. Our own false descriptions to counter the falsehood invented about us, concealing for reasons of security our secret selves (SV, 49).

In this passage the narrator outlines a number of possible ways in which Saladin's willed metamorphosis may be perceived: the first explanation condemns the project as blasphemous through a religious discourse, the actual creation of humans being the prerogative of God. The next explanation sees Saladin through a tragic discourse, in which man risks death in a heroic struggle. The last explanation understands Saladin's self-constructions as socio-political, as a defence against the false constructions created by power discourses. The explanations are not presented as hierarchically differentiated, all three – the dissociative, the admiring, and the sympathising explanation – appear as plausible ways in which to comprehend Saladin.

When Saladin visits his family in Bombay after his stay on the boarding school and before commencing his university studies, his transformation into an English gentleman is at an advanced stage and his bitterness towards his father and everything Indian is steadily growing. At the same time his mother passes away, which triggers a complete exposure of the fragility of the tie between father and son. When Changez marries Nasreen II without prior notice one year after Nasreen's death, the relationship between father and son deteriorates and is finally terminated.

After graduating from university, Saladin settles in London and goes on the stage. Returning to Bombay during a tour, he experiences several heavy confrontations with his past, which causes his present mask to crack. Visibly distressed by the lack of self-control, Saladin confides in his friend, the doctor and art critic Zeenat Vakil: "When he was young, he told her, each phase of his life, each self he tried on, had seemed reassuringly temporary. Its imperfections didn't matter, because he could easily replace one moment by the next, one Saladin by another. Now, however, change had begun to feel painful; the arteries of the possible had begun to harden" (SV, 63). The former ease with which Saladin could jump from one role to another, from one mask to another, yields to encumbrance. The past resurfaces in, for instance, Saladin's speech, which up until now has poshly manifested itself as the Queen's English, but gives way to his old Indian-English idiom on the flight back to London from Bombay. When a stewardess wakes him from a slumber to offer him drinks, Saladin semi-consciously exclaims: "'Achha, means what?' he mumbled. 'Alcoholic beverage or what?' And, when the stewardess reassured him, whatever you wish, sir, all beverages are gratis, he heard, once again, his traitor voice: 'so, okay, bibi, give one whiskysoda only'" (SV, 34). Here, the nature of metamorphosis is staged through the material properties of language, denoting the mental condition of the character through idiom as an intermezzo between Indian and English identity, between past and present, between self-control and inevitable capitulation.

Above all, it is Zeeny who sees through Saladin's project and criticises his attempt to escape the past: "You know what you are, I'll tell you. A deserter is what, more English than, your Angrez accent wrapped around you like a flag, and don't think it's so perfect, it slips, baba, like a false moustache" (SV, 53). This outburst does not mean that Zeeny advocates Indian nationalism, on the contrary, she supports a form of pragmatic eclecticism: "She was an art critic whose book on the confining myth of authenticity, that folkloristic straitjacket which she sought to replace by an ethic of historically validated eclecticism (...) had created a predictable stink" (SV, 52).[34]

---

34   Zeeny's importance in the novel is supported by Rushdie's own assertion of eclecticism: "The rest of us understand that the very essence of Indian culture is that we possess a mixed tradition, a mélange of elements as disparate as ancient

At one time in a pub with Zeeny and some of her friends, Saladin begins to feel sick due to the imposing Indianness that surrounds him: "Chamcha clutched his glass as the noise level rose, and the air seemed to thicken, gold teeth flashed in his face, shoulders rubbed against his, elbows nudged, the air was turning into soup, and in his chest the irregular palpitations had begun" (SV, 57). The bombardment of the senses and the violent signs undermines Saladin's self-control and unlocks the past: "He had to accept the fact that his blood no longer contained the immunizing agents that would have enabled him to suffer India's reality" (SV, 57).

When Saladin visits his father in the home of his childhood, he feels overpowered by the past once again: "Saladin felt the past rush in like a tide, drowning him, filling his lungs with its revenant saltiness. *I'm not myself today*, he thought. The heart flutters. Life damages the living. None of us are ourselves. None of us are *like this*" (SV, 65). The feeling of necessity in the constitution of human identity, which crops up in the contingent encounter with an Outside, for example the childhood home, questions Saladin's "heroic" project of creating his own masks independent of past experiences. This explains why Saladin is out of balance, and increasingly so, when he is faced with the scenario his father inhabits with the old servant couple, Vallabh and Kasturba. As it transpires, Changez maintains due respect towards his late wife Nasreen I, on the one hand, by preserving the house exactly the way it was when she died, and, on the other hand, by having Kasturba dressed in Nasreen's old saris and perform the role of the lady of the house in any conceivable way. The perversity of this arrangement stirs Saladin's irreconcilable anger at his father, causing him once again to break up their relationship. Hence, Saladin boards the plane to London with highly complex motives and feelings: the once repressed past re-imposes itself (illustrated, for example, by the slip of tongue on the plane), but at the same time this

Mughal and contemporary Coca-Cola American. To say nothing of Muslim, Buddhist, Jain, Christian, Jewish, British, French, Portuguese, Marxist, Maoist, Trotskyist, Vietnamese, capitalist, and of course Hindu elements. Eclecticism, the ability to take from the world that seems fitting and to leave the rest, has always been a hallmark of the Indian tradition, and today it is at the centre of the best work being done both in the visual arts and in literature" (IH, 67).

uncontrollable pressure prompts Saladin once and for all to cut the anchor chain, and the experience of the surrealist scenario in his childhood home underpins the necessity of this decision.

Thus, we have seen how Gibreel and Saladin each suffers from deep divisions, a sacred and a profane division, and we have seen how these divisions have developed and consolidated themselves as the determining factors of their identities. Onboard the plane Saladin's division also manifests itself in the contrast between (Indian) superstition and (English) rationality as a nightmare he has had about hijacking starts to become real; this is one of the examples of how ontological boundaries are blurred in the novel. In the thrall of his internal division and clinging to English virtues, such as common sense and rational explanations, or simply by repressing the connection between his dream and reality, Saladin tries to dismiss the increasingly forceful indications that the figments of his imagination are materialising around him.

As for Gibreel, the serial dreams begin to haunt him during the 111 days long hijack: "The dreams had begun that very night. In these visions he was always present, not as himself but as his namesake, and I don't mean interpreting a role, Spoono, I am him, he is me, I am the bloody archangel, Gibreel himself, large as bloody life" (SV, 83). The text does not explain the dreams unequivocally, but suggests that they may be perceived as true revelations as well as they may be a deflection of Gibreel's megalomania. Besides, the passage is an example of free indirect discourse, the idioms of the narrator and the character leaking into each other.

When the uncompromising Tavleen, the (metaphorical and literal) sex bomb pulls the string that sets off the explosion that blows up the plane, one of these threshold situations between the old and the new order comes to light, a destruction containing a construction. Gibreel hovers in an intermezzo between a waking and a dreaming state, a schizophrenic process has started, the course of which is directed by doubt, religion, and love. Saladin floats in an intermezzo between India and England, between past and present, at one at the same time fervently intent on flight and helplessly deadlocked by remnants of memory squeezing his superficial skin.

The time is New Year's day, or thereabouts, a symbol of the transition from the old to the new where things gather speed, like the midnight hour in *Midnight's Children*. The place is in the air space above England: "Out of thin air: a big bang, followed by falling stars. A universal beginning, a miniature echo of the birth of time… the jumbo jet *Bostan*, Flight Al-420, blew apart without any warning, high above the great, rotting, beautiful, snow-white, illuminated city, Mahagonny, Babylon, Alphaville" (SV, 4). We meet Gibreel and Saladin at the beginning of the novel, falling through the air as seats, headphones, dutyfree videogames, sheets, oxygen masks, untranslatable jokes, and revealed secrets are whizzing by:

> but for whatever reason, the two men, Gibreelsaladin Farishtachamcha, condemned to this endless but also ending angelicdevilish fall, did not become aware of the moment at which the processes of their transmutation began.
> Mutation?
> Yessir, but not random. Up there in air-space, in that soft, imperceptible field which had been made possible by the century and which, thereafter, made the century possible, becoming one of its defining locations, the place of movement and war, the planet-shrinker and power-vacuum, most insecure and transitory of zones, illusory, discontinuous, metamorphic, – because when you throw everything up in the air anything becomes possible – wayupthere, at any rate, changes took place in delirious actors that would have gladdened the heart of old Mr Lamarck: under extreme environmental pressure, characteristics were acquired (SV, 5).

In this transitory, illusory airspace properties are transferred between our two heroes while at the same time a number of new properties are conferred to them: "But they had fallen through the transformations of the clouds, Chamcha and Farishta, and there was a fluidity, an indistinctness, at the edges of them" (SV, 8). In this zone their bodies become permeable and open to new flux and intensities, the boundaries of their bodies are liquid and receptive to molecular micro-forces, deterritorialising the once solid organism by discharging new lines of flight.

The cause of the metamorphosis is ambiguous.[35] The text catalogues various frames of explanation, primarily through intertextual references: The theory of evolution is suggested through the comparison with The Big Bang and the allusion to Lamarck. In addition, a religious interpretation is allowed for as the name of the plane, Bostan, is the name of one of the gardens of Paradise in the Koran. Hence the fall may be read as a secularised parallel to the story in the Koran about Iblis' expulsion from Heaven (Sûra 15, verses 31-36) or the story in the Bible about Satan's banishment from Heaven. A third reading of the metamorphosis centres on airspace as a symbol of the migrant's conquest of gravity, Saladin and Gibreel's fall reflecting the movement and hybridisation of the migrant in an intensified sense. In addition, the novel reflects a notion of the borderlessness of imagination, stated through "anything becomes possible," and the imperative behind this reflection being one of pushing art to the limits of the thinkable.

Similarly, there is a connection between the dream tracks and the novel's metamorphosing quality, which opens the possibility of a psychological interpretation of the constitution of the metamorphosis. Yet, the psychological interpretation, which has been deployed in the defence of Rushdie in the Affair, is problematic because the composition of *The Satanic Verses* is of such a complex nature that it is often impossible to maintain a clear distinction between dream and reality. The argumentation of the defence depends on a separation of the novel's ontological levels: "But the blasphemous sections are just dreams," the argument goes. However, this is only partially correct because the "echo-effect" breaks down the boundaries between the ontological levels, for instance through the convergence of names: Ayesha penetrates the internal boundaries between three dream tracks, as she is the name of the Imam's enemy (the C-line), the butterfly girl (the C-line), and Mahound's favourite wife (the B-line). As has been shown, the boundaries between dream and reality are questioned in the case of Hind who is both Muhammad

---

35   As regards the idea of the ambiguous cause of the metamorphosis, I am indebted to Leif Bonderup and his unpublished dissertation *Refleksivitetens materielle vej i* The Satanic Verses: *Om romangenre, metamorfose og Rushdie-affæren (The Material Way of Reflexivity in* The Satanic Verses: *On the Genre of the Novel, Metamorphosis and the Rushdie Affair)*, pp. 55-82, from Aarhus University, 1998.

Sufyan's wife (the A-line) and Abu Simbel's wife (the B-line). Added to that, London's topographical evanescence (the A-line) recurs in that of Jahilia, built of sand (the B-line).

Whereas Hind and London-Jahilia may be explained as residues from the dreams, there are other echoes which must be determined as schizophrenic manifestations: for instance, the prostitutes appear in the dream of Jahilia (the B-line) and subsequently they turn up in the next chapter during Gibreel's roamings around London (the A-line). The residues are characterised by elements from the odd-numbered chapters (the A-line) emerging in even-numbered chapters (the B- and C-lines), whereas Gibreel's schizophrenia manifests itself when elements from the even-numbered chapters appear in the odd-numbered chapters. However, the distinction between residues and schizophrenia is determined by the precondition that the novel is chronological, but the temporal relation between the chapters is often unspecified, which makes it difficult to maintain a clear distinction between residue and schizophrenia. Each of the three lines progress along a relatively chronological line of narration, but the dream tracks are almost impossible to place in time in relation to the A-line. So, the psychological analysis that defends Rushdie is problematic primarily because it does not take the compositional complexity into consideration and, secondly, because it excludes the other explanations of the metamorphosis.

*

Gibreel and Saladin survive the fall miraculously and land on the English coast where Rosa Diamond invites them to stay in her house. Saladin and Gibreel have been reborn and find themselves in a kind of virginal state, characteristic of the migrant position: "Then nothing existed. He was in a void, and if he were to survive he would have to construct everything from scratch, would have to invent the ground beneath his feet before he could take a step" (SV, 132). By now their bodily transformations are at an advanced stage:

> And around the edges of Gibreel Farishta's head, as he stood with his back to the dawn, it seemed to Rosa Diamond that she discerned a faint, but distinctly golden, *glow*.

> And were those bumps, at Chamcha's temples, under his sodden and still-in-place bowler hat?
> And, and, and (SV, 133).

The finishing line in this quotation is interesting as it reminds us of Deleuze and Guattari's characterisation of rhizome-literature as an and-literature. As has been noted before, Rushdie's novels also progress via conjunctions rather than attributions, and the "and, and, and" indicates exactly the continuous proliferation of the metamorphoses of our two main characters: it is the conjunction, or the clash, between India and England and between faith and doubt that determines Saladin and Gibreel respectively.

After Saladin has been arrested Gibreel stays with Rosa Diamond where he is magnetically sucked into the magical-realist stories of her past in Argentina in the 1930s. It is also during his stay with Rosa that it becomes increasingly difficult for Gibreel to sustain the distinction between dream and reality: "the universe of his nightmares had begun to leak into his waking life" (SV, 144). On her deathbed, Rosa tells him about her relationship with Martín de la Cruz, a story that refuses to choose between several diverse versions of the chain of events. Did Rosa shoot Martín? Did Martín shoot Rosa's husband, Henry? Did Rosa turn down Martín's sexual advances, with rape as a consequence? Did she give in to her passions and make love to Martín? As regards the last two questions, the narrator notes: "the two possibilities kept alternating, while dying Rosa tossed on her bed, did-she-didn't-she, making the last version of the story of her life, unable to decide what she wanted to be true (...) so that it was not possible to distinguish memory from wishes, or guilty reconstructions from confessional truths" (SV, 152-53). Margareta Petersson correctly sees the frame story of Rosa Diamond as a prism with metafictive overtones as it contains a reflection on the difficulty in establishing an unequivocal picture of the ontology of the novel's fictive universe.

While Gibreel is enjoying life at Rosa's, Saladin goes through a terrible time of police violence, racism, painful metamorphoses, and humiliations: "His thighs had grown uncommonly wide and powerful, as well as hairy. Below the knee the hairness came to a halt, and his legs narrowed into tough, bony, almost fleshless calves, terminating in a pair of shiny, cloven hoofs, such as one might find on any billy-goat. Saladin was also taken aback by the sight of his phallus, greatly enlarged and embarrassingly erect, an organ that he had the greatest difficulty in acknowledging as his own" (SV, 157). Rushdie projects a number of outstanding scenes with striking dialogues among the policemen, the underlying motives aiming at a portrayal of pitiless racism, the crudeness of herd mentality, and the self-feeding effect of violence. When the policemen finally recognise their mistake of arresting a respectable British citizen, the auto-protective power mechanisms of the state machinery are activated through a cover-up, drowning out any potential protest by the individual.

Saladin is admitted to a hospital where other monstrous creatures, such as manticores and glass-beings, are hospitalised. The patients all suffer from Western orientalism: "They have the power of description, and we succumb to the pictures they construct" (SV, 168). This is a recurrent theme in Rushdie, to whom the invention of new counter-images to established ideas is the prime purpose of art.[36] To the patients in the hospital, the stranger's (colonial) gaze has become the constituting factor of their self-understanding and self-image. However, the patients escape together and thus they literally project a line of flight that deterritorialises the colonisers' past concentration of power and produce an iconoclastic problematisation of the demonisation of the immigrant: "To migrate is certainly to lose language and home, to be defined by others, to become invisible or, even worse, a target; it is to experience deep changes and wrenches in the soul. But the migrant is not simply transformed by his act; he also transforms his new world. Migrants may well become mutants, but it is out of such hybridization that newness can emerge" (IH, 210). The active role of the migrant is suggested in the novel through the

---

36   "We live in ideas. Through images we seek to comprehend our world. And through images we sometimes seek to subjugate and dominate others. But picture-making, imagining, can also be a process of celebration, even of liberation. New images can chase out the old" (IH, 147), says Rushdie about the double movement in the creation of images. In the same essay, "Home Front," he adds: "The imagination can falsify, demean, ridicule, caricature and wound as effectively as it can clarify, intensify and unveil" (IH, 143).

image of the migrant as sperm cells: "yes, the father ship, an aircraft was not a flying womb but a metal phallus, and the passengers were spermatoza waiting to be spilt" (SV, 41). During the escape Saladin is struck by the same ontological "flicker" that haunts Gibreel as the distinction between sleep and being awake is erased as "states that flowed into and out of one another to create a kind of unending delirium of the senses" (SV, 169). Gradually, the novel assumes an increasingly schizoid and rhizomatic character, in which the centre is in constant movement, relations of time and space dissolve into irrational configurations, and causality operates according to an unusual logic.

After the escape from the hospital, Saladin calls on his wife Pamela Lovelace (clearly a Richardsonian simulacrum), with whom he finds his old study mate, Jumpy Joshi, dressed in a pyjama. Pamela refuses to recognise Saladin's presence and survival and Jumpy, stirred by a mixture of pity and shame, escorts Saladin to the Shaandaar Café where he is given shelter. Saladin's marriage with Pamela is characterised by two lines of flight crossing each other as both of them had tried to escape their backgrounds by marrying their opposites. Fleeing his Indian past, Saladin had seen Pamela as the incarnation of the English upper-class life that he strove to be part of, whereas Pamela in her effort to snub the aristocracy had thrown herself into the arms of the dark Indian with the outlandish customs and the exotic name (which used to be Salahuddin Chamchawalla).

Jumpy has lived with Pamela since the news of the plane crash and one night, grieving the assumed death of Saladin, he pays a nostalgic visit to his friend's room: "Chamcha's room struck the sleepless intruder as contrived, and therefore sad: the caricature of an actor's room full of signed photographs of colleagues, handbills, framed programmes, production stills, citations, awards, volumes of movie-star memoirs, a room bought off the peg, by the yard, an imitation of life, a mask's mask" (SV, 174). This description supports the former image of Saladin as the sycophant who, as Jumpy notices, would "change into any shape, if it earned him a loving word" (SV, 174). The depiction of the room imitates postmodern terminology and the reader may sense a certain amount of criticism of the kind of postmodernism that takes no root in life and merely stages an empty masquerade without substance.

While Saladin is dismissed from his own home, Gibreel is on his way to London, which greets him as an evasive and illusory city that insistently stands up against him: "It's A, I'm off my head, or B, baba, somebody went and changed the rules. (...) Fictions were walking around wherever he went, Gibreel reflected, fictions masquerading as real human beings" (SV, 189, 192). With the map "London from A to Z" as his guide, Gibreel has to realise that his dreams are about to take control of his personality: "Even the serial visions have migrated now; they know the city better than he. And in the aftermath of Rosa and Rekha the dream-worlds of his archangelic other self begin to seem as tangible as the shifting realities he inhabits while he's awake" (SV, 205).

Thus, both Saladin and Gibreel have lost hold of their lives. Saladin, who is baffled about the metamorphoses he goes through, sides with Lucretius in an attempt to understand himself: "The inconstant soul, the mutability of everything, das Ich, every last speck. A being going through life can become so other to himself as to *be another*, discrete, severed from history" (SV, 288). In the meantime, Gibreel is playing the role of the rescuing angel, while his fierce and messy looks are scaring people off: "Mr Gibreel Farishta, transformed into the simulacrum of an angel as surely as he was the Devil's mirror-self" (SV, 294). Opposites, like rescuer and devil, the good and the bad, Ovid and Lucretius, seem to get mixed up in the novel and become mutually dependent.

Saladin realises that the moral categories with which man is described are really internal matters rather than eternal and externally determined truths; evil is an immanent part of man just as kindness is.[37] Having recovered his human body, Saladin is happy to be transformed back to his old self, but soon he also realises that the entire process of his metamorphosis into a goat is part of him: "What Saladin Chamcha understood that day was that he had been living in a state of phoney peace, that the change in him was irreversible" (SV, 418). As he is confronted

---

37   In "In Good Faith" Rushdie says: "If migrant groups are called devils by others, that does not really make them demonic. And if devils are not necessarily devilish, angels may not necessarily be angelic... From this premise, the novel's exploration of morality as internal and shifting (rather than external, divinely sanctioned, absolute) may be said to emerge" (IH, 402-03).

with Gibreel again, evil flares up in him in the form of vindictiveness, but this time his hatred is aimed at an object whereby he keeps his human shape: "*humanized* – is there any option to conclude? – by the fearsome concentration of his hate" (SV, 294).

Gibreel, on the contrary, oscillates between exhausting spells of drifting, during which his schizophrenia spurs him on as the rescuing archangel, and periods of recovery in Allie's embrace: "'The craziness is in here and it drives me wild to think it could get out any minute, right now, and *he* would be in charge again.' He had begun to characterize his 'possessed,' 'angel' self as another person: in the Beckettian formula, *Not I. He.* His very own Mr Hyde. Allie attempted to argue against such descriptions. 'It isn't *he*, it's you, and when you're well, it won't be you any more'" (SV, 340). In the course of his wanderings round London, Gibreel realises that the problem of London is meteorologically determined, after which he proceeds to tropicalise the city, cataloguing and estimating the pros and cons of the effect of its tropicalisation:

> Gibreel enumerated the benefits of the proposed metamorphosis of London into a tropical city: increased moral definition, institution of a national siesta, development of vivid and expansive patterns of behaviour among the populace, higher-quality popular music, new birds in the trees (macaws, peacocks, cockatoos), new trees under the birds (coco-palms, tamarind, banyans with hanging beards). Improved streetlife, outrageously coloured flowers (magenta, vermilion, neon-green), spidermonkeys in the oaks. A new mass market for domestic air-conditioning units, ceiling fans, anti-mosquito coils and sprays. A coir and copra industry. Increased appeal of London as a centre for conferences, etc.; better cricketers; higher emphasis on ball-control among professional footballers, the traditional and soulless English commitment to "high workrate" having been rendered obsolete by the heat. Religious fervor, political ferment, renewal of interest in the intelligentsia. No more British reserve; hot-water bottles to be banished forever, replaced in the foetid nights by the making of slow and odorous love. Emergence of new social values: friends to commence dropping in on one another without making appointments, closure of old folks' homes, emphasis on the extended family. Spicier food; the use of water as well as paper

in English toilets; the joy of running fully dressed through the first rains of the monsoon.

Disadvantages: cholera, typhoid, legionnaires' disease, cockroaches, dust, noise, a culture of excess (SV, 354-55).

Rushdie is obviously playing with stereotypes in this wonderful passage. Whereas Gibreel wants to transform London to make it suit his identity, Saladin wants to transform his identity to make it suit the city, at least as it is depicted in the official images of it. In the chapter "A City Visible but Unseen", voicing the deviant lives of London, the subculture and the underground, Rushdie brilliantly succeeds in projecting an unofficial picture of London.

A significant cause of Gibreel's illness is his extremely jealous mind, and Saladin exploits this to drive him mad. Saladin starts calling Allie and Gibreel on the phone, pretending by means of his 1001 voices to be Allie's endless number of lovers – all invented by Saladin. Thus Saladin repeats the motif of the satanic verses, which, instead of arising out of a religious discourse, unfolds as a drama of love and revenge. As a consequence of Saladin's satanic verses and Gibreel's jealousy, Allie leaves Gibreel. When Gibreel learns that Saladin is behind the verses, he literally plays the role of the rescuing archangel, saving him from the sea of flames in the Shaandaar Café. However, Gibreel is not cured by his act of mercy, he continues to be locked in a pathological dead-end, which finally drives him to kill both S.S. Sisodia and Allie, whereupon he seeks out Saladin and commits suicide.

In contrast, and as indicated before, Saladin seems well on the way to become a "whole" person, and the episode in the Shaandaar Café, where he is rescued by the victim of his own smear campaign, helps him in the process. When Saladin decided in anger to make a definitive break with his past and his father, he asked his father to chop down the walnut tree planted by his father in the family garden on the occasion of Saladin's birth. The walnut tree was a symbol of Saladin's rootedness and Saladin's father was convinced that the tree contained Saladin's lost soul. Needless to say, the felling of the tree was a clear indication of Saladin's escape from home and Saladin has been tormented by this symbolism throughout the novel, but one day when he is watching a TV programme featuring a chimera, a grafted tree, he senses the possibility of new cohesion: "There it palpably was, a chimera with roots, firmly planted in and growing vigorously out of a piece of English earth: a tree, he thought, capable of taking the metaphoric place of the one his father had chopped down in a distant garden in another, incompatible world. If such a tree were possible, then so was he; he, too, could cohere, send down roots, survive" (SV, 406). The chimera seems to become a symbol of the acceptance of both his English and his Indian identity, of identity as a network of roots in preference to complete rootlessness or entrenched rootedness.

In a long passage the narrator explicitly reflects on the difference between the novel's two main characters:

> Should we even say that these are two fundamentally different *types* of self? Might we not agree that Gibreel, for all his stage-name and performances; and in spite of born-again slogans, new beginnings, metamorphoses; – has wished to remain, to a large degree, *continuous* – that is, joined to and arising from his past; that, in point of fact, he fears above all things the altered states in which his dreams leak into, and overwhelm, his waking self, making him that angelic Gibreel he has no desire to be; – so that his is still a self which, for our present purposes, we may describe as "true"... whereas Saladin Chamcha is a creature of *selected* discontinuities, a *willing* re-invention; his *preferred* revolt against history being what makes him, in our chosen idiom, "false"? And might we then not go on to say that it is this falsity of self that makes possible in Chamcha a worse and deeper falsity – call this "evil" – and that this is the truth, the door, that was opened in him by his fall? – While Gibreel, to follow the logic of our established terminology, is to be considered "good" by virtue of *wishing to remain*, for all his vicissitudes, at bottom an untranslated man (SV, 427).

There is a certain truth to the narrator's account. So far we have also employed a terminology along the lines of the above in our analysis, but at the same time we have also made the suggestion that the distinction between truth and falseness or goodness and evil cannot be maintained because the novel stipulates that the difference between these opposites is not essential or externally determined; rather, it is accidental and internally motivated by each of the novel's characters. The narrator adds: "Such distinctions, resting as they must on an idea of the self as being (ideally) homogeneous, non-hybrid, 'pure' – an utterly fantastic notion! – cannot, must not, suffice" (SV, 427). Who says that truth is to remain the same and to change is a matter of deceit? Thus, what seems to be crystallising here is an affirmation of identity as heterogeneous and complementary, as impure and hybrid, not without roots, but with roots planted in several places.[38] Saladin appears as one of the rare species in Rushdie's universe who is allotted with bright prospects. Of course it is also the first novel that does not end apocalyptically. As I mentioned earlier, the novel completes Rushdie's project of examining the range of possible identities that migration may give rise to. In the case of Saladin, Rushdie seems to have explored new territories for the potential paths of his own life in a character that is otherwise very much based on autobiographical detail. As opposed to Rushdie, Saladin has a decisively assimilationist relation to England, at least to begin with and, secondly, Rushdie examines the possibilities of returning to India, to the city of his childhood, Bombay, a possibility Rushdie has not chosen to make use of himself.[39]

Saladin seems to experience relief primarily through the understanding he gains of his hybrid nature, acknowledging his history and his past. Saladin's insight is triggered by episodes like the fire in the Shaandaar Café and the wedding between Mishal Sufyan and Hanif Johnson (two examples of "survivors" among the immigrants), but the actual conversion happens when he receives the letter about his father's imminent death: "Only a few days ago that back home would have rung false. But now his father was dying and old emotions were sending tenta-

---

38 I thus agree with Dutheil's conclusion on the problem of human identity when she says: "If Rushdie avoids final answers on the issue of whether one remains at bottom continuous or discontinuous with one's self in the process of migration, he clearly states his belief in the heterogeneous, self-contradictory nature of identity. He thus refutes the notion of self as stable and static and accordingly refuses the traditional definition of character as a coherent whole" (Dutheil, 119).
39 "So, in both senses, he's different. It's much more interesting to write about the other possibilities that you didn't take, than simply to write about who you are" (Meer, 122), Rushdie replies to Amina Meer's question about the similarity between Saladin and Rushdie.

cles out to grasp him" (SV, 514). The last part of the novel is written with love and reconciliation as pivotal principles, but it is also in the closing parts of the novel that Gibreel dramatically brings his life to an end. Yet, for Saladin's part a positive conversion seems to take place as he recovers a kind of wholeness: "Although he kept it quiet, however, Saladin felt hourly closer to many old, rejected selves, many alternative Saladins – or rather Salahuddins – which had split off from himself as he made his various life choices, but which had apparently continued to exist, perhaps in the parallel universes of quantum theory" (SV, 523).[40] Saladin regains the ability to love. He falls in love with Zeeny, he can now forgive his father and, finally, it becomes possible for him to receive his father's and Zeeny's love and forgiveness in return: "Yes, this looked like the start of a new phase, in which the world would be solid and real" (SV, 534). The novel ends with a passage that in many ways contains echoes of the novel's recurrent images, motifs and themes:

> He stood at the window of his childhood and looked out at the Arabian Sea. The moon was almost full; moonlight, stretching from the rocks of Scandal Point out to the far horizon, created the illusion of a silverpathway, like a parting in the water's shining hair, like a road to miraculous lands. He shook his head; could no longer believe in fairy-tales. Childhood was over, and the view from this window was no more than an old and

---

[40] Accordingly, I disagree with Pernille Bramming's conclusion that Rushdie chooses Lucretius in preference to Ovid: "Salman Rushdie chooses the mutant-model: A person is capable of turning into a new person, entering into new, different relations with his/her fellow human beings" (Bramming, 19). Assuming that Saladin represents Rushdie's voice (he is the character Bramming bases her entire interpretation upon), the opposite seems to be the case. The point is, rather, that Rushdie chooses both models as modes of existence. In the interview with Meer, Rushdie actually seems to be personally committed to Ovid: "That's right, you see it's the old debate about whether the soul changes, or whether it doesn't. Whether it's the same thing all along or whether there's kind of choice to make – about what you think human beings are like – whether social conditions can make such a revolution in the self that there's nothing left of the original self, or whether there is always that irreducible thing. I go more along that line myself. That there is something. In another way, that's what the novel's about" (Meer, 115).

sentimental echo. To the devil with it! Let the bulldozers come. If the old refused to die, the new could not be born.

"Come along," Zeenat Vakil's voice said at his shoulder. It seemed that in spite of all his wrong-doing, weakness, guilt – in spite of his humanity – he was getting another chance. There was no accounting for one's good fortune, that was plain. There it simply was, taking his elbow in its hand. "My place," Zeeny offered. "Let's get the hell out of here."

"I'm coming," he answered her, and turned away from the view (SV, 547).

As for the villagers and as for Gibreel and Saladin during the fire, a path opens for Saladin and Zeeny that promises a new and better place, but Saladin partly rejects the pulling power of fairy tales to rely on the tangible and real situation at the present with Zeeny by his side. Deciding to have his childhood home torn down, Saladin picks up the thread from the opening quotation of the novel: in order for the new to be born, the old has to die. The novel has produced many interpretations of this idea, however. May parts of the old order be allowed to survive? Or does the old have to die completely? We have seen examples of both.

If we are to differentiate between *Midnight's Children*, *Shame*, and *The Satanic Verses* with respect to their rhizomatic status, the conclusion is that the latter is no less than the epitome of the rhizome. *The Satanic Verses* is a schizo-novel, in constant movement, in which composition and enunciation render any kind of centralisation of types of discourse, narrative voices, and stories impossible. The novel is anti-hierarchical and anti-genealogical as any form of origin proves to be a construction and therefore open to re-interpretation. Ontological complementarity and ambiguity are generated primarily by allowing the three lines to leak into one another via metamorphoses and echoes, making dream and reality indistinguishable. The question of human identity has also supported the overall rhizomatic character of the novel in that identity is portrayed as heterogeneous and complementary, as processual and decentred, and as hybrid and impure. In the next sub-chapter the rhizomatic character of the novels will be emphasised through an analysis of the role of metaphor and metonymy.

METAPHOR AND METONYMY

> "In short: Metaphors say something new about reality."
> – Jan Kjærstad: *Menneskets felt* (*The Human Zone*)

Metaphor and metonymy are tropes and at the same time also dichotomous concepts that indicate how language works. In Rushdie's novels, metaphor represents a unifying and creative strategy whereas metonymy represents a distributive strategy. Metaphor is closely related to simile and analogy and means transfer or translation: one area of meaning is transferred to another area of meaning through a relation of similarity. In a speech act metaphor denotes the selection a language user may make on the paradigmatic level: in a sentence words may be replaced with synonyms that, being included in the same group of words, carry a likeness to the primary word. In contrast, metonymy denotes a combination of words that makes up the sentence as a chain or a syntagma. In distinction from the relation of similarity in metaphors, metonymy operates through a relation of contiguity. So, whereas metaphor is linked to concepts such as similarity, selection, group, and paradigm, metonymy is related to concepts such as contiguity, combination, chain, and syntagma.

In relation to metaphor, it is important to note that modern metaphor theory, as developed by for instance I.A. Richards, Max Black, and Paul Ricoeur, adds as much importance to the fundamental difference between two heterogeneous areas as they do to the relation of similarity. In this way modern metaphor theory differs from the understanding of metaphor in classical rhetoric by granting the metaphor a basic untranslatability, whereas in classical rhetoric (e.g. Cicero) metaphor was only regarded as an ornamental wrapping of a pre-existing thought that would always remain the same regardless of the nature of its wrapping. Content was seen as independent of the nature of its form and as prior to the making of form as well. In contrast, untranslatability derives from the idea that metaphor does not operate unidirectionally, but is bi-directional in a transversal communication between the two parts; hence, the two areas brought together interact with each other, transferring meaning in both directions. In doing so, a production of meaning occurs and the function of metaphor becomes cognitive. The production of meaning depends partly on the similarity between the two parts of the metaphor, without which the cognitive function would be impossible, and partly on the difference between the parts, without which the cognitive function would result in stasis and mechanical repetition. I would like to emphasise, though, that my definition of metaphor and its function is not limited to the formation of tropes on a linguistic micro-level. In my deployment of the term metaphor works on the macro-level of composition where large elements may be joined in conflictual clashes, as for instance in the three heterogeneous lines of composition in *The Satanic Verses*.

When Deleuze claims in regard to Proust that "metaphor is essentially metamorphosis and indicates how the two objects exchange their determinations, exchange even the names that designate them, in the new medium that confers the common quality upon them" (PS, 48), he does so in extension of modern metaphor theory. The same goes for the Saleem-India relation, in which the two parts can be understood as immediate metaphors of each other, but, as it turns out, the natures of both are changed through their shared qualities. In metaphor understood as metamorphosis, a concept which has been pulled out of its usual domain and is thus deterritorialised is used to reterritorialise a concept belonging to another domain. Consequently, metaphor as metamorphosis causes a surplus of meaning in the tension between repetition and difference.

Rushdie recognises the metamorphic nature of metaphor in the following quotation about migration as one of the richest metaphors of our time: "The very word *metaphor*, with its roots in the Greek words for *bearing across*, describes a sort of migration, the migration of ideas into images. Migrants – borne-across humans – are metaphorical beings in their very essence; and migration, seen as metaphor, is everywhere around us. We all cross frontiers; in that sense, we are all migrant peoples" (IH, 278-79). Transfer is a double-edged process of gain and loss, as is illustrated in the following citation: "It is generally believed that something is always lost in translation; I cling to the notion (...) that something can also be gained" (S, 29). The passages I have quoted elaborate on our earlier examination of Rushdie's theory on the subject whose terms of existence are determined by geographical and, not least, mental migrations. In this way the migrant becomes the epitome of metamorphosis. However, metamorphosis is to Rushdie as well as to Deleuze also the "driving force of art": "Of all the opposed pairs of ideas by which human beings have sought to understand themselves, perhaps the oldest and deepest-rooted are the eternally warring myths of stasis and of metamorphosis. Stasis, the dream of eternity, of a fixed order in human affairs, is the favoured myth of tyrants; metamorphosis, the knowledge that *nothing holds its form*, is the driving force of art" (IH, 291), Rushdie says.

The metaphorical technique in *Midnight's Children* progresses through the connections and correspondences the narrator creates via a vigorous subjective and rational effort which is supposed to counteract absurdity. The connection between past and present may, for instance, be established through the weather, as in the case when Saleem reflects on similarities and differences between his current self and his past self: "Different and similar, we are joined by heat. A shimmering heat-haze, then and now, blurs his then-time into mine... my confusion, travelling across the heat-waves, is also his" (MC, 167). Continuity is marked by both similarity and difference and at the same time the quotation shows the narrator's controlling and engineering role in the projection of the connecting transversal. Another mode of connection between past and present is the culinary one which has a great structuring significance throughout the novel: "Pickle-fumes, heavily oppressive in the heat, stimulate the juices of memory, accentuating similarities and differences between then and now" (MC, 166).

Connections are not always created between past and present only, the connection between Saleem and India, for example, is set up on the basis of a principle of simultaneous correspondence. As Saleem enters the world the moment India is born as an independent nation, simultaneity obviously becomes the governing idea: "thanks to the occult tyrannies of those blandly saluting clocks I had been mysteriously handcuffed to history, my destinies indissolubly chained to those of my country" (MC, 9). Hence, the governing principle of the novel's structure is the connection between story and history, a metaphorical connection which is almost intensified into a 1:1 relation by Saleem himself, but also by Jawaharlal Nehru, India's Prime Minister, who (in the novel) sends the following letter of congratulation to Saleem: "Dear Baby Saleem, My belated congratulations on the happy accident of your moment of birth! You are the newest bearer of that ancient face of India which is also eternally young. We shall be watching over your life with the closest attention; it will be, in a sense, the mirror of our own" (MC, 122). A structure like this, in which a macrocosmic structure is mirrored in a microcosmic structure in a 1:1 relation, is in *Midnight's Children* a kind of ideal state which is impossible to maintain in the novel's overall aesthetics as the relation is entirely based on a relation of similarity. Saleem and Nehru express a desire to enter such a state, but as the story evolves Saleem realises the metaphysical illusion behind an ontology in which difference is neglected. Still, this does not prevent the Saleem-India relation from being the overall skeleton that often binds together the chaotic confusion of stories, motifs, and incidents.

Operating through fusions, connections, and transversals, metaphor contributes to the establishment of order and the integration of "the world." In the face of differences, it focuses on correlations, links, and similarities, making the world cohere. As we have already seen, the perforated sheet is a metaphor of both narrative technique and epistemology. As the sheet resurfaces throughout the novel it connects the grandfather Aadam with his daughter Naseem as well as with Jamila Singer, and thus the sheet legitimises a continuity and natural cohesion in the family story in defiance of differences.

Furthermore, the metamorphosing nature of metaphor means that it is through metaphor that newness is created. Metaphor as metamorphosis is above all determined by difference. In other words, newness only occurs by virtue of the difference that will always be there prior to human-induced similarities. Jan Kjærstad touches on the same thing in *Menneskets felt* (*The Human Zone*):

> By use of language we are able to experience and think new things. Metaphor is a window to the enigma of creativity. To Ricoeur, the key to the renewing capacities of language lies in the possibility of deliberate linguistic transgressions, in the conflict they cause. Such collisions of

language create a kind of semantic state of shock, a disoriented state holding the occasion for a reorientation of thought. In Ricoeur, conflict, not similarity, is the most important characteristic of metaphor. A good metaphor calls for taxing mental activity. If one still maintains that metaphor is founded on similarity, it is a similarity that allows for *leaps* (Kjærstad, 34).

Whereas the focus on similarity results in coherence and order, the focus on difference means that the collision between traditionally heterogeneous elements is brought to light. Collision causes conflict and conflict provokes disorientation which in turn produces leaps and leaps lead to renewal. According to Kjærstad, renewal is the *raison d'être* of art: "literature, as Ezra Pound insists, must 'Make It New.' To me this is actually the principal criterion of good literature. It renews the world. Metaphor does not mirror reality, it *creates* reality. Perhaps metaphors have something to do with connections rather than with similarity – creating or seeing connections where there are no connections" (*ibid.*, 34). Kjærstad gives expression to the point that we have made earlier, namely that connections are constructed by subjective volition, which emphasises that the world is always to be understood through a medium, such as language for example, and that language, for that reason, contributes to the definition of – but also the expansion of – our understanding of the world.

The question of how newness occurs is an explicit theme in *The Satanic Verses*: "How does newness come into the world? How is it born? Of what fusions, translations, conjoinings is it made?" (SV, 8). The quote points to the idea that newness occurs through operations we have already identified as crucial to Rushdie's aesthetics (practice) and poetics (intention), that is, fusions, translations, conjunctions. As we have seen, the etymological meaning of metaphor is translation, or transfer, and it is in view of this that Rushdie determines the migrant as a metaphorical being and as a metaphor of humanity: we are all translated beings, borne across, physically or mentally; we all step across lines in a process of becoming, which may happen at a high or low velocity, but is at all times indisputable. We have also touched on conjunctions as zones of uncertainty, in which things pick up speed and intensity occurs: we have seen a zone of religious uncertainty in connection with Aadam Aziz, who found himself unable to worship God while at the same time he could not stop believing in God, and we have seen it in connection with Gibreel, where the zone results in an unfortunate blocking of the process in a pathological dead-end. Fusion is another concept belonging to the terminology of metaphor; it is itself a metaphor of the function of metaphor, a metaphor adopted from nuclear physics where fusion denotes the process that occurs when two atomic nuclei melt together and release a considerable amount of energy. I will return to fusion below with examples from *The Satanic Verses*, but before that I would like to go back to the concept of conjunction which Deleuze introduces in *Logic of Sense* where he links connection, conjunction, and disjunction as three principles of composition.

The connective synthesis is constructed by one series and proceeds as an "if-then." This kind of synthesis reflects homogeneity and traditional causality within the fictive universe. Ambiguity is toned down in favour of a more rational logic and argumentation. This may be exemplified by one of the series that constitute the frames of explanation of Gibreel's metamorphosis. The childhood series, which is presented through the narrator's relatively realistic mode of description and is composed by the background elements from Gibreel's childhood, progress, when viewed in isolation, as an if-then logic: if Gibreel is unsuccessful with girls, then he throws himself at a reading of myths and religion, which later develops into a constituent element of the dream tracks and thus the metamorphoses; if Gibreel's mother used to call him her little angel, then it is only natural that Gibreel calls himself Farishta, which also becomes a constituent element of the dreams and, with that, the metamorphoses.

The conjunctive synthesis is constructed by converging series and progresses as a logic of "and." This kind of synthesis maintains a relatively homogeneous fictive universe, but inclusivity is orchestrated through the conjunction. The conjunctive synthesis may be said to function as a principle of coordination within diversity. It may be said that "and... and... and..." becomes cuts or provisional points of assemblage in the continued process of heterogeneity. An example of this is the coordination of the frames of explanation of the cause of metamorphosis in *The Satanic Verses*, where conjunction constitutes a paratactical listing of evolution theory and secular Fall and a condensed zone of the hybridising capacities of transfer and... and... and...

The disjunctive synthesis distributes the diverging series following an inclusive "either-or" logic which, in contradistinction to the exclusive use of disjunctive synthesis, does not exclude any predicates in favour of the identity of a concept. Disjunction cannot be reduced to conjunction as it is not based on convergence, but on divergence. Divergence becomes a confirmation and not a negation, either-or becomes inclusive and sheer affirmation, as in for example the complementary description of Rosa Diamond's life story where she was either raped or allowed herself to be seduced, or in the story of the pilgrimage of the villagers where the ocean either parted for the chosen ones or did not part for anyone at all, or in the story of Gibreel's tropicalisation of London where Gibreel is either a victim of self-deception or in actual fact has an influence on the weather of the city, or... In this way, the disjunctive synthesis forms an aesthetics of complementarity in which irreconcilable versions of reality may exist simultaneously. The result is ontological "flicker."

Deleuze summarises the mutual performance of the three functions like this: "a disjunction which had become a synthesis introduced its *ramifications* everywhere, so that the conjunction was already *coordinating* in a global way divergent, heterogenous, and disparate series, and that, affecting the details, the connection already *contracted* a multitude of divergent series in the successive appearance of a single one" (LS, 175). Therefore one can perform various incisions into the fictive universe where the focus on connection also carries the seeds of the coordinating conjunction and the distributing disjunction, or one may choose to use one of the latter as a point of departure and find elements of the two others there.

To summarise: Metaphor seems to have two functions. First, it has a gathering and ordering function where focus is on similarity, and, secondly, it has a metamorphic function of renewal where focus is on difference and conflict. The two sides to metaphor are inseparable and operate simultaneously: connection refers to both similarity and difference. Likewise, concepts like transversal, conjunction, disjunction, fusion, and transfer can be said to belong to the terminology of metaphor.

Whereas the metaphor as a trope is characterised by a relation of similarity (and thus also a relation of difference), metonymy is characterised by a relation of contiguity. Metonymy means that a whole is indirectly represented by a part of the whole, or that a cause is indirectly represented by the effect. As a linguistic mode of operation metonymy functions through combination and displacement. According to Lis Møller, it is characteristic of a metonymical writing style that details pile up without ever clarifying the whole or causality: "Thus metonymy focuses on effects rather than causes and deals with parts rather than wholes. The path from an effect to a cause and from a part to a whole is quite often rather hazy or even blocked; details amass, but are never gathered to form a whole. The result is 'impressionistic' or deliberately fragmented. As a figure of thought, metonymy may be employed to display the obscure, the ephemeral, and the chaotic" (Møller, 174). In light of this, the perforated sheet may be seen as a metaphor of Rushdie's fragmentary and metonymical narrative technique. Condemned to perceive the world through the perforated sheet, Saleem is condemned to experience and recognise the world in fragments, wholeness being unattainable: "that perforated sheet, which doomed my mother to learn to love a man in segments, and which condemned me to see my own life – its meanings, its structures – in fragments also" (MC, 107). Perception depends on metonymy as perception logs on to the world passing by as flux. In reflecting on the world, one uses metaphor with the purpose of cutting up the world and establishing coherence and order in the stream of perception.

Metonymy helps indicating the distributive forces of the world through its endless, dynamic, and displacing qualities. Whereas metaphor distributes and renews through the complex relation between similarity and difference, the distributive force of metonymy works through an interminable logic of fragmentation. The following example illustrates the distributive logic of metonymy, but at the same time it contains a unifying summation: "close-up of my grandfather's right hand: nails knuckles fingers all somehow bigger than you'd expect. Clumps of red hair on the outside edges. Thumb and forefinger pressed together, separated only by a thickness of paper. In short: my grandfather was holding a pamphlet. It had been inserted into his hand (we cut to a long-shot – nobody from Bombay should be without a basic film vocabulary) as he entered the hotel foyer" (MC, 32-33). The narrator's point of view assumes the form of a camera eye which at first moves from detail to detail in a close-up perspective, then it moves on to gather all the details in a conclusive description; after that, the narrator reaches back in time to give us the cause (the pamphlet was put in the grandfather's hand) of the effect we have just been presented with (the detailed description of the hand), and as the cause is presented to us, the point of view cuts from close-up to a panoramic view.

The distributive logic of metonymy, in which language works as a centrifugal force, is not always succeeded by a unifying conclusion. In Rushdie human identity is often projected in terms of metonymy: Wee Willie Winkie is described as "Talldarkhandsome" (MC, 101); Saleem describes himself as "Snotnose, Stainface, Sniffer, Baldy, Piece-of-the-moon" (MC, 118) and as "cucumber-nose stainface chinlessness horntemples bandy-legs finger-loss monk's-tonsure" (MC, 301). Metonymical descriptions like these, in which details are piled up in a paratactical logic, distributing traits rather than collecting them, support the examination we made earlier of human identity as rhizomatic and processual; the rhizome is an open system just as metonymy is interminable.

Another syntactical technique we come across in Rushdie is his inclination to bundle words in heaps: "whatdoyoumeanhowcanyousaythat" (MC, 227), or his employment of asyndeta, in which the joining conjunctions are missing: "their heads were full of all the usual things, fathers mothers money food land possessions fame power God" (MC, 228-29). Paradoxically, the technique has both a gathering and a distributive function. The enumeration of words indicates a complete inventory while at the same time it contains the seeds to infinitude by indirectly pointing to the further continuation of the list. We find a striking example of cataloguing in Shame in connection with the three mothers' decision to isolate themselves in Nishapur. They arrange for the construction of an ingenious elevator which makes it possible to stay out of visual contact with the surrounding world when goods are received and dispatched. The narrator recounts the agreements the mothers make with the businessmen in town, including the following catalogue: "the selected vendors of meats, fruits, haberdashery, flowers, stationary, vegetables, pulses, books, flat drinks, fizzy drinks, foreign magazines, newspapers, unguents, perfumes, antinomy, strips of eucalyptus bark for tooth-cleaning, spices, starch, soaps, kitchen utensils, picture frames, playing cards and strings for musical instruments" (S, 18). The passage is a brilliant example of Rushdie's attempts to indicate diversity and fragmentation, but at the same time it also implies a desire for wholeness.[41]

Accordingly, Rushdie writes in a distributive and conjunctive rather than in an attributive manner. In the chapter "Lucretius and the Simulacrum" in *The Logic of Sense*, Deleuze states the following, which may serve as an illustration of a Rushdian aesthetics: "*Physis* is not a determination of the One, of Being, or of the Whole. Nature is not collective, but rather distributive, to the extent that the laws of Nature (...) distribute parts which cannot be totalised. Nature is not attributive, but rather conjunctive: it expresses itself through 'and,' and through 'is.' This *and* that – alternations and entwinings, resemblances and differences, attractions and distractions, nuance and abruptness (LS, 267). Rushdie also focuses on the conjunctive mechanism of "and" which is either directly represented or implied as a missing conjunction in metonymical constructions. Saleem is both a snotnose and a stainface and a sniffer and... Aadam is both a non-believer and a believer; he is both incapable of believing in God and incapable of denying God's existence. As in Lucretius's Epicurean inspired Naturalism and sense aesthetics, we find a logic in Rushdie which is based on similarities and differences, collecting and distributing elements, accordingly; diversity is projected as a sum which never takes the form of a closed totality, however. Difference distributes, or, in other words, simulacrum does, which in Lucretius as-

---

41   Jan Kjærstad sees Borges's catalogues as an attempt to establish order: "When Borges catalogues the world, it is not the result of a penchant for fragmentation, on the contrary, it is an expression of a desire to bring things together. His catalogues do not pay testimony to any disillusion caused by chaos, they attest to an attempt to establish a secret order" (Kjærstad, 265). In addition, he says: "A catalogue is an expression of concentration, of compression" (*ibid.*, 267). As is apparent in the above, I only partially agree with Kjærstad. I insist that the catalogue expresses a double movement: an amassing movement, as the catalogue becomes a metaphor of wholeness, and a distributing movement, as the catalogue fragmentarily piles up details in an interminable paratactical logic. Perhaps it is possible to see the distinction between the distributive and amassing function of the catalogue as a distinction between the strategies, or, rather, mentalities, of postmodernism and modernism?

sumes the status of the sounds, smells, aromas, forms, colours, and light, ceaselessly emitted by the world. Simulacrum cannot be referred to a Platonic sphere of ideas, on the contrary, it assumes a character of sensuousness and it confirms singularity in the flux of events.

Analepsis, prolepsis, and the syntactical techniques described above function as unifying strategies in Rushdie, but through the very presence of this style, the centrifugal force of diversity that necessitates such a style is hinted at concurrently. This is the paradoxical double movement between the indication in the style of the continued process of diversity (and... and... and...) and the indication in the style of the necessity of cutting up the world by means of provisional attributes and artificial repetitions.

As we have seen, the metaphorical and metonymical techniques serve different (but at times also the same) purposes in the projection of the fictive universe. Via its focus on relations of similarity, metaphor is charged with establishing coherence and order in an otherwise chaotic world. In *Midnight's Children*, for instance, metaphor is orchestrated through the narrator as a subjective act of will with an aim to create meaning. In addition, metaphor is the locus of metamorphosis as it creates unexpected connections between heterogeneous elements (conjunction) via its transversal mode of operation; newness may occur by focusing on conflictual collision and difference.

Metonymy does not unite things, it distributes them. The distributive function of metonymy is also orchestrated through a conjunctive logic (both-and) when Rushdie exploits the centrifugal forces in syntax and language; distribution is projected through metonymy's displacing and combinatory relation of contiguity. One could also say that metaphor operates through fusion whereas metonymy operates through fission.

A pure metonymical style is not possible because language is metaphorically constituted; meaning only occurs with metaphor. Without metaphor, metonymy would be a meaningless process, but, the other way round, metaphor would develop into a static freezing of the distributive forces of the world without metonymy. Yet, Rushdie is still tied to the construction of metaphors by subjectivity via connections, repetitions, forms, and fusions due to the subjacent metonymical ontology: "As a people, we are obsessed with correspondences. Similarities between this and that, between apparently unconnected things, make us clap our hands delightedly when we find them out. It is a sort of national longing for form – or perhaps simply an expression of our deep belief that forms lie hidden within reality; that meaning reveals itself only in flashes" (MC, 300). Without metaphor there is no meaning and the subject risks succumbing to the dizziness of absurdity: "O dizzying early days before categorization! Formlessly, before I began to shape them, the fragrances poured into me" (MC, 316-17), Saleem exclaims when his olfactory skills are still new to him. This is why he finds himself in a metonymical condition with singular smells that make no sense because they have yet to be connected with other semantic fields. Gradually, meaning takes shape, however, so that different smells are connected with psychological conditions.

To Rushdie and Saleem, form becomes a question of survival: "Reality can have metaphorical content; that does not make it less real. (…) Everything has shape, if you look for it. There is no escape from form" (MC, 200, 226). Saleem recognises the fact that the metaphorical style is connected with the subject's longing for meaning as he doubts his own metaphorical and transversal constructions in the novel: "but perhaps it was all an illusion, born of my attempt to bind him to the threads of my history by an effort of sheer will" (MC, 426). The world does not only progress through fusions (material or subjectively constructed), but also through fissions: "our ancient national gift for fissiparousness had found new outlets" (MC, 399), is Saleem's comment on the divided Communist fractions in the ghetto. The process of fission also applies to the divided Pakistan as well as to the divided India, the divided Sinai family and Saleem's condition at the end of the novel where his fission symbolises the transition from narrator to novel: the stories in *Midnight's Children* are pouring out from Saleem's cracks and crevices. In this way the novel may be said to oscillate between fusion and fission, between unifying and distributing passages, and between metaphorical and metonymical techniques.

There is an interesting notion of the status of the metropolis in *The Satanic Verses*, expressed by Alleluia Cone's father, the Polish immigrant, Otto Cone. Otto does not believe the world to be a homogenous continuum, which he ardently tries to lecture Allie about: "'Anybody ever tries to tell you how this most beautiful and most evil of planets is somehow homogeneous, composed only of reconcilable elements, that it all *adds up*, you get on the phone to the straitjacket tailor,' he advised her, managing to give the impression of having visited more planets than one before coming to his conclusions. 'The world is incompatible, just never forget it'" (SV, 295). *The Satanic Verses* does not appear as an organism, either, whose totality constitutes the sum of its parts. Complementarity, the irreconcilable but still equal elements and descriptions, turns the novel into an open totality whose heterogeneity is the most conspicuous thing about *The Satanic Verses*, according to Tygstrup:

> If we stick to a formal-typological register in the first instance, heterogeneity is what catches the eye; it is possible to distinguish between a number of "levels" in the novel: there is a realistic storyline with characters, environments, and developments, there is a number of dream sequences, which constitute fragments of a religious discourse with quotes from the Koran and more or less authorised, narrated sequences from it accompanied by comments, there are "fantastic" sequences and scenes; in addition, there are myriads of languages, blending with each other, and of tenses, foci, and perspectives (Tygstrup, 1995, 184).

Heterogeneity is not joined by an omniscient consciousness, but retains its mark of incompossibility throughout one's reading of the novel, the disjunctive synthesis confirming diversity as a positive principle.

Otto Cone elaborates on his worldview one day when the family is gathered for dinner:

> "The modern city," Otto Cone on his hobbyhorse had lectured his bored family at table, "is the locus classicus of incompatible realities. Lives that have no business mingling with one another sit side by side upon the omnibus. One universe, on a zebra crossing, is caught for an instant, blinking like a rabbit, in the headlamps of a motor-vehicle in which an entirely alien and contradictory continuum is to be found. And as long as that's all, they pass in the night, jostling on Tube stations, raising their hats in some hotel corridor, it's not so bad. But if they meet! It's uranium and plutonium, each make the other decompose, boom" (SV, 314).

Otto Cone's idea about the incompatible continuums corresponds to the modern Leibnizianism reflected on by Deleuze in *Proust* and *Signs* and in *The Fold: Leibniz and the Baroque*. In Leibniz, compossibility and homogeneity are warranted through the pre-established harmony of the monads, guaranteeing that everyone sees the world through the same perspective. The "pre-established harmony" and the unity within multiplicity ensue from God as unifying principles.[42] Deleuze's rethinking of Leibniz is, among other things, a consequence of the death of God and Nietzsche's philosophy: "Nietzsche's perspectivism – his perspectivism – is a much more profound art than Leibniz's point of view: for divergence is no longer a principle of exclusion, and disjunction no longer a means of separation. Incompossibility is now a means of communication" (LS, 174).[43] To Otto Cone and to Rushdie, there is no pre-established harmony univocally guaranteeing the "reality in our perceptions." To Rushdie neighbours may be separated by such fundamental differences that their worlds are incompatible, which is a thought that may have increased in significance and relevancy after the lesson of the Rushdie Affair with its irreconcilable worldviews. Yet, incompatibility does not entail purity, on the contrary, it gives rise to a new form of communication which does not cancel out the differences between the heterogeneous elements.

At the same time Otto Cone gives us an answer to the novel's question of how newness occurs, and, as we have seen before, the answer is fusion. The novel generates fusions on many levels: between ages of time, between languages, between genres, between places, between characters (the relation between Allie and Gibreel is an example of incompatible worlds as Allie has quite simply ended up in the wrong story), and within single sentence constructions between consciousnesses (free indirect speech), and between tragic and comic languages. According to Kjærstad, it is this impurity that remains the emblem of *The Satanic Verses*: "Yet it is Salman Rushdie who provides the actual paradigm of

---

42 In *Discourse on Metaphysics* Leibniz writes: "Thus God alone constitutes the relation or communication between substances. It is through him that the phenomena of the one meet and accord with the phenomena of the others, so that there may be a reality in our perceptions" (Leibniz, XXXII).
43 One might say that in a certain way Nietzsche's philosophy anticipates Bohr's quantum physics.

impure literature, a novel that mixes everything together; place, time, different logics, different religions, dream and reality. This is particularly the case of *The Satanic Verses*, undoubtedly the most important book of the 1980s" (Kjærstad, 18).

Kjærstad proceeds to reflect on the nature of the impure novel as monstrosity, a monstrosity achieved through a virus-evolution, which directs our thoughts to Deleuze and Guattari's idea of a-parallel lines of evolution:

> The impure novel is not attractive on the face of it, now and then it may cause alarm as if leprous, or because it is *infected* with the viruses that prevail in society. The impure novel is a book without absolutes, a novel that guarantees us nothing whatsoever, other than its desire to present human possibilities. The impure novel does not discuss the problems everyone else is discussing; it formulates and discusses the problems that have not been raised yet (*ibid.*, 17-18).

The novel is a fantastic chimera that adopts a bit of this and a bit of that, and it is no accident either that Otto Cone has planted a chimera in his garden, "the central, symbolic tree, a 'chimeran graft' of laburnum and broom" (SV, 298-99). Therefore I think that Goonetilleke misunderstands the significance the chimera has for Saladin and Otto: "The chimeran graft is played off against the walnut tree, the former a symbol of hybridity. Rushdie, however, entertains a doubt and worry regarding hybridity, though it is a major (in his case too) and widely accepted positive today. Saladin, in the end, turns his back on it. Otto turns his back *via* suicide" (Goonetilleke, 82). As I see it, Saladin accepts the chimera and hybridity by recognising his Indian roots without turning his back to his English experiences for that reason. It is true that Otto Cone commits suicide, but in spite of his theoretical considerations of the chimera and in spite of the fact that he has planted a chimera in his garden, his life develops as one prolonged rejection of his own roots; like Saladin at the beginning of the novel, his attitude to England is assimilationist (he changes his name, for example, from Cohen to Cone). A reading that, based on Otto Cone's destiny, concludes that Rushdie and the novel are sceptical towards hybridity and the chimera as a figure is thus a misinterpretation since Otto

Cone leads the opposite of a hybrid life in practice. According to his wife Alicja, Otto is trying to live an imitation of life. It is also Goonetilleke who produces comments like these in relation to Saladin: "a return to his original identity (...) found himself (...) completes his process of regeneration" (Goonetilleke, 90-91). Saladin does not return to his original self (whatever that might have been?), and regressive movements are impossible, which was illustrated in the passage quoted earlier about the irreversibility of process. Goonetilleke's idea of the completion of rebirth is also wrong: as we have seen, completion is an illusory thing in Rushdie's universe.

With the above, a certain ethics emerges from the aesthetic form. In all of the novels there is a general agreement between form and content, or between what they do and what they say. But what is it then that they do? Through the agency of the metaphorical ploy, orchestrating newness and metamorphosis, and through the agency of the metonymical ploy, indicating distribution and process, the novels "perform" an ethics which is primarily related to democratism. Processuality and nomadism mean that one's grasp of the world will never be more than a provisional grasp and thus truth will never be captured definitively; it has to be reconstructed repeatedly. In this way Rushdie's writings oppose all kinds of dogmatism and hegemony which are to be found for instance in theocratic countries like Iran but also manifest themselves in Western societies where democratic ideology is often superimposed by a capitalist economy.

Furthermore, the radical Nietzschean inspired perspectivism in Rushdie seems to verge on a kind of individualism and solipsism as there is no pre-established harmony guaranteeing each individual the same world. The reason for the absence of harmony is, apart from the death of God, that the world no longer appears as a positivist entity that may be weighed and measured objectively. Quite the opposite, it is now entangled with a language that is never neutral, but always charged with value. Between man and the world, there is the sign with one half starting from the subject and the other half starting from the object, in addition to being extremely unstable and ambiguous. But does this perspectivism, solipsism, and relativism result in a kind of nihilism in Rushdie? If we are all looking at a different world and if the world is impossible to capture objectively, is everything then not of equal value and hence of no consequence? Is it not too easy to profess this relativism? On the contrary, relativism is in many ways harder to live with than absolutism, and at the same time relativism guarantees the continuation of doubt and reflection, which, when expressed in art, furnishes us with the best possible means of generating intersubjective perspectives that may lift us out of solipsism and individualism. At the same time, the constant doubt that is warranted by the world as an open becoming is the basis of perpetual dialogue and critical debate. In this way, through their webs of stories without beginnings and ends, and through their flat cartographies, in which no stories are allowed a hegemonic status, Rushdie's novels project complex polyphonies and multiplicities, charting a pluralistic ethics based on human understanding and social responsibility.

TOWARD A MINOR LITERATURE

> "One's always writing to bring something to life, to free
> life from where it's trapped, to trace lines of flight."
> – Gilles Deleuze: *Negotiations*

In connection with their reading of Kafka's writings Deleuze and Guattari introduce the concept of "minor literature." Minor literature is rhizomatic and three characteristics are assigned to it: "the deterritorialisation of language, the connection of the individual to a political immediacy, and the collective assemblage of enunciation" (K, 18). In this sub-chapter I will make use of Rushdie's essays as a source of explanation and support to a greater extent than previously because his poetics largely appear to overlap with Deleuze and Guattari's characterisations of minor literature. However, I will still draw examples from his fictive works which are, of course, my primary object of analysis.

The deterritorialisation of language means that forms of expression and language systems are set in motion and pushed out of balance. In Rushdie's case, the English language is brought out of balance as his status as both an outsider and insider provides him with an essential and prolific double vision. He functions as a "difference within" in relation to both England and India. To Rushdie the English language carries a metaphysics which contributes to the fortification of imperial dominance of the former colonies (coca-colonisation). Language is the most important instrument in the construction, or understanding, of reality, and to Rushdie it is of paramount importance that English is deterritorialised from within: "What seems to me to be happening is that those peoples who were once colonized by the language are now rapidly remaking it, domesticating it, becoming more and more relaxed about the way they use it – assisted by the English language's enormous flexibility and size, they are carving out large territories for themselves within its frontiers" (IH, 64). Deterritorialisation, and thus liberation and the mapping of new territories, happens through the collisions Rushdie creates between the

Indian and the English language and within the English language itself: "To be a sort of stranger within [one's] own language" (K, 26), Deleuze and Guattari proclaim.[44]

One is a stranger in one's own language when one causes the language to move, for instance, by exploiting the polylingual nature of language: "To make use of the polylingualism of one's own language, to make a minor or intensive use of it, to oppose the oppressed quality of this language to its oppressive quality, to find points of nonculture or under-development, linguistic Third World zones by which a language can escape, an animal enters into things, an assemblage comes into play" (K, 27). In Rushdie's novels, a heteroglossia is orchestrated in which countless types of discourse encounter each other, contaminating official or imperial English. Rushdie typically moves about in linguistically heterogeneous localities, such as Bombay, London, and New York. In Kafka's case, the German spoken in Prague had already been deterritorialised (according to Deleuze and Guattari), and in a conversation with Günter Grass in connection with the post-war German writers, Rushdie says: "The practitioners of 'rubble literature' – Grass himself being one of the most prominent of these – took upon themselves the Herculean task of reinventing the German language, of tearing it apart, ripping out the poisoned parts, and putting it back together" (IH, 279). Likewise, it may be argued that Afro-Americans and Hispanics in the USA today are in the process of deterritorialising American-English: "English has always been worked upon by all these minority languages, Gaelic-English, Irish-English, etc., which are like so many war-machines against the English" (D, 58).

In *The Satanic Verses* we find an example of linguistic deterritoriali-

---

44   In *Dialogues* we find the following normative statement: "We must be bilingual even in a single language, we must have a minor language inside our own language, we must create a minor use of our own language" (D, 4). And it continues: "We must pass through [passer par] dualisms because they are in language, it's not a question of getting rid of them, but we must fight against language, invent stammering, not in order to get back to a prelinguistic pseudo-reality, but to trace a vocal or written line which will make language flow between these dualisms, and which will define a minority usage of language, an inherent variation as Labov says" (D, 34).

sation brought about through the sound of language in connection with S.S. Sisodia whose stuttering produces unexpected collisions between elements that are usually kept apart: "The top gogo goddess is absolutely Lakshmi" (SV, 512). Sisodia's articulation creates an encounter between gogo-girls and the goddess Lakshmi, Rushdie thus producing a creative metamorphosis through the materiality of language (sound) and its sociality, which in this case circumvents the experience of the character, or superimposes it so to speak. Sisodia also asks Saladin: "What lie lie line are you in?" (SV, 512). Here the concepts of "lying" and "profession" are brought together – unintentionally by Sisodia, but intentionally by the implicit narrator as an allusion to Saladin's activities as dishonest and deceitful (his job, his identity, his satanic verses). Once again linguistic creativity is produced through the sound and sociality of language rather than through the experience of the character, and in both examples it is the reader who completes the creativity. The first example plots the theme of profanity-sacredness, the latter the theme of deceit-honesty, and both reflections feature as variations within the overall thematic structure of the novel. However, the examples also show that it is insufficient for any interpretation of the novel only to base itself on an analysis of the characters and their experience. In order to draw a qualified picture of the novel's overall aesthetic form, as such, it is necessary to include the material level of, for instance, the language, since the meaning that is produced on this level escapes the experience of the characters, as the above examples show.

Language has a special status in minor literature as it seeks to undermine the prevailing metaphysics sustained through allegorical and symbolic uses of the dominant language. To Rushdie, for example, religious discourse occupies a particularly strong position in dictatorial-theocratic regimes: "Autocratic regimes find it useful to espouse the rhetoric of faith, because people respect that language, are reluctant to oppose it. This is how religions shore up dictators; by encircling them with words of power, words which the people are reluctant to see discredited, disenfranchised, mocked" (S, 251). Minor literature attempts to trick language by writing anti-mimetically or anti-referentially, whereby the official language ceases to innocently represent the objects it pretends to be speaking about. Language ceases to function by means of an as-conjoining mechanism, which means that focus is moved from a meaning-making relation of similarity integral to the metaphorical technique to an intensity-producing, replenishing relation of difference: "There is no longer a designation by means of a proper name, nor an assignation of metaphors by means of a figurative sense. But *like* images, the thing no longer forms anything but a sequence of intensive states, a ladder or a circuit for intensities that one can make race around in one sense or another, from high to low, or from low to high" (K, 21-22).

Language is no longer literal or figurative as the collision between the two parts of the metaphor brings about a purely metaphoric and intensive state in language. Language use in minor literature follows the a-signifying, intensive lines constituted by sounds and smells, by light and tactility, by the free shapes of imagination, and by elements from dreams or nightmares. Here the point is to escape the straightjacket of meaning by means of the flux that is produced by a yet formless matter. But sounds (e.g. Jamila Singer's song), smells (e.g. the smell of grasshopper-green chutney leading Saleem on track of his childhood in a Proustian moment), tactility (e.g. the almost physical encroachment of the Sundarban jungle), and elements of nightmares (e.g. the nightmare of the green-black widow) are of course only conveyed through language. However, the idiosyncratic use of language that escapes doxa manages to create these exceptional conditions through the internal tensions of language: "Generally, we might call the linguistic elements, however varied they may be, that express the 'internal tensions of a language,' intensives or tensors" (K, 22). By referring to the border zones of a language and its paradoxical intrinsic possibilities, minor literature escapes a mere representative use of language which preserves the world in a locked position and blocks human becoming: "Language stops being representative in order to now move toward its extremities or limits" (K, 23).[45] In other

---

45   In the interview with Durix Rushdie speaks of the syntactical-technical sides of his own distinctive use of language, admitting his indebtedness to Desai's *All About H. Hatterr*: "it showed me that it was possible to break up the language and put it back together in a different way. To talk about minor details, one thing it showed me was the importance of punctuating badly. In order to allow different kinds of speech rhythms or different kinds of linguistic rhythms to occur in the book, I found I had to punctuate it in a very peculiar way, to destroy the natural rhythms of the

words: the way things are expressed is not only more important than the content, it actually produces a content which usually does not carry any meaning in the traditional sense, but rather provokes a flux of intensity within the reader who passes through a number of becomings. These affects, which are a-conscious and a-personal, only turn into affections once the individual, by use of reason and consciousness, begins to reflect on them and thus contextualises them within more conventional semantic frames. The examples above, in which the implicit narrator backstabs the characters by means of the materiality of language, precisely demonstrate the potential of an a-conscious material.

In minor literature everything is political, Deleuze and Guattari say. In major literature the individual sphere (the familial sphere, the marital sphere, etc.) seems to merge with other spheres which are no less individual, reducing the social sphere to a mere milieu or background. In minor literature the individual sphere is directly joined with the socio-political sphere as it proves impossible to sustain an illusion of the individual as an isolated island in the world. History has become a monster, as Kundera has said, and can no longer be tamed or trained to serve merely as background. In *Midnight's Children*, the blending of story and history forms the very structuring principle of the novel where it turns out, at the same time, that Saleem is subject to the macrocosmic forces he at times thought he was in control of: "The individual concern thus becomes all the more necessary, indispensable, magnified, because a whole other story is vibrating within it. In this way, the family triangle connects to other triangles – commercial, economic, bureaucratic, juridical – that determine its values" (K, 17). Saleem's individual sphere has been magnified through the microscopic point of view that is usually employed by the

English language; I had to use dashes too much, keep exclaiming, putting in three dots, sometimes three dots followed by semi-colons followed by three dashes... That sort of thing just seemed to help dislocate the English and let other things into it" (Durix, 2000, 10). In addition we find a comment on the peculiar and intensifying texture of the Sundarban chapter in the interview with Haffenden: "It seemed to me that if you are going to write an epic, even a comic epic, you need a descent into hell. That chapter is the inferno chapter, so it was written to be different in texture from what was around it. Those were among my favourite ten or twelve pages to write, and I was amazed at how they divided people so extremely" (Haffenden, 37).

narrator when he tells the story about the Sinai family. Yet at the same time, the microscope tells another story, that of history which, by reason of its religious, juridical, commercial, and political (foreign and domestic) stories, plays a role in determining the values in Saleem's individual story, but also reveals the individual as caught in a trap. In *Shame*, Omar is also linked to the political sphere, although he has the status of a peripheral hero: "it was the fate of Omar Khayyam Shakil to affect, from his position on the periphery, the great events whose central figures were other people but which collectively made up his own life" (S, 108).

Rushdie's novels are indisputably political, but this does not mean that they propagandise a certain political message. It means, first of all, that they portray a world in which the hero is hooked up to a political-historical machine which he or she is unable to control. Secondly, it means that the novels inscribe themselves in the actual, contemporary political sphere, accommodating and acknowledging an influential and subversive force (the aesthetic form that transcends the fate of the individual), which may very well be categorised as a utopian element: "I must say first of all that description is itself a political act" (IH, 13), Rushdie admits and points out the antagonistic relation between the writer and the politician as well: "Writers and politicians are natural rivals. Both groups try to make the world in their own images; they fight for the same territory. And the novel is one way of denying the official, politicians' version of truth" (IH, 14). With reference to Deleuze, it may be said that Rushdie's novels work as literary machines, engaging with the political machine, which the Rushdie Affair is a clear example of. There is no paradox in perceiving the novel as an art form which is radioactive with history and politics, but whose primary question is nevertheless about the status of the individual exactly because this is determined by his or her interconnection with history.

In the famous essay "Outside the Whale" Rushdie carries on a controversy against George Orwell's quietism as expressed in Orwell's equally famous essay "Inside the Whale."[46] I will briefly go through the

---

46   It must be pointed out that Rushdie admits in the preface of *Imaginary Homelands* that his criticism in the essays on Orwell and Miller is a bit unfair: "but I should say that, seven years on, I find 'Outside the Whale' a little unfair to George

main points in the two essays. Orwell writes his essay in 1940 at a time when the world is in the midst of one of its worst crises, and the starting point of his essay is a review of Henry Miller's *Tropic of Cancer*. Miller's novel is praised as a small masterpiece, in spite of the fact, or perhaps precisely because of the fact that it does not take place in any of the hot spots of the world, Berlin, Moscow, or Rome, but unfolds in the introvert artistic society in Paris in the 1930s among shabby immigrants, "people living the expatriate life, people drinking, talking, meditating, and fornicating" (Orwell, 12). Orwell raises a bit of criticism against Miller, however, as he sees it as a drawback that the novel keeps a restricted focus on the everyday life of the exile: "That is the penalty of leaving your native land. It means transferring your roots into shallower soil. Exile is probably more damaging to a novelist than to a painter or even a poet, because its effect is to take him out of contact with working life and narrow down his range to the street, the café, the church, the brothel and the studio" (*ibid.*, 12). Orwell certainly has a different idea of the migrant than Rushdie.

Orwell sees a tendency in Miller's writings, which may neither be classified as part of the increased attention in the 1920s to the technical and stylistic features of the literary work, nor as part of the distinctly political literature of the 1930s, which Orwell associates with propaganda written by "cocksure partisans telling you what to think" (*ibid.*, 18). In contrast, he describes Miller's works as "non-political, non-educational, non-progressive, non-co-operative, non-ethical, non-literary, non-consistent, non-contemporary," giving voice to "the ordinary, non-political, non-moral, passive man" (*ibid.*, 19). Still Orwell admits that no book may ever be neutral, which is a reservation Rushdie seems to overlook in his criticism of Orwell.

Orwell's point about an a-political quietist literature is made primarily as a reaction against political literature, which was firmly anchored in Communist orthodoxy when it comes right down to it: "The atmosphere of orthodoxy is always damaging to prose, and above all it is completely ruinous to the novel, the most anarchical of all forms of

Orwell and to Henry Miller, too" (IH, 3). However, this does not mean that we cannot use this essay to establish a clearer insight into Rushdie's view on the role of literature in society.

literature. (...) The novel is practically a Protestant form of art; it is a product of the free mind, of the autonomous individual" (*ibid.*, 39). Rushdie cannot disagree with this, given that he also celebrates the idea of the free movement of thought. But Rushdie opposes Orwell's poetics of irresponsibility. Orwell sees this particular poetics at work in Miller who, according to Orwell, neither ignores the processes of history, as did the *l'art pour l'art* movement of the 1920s, nor disputes these processes, as did the orthodoxy-literature of the 1930s. What is new in Miller is the weighting of passivity, acceptance, endurance, and a simple registering of subjective truth: "Progress and reaction have both turned out to be swindles. Seemingly there is nothing left but quietism – robbing reality of its terrors by simply submitting to it. Get inside the whale – or rather, admit you are inside the whale (for you *are*, of course). Give yourself over to the world-process, stop fighting against it or pretending that you control it; simply accept it, endure it, record it" (*ibid.*, 48-49). Orwell simply does not believe in a novel that strives to move in more positive or constructive directions, and the reason for this is obviously the worldly political situation and development he is surrounded by.

Rushdie shows sympathy for Orwell's pessimism and resignation, but he does not accept it: "Sit it out, he recommends; we writers will be safe inside the whale, until the storm dies down. I do not presume to blame him for adopting this position. He lived in the worst of times" (IH, 96-97). To Rushdie resignation means that the artist surrenders and leaves it to the politicians to be the only cartographers of the world, whereby truth is manipulated:

> It seems to me imperative that literature enter such arguments, because what is being disputed is nothing less that what is the case, what is truth and what is untruth. If writers leave the business of making pictures of the world to politicians, it will be one of history's great and most abject abdications.
>
> Outside the whale is the unceasing storm, the continual quarrel, the dialectic of history. Outside the whale there is a genuine need for political fiction, for books that draw new and better maps of reality, and make new languages with which we can understand the world. Outside the

whale we see that we are all irradiated by history, we are radioactive with history and politics (IH, 100).

In Orwell the artist may isolate him-/herself from the historical processes, so to speak, by hiding inside the whale, which is still a transparent whale. In Rushdie's universe the separation of the subject and history is an impossibility, which his novels testify to. Thus there is no whale in Rushdie's universe. Hiding places have proved themselves impossible and the desire to return to the womb is a dangerous illusion:

> The truth is that there is no whale. We live in a world without hiding places; the missiles have made sure of that. However much we may wish to return to the womb, we cannot be unborn. So we are left with a fairly straightforward choice. Either we agree to delude ourselves, to lose ourselves in the fantasy of the great fish, for which a second metaphor is that of Pangloss's garden; or we cannot do what all human beings do instinctively when they realize that the womb has been lost for ever – that is, we can make the very devil of a racket (IH, 99).

When Orwell suggests passivity, Rushdie suggests agency; when Orwell suggests an a-political literature, Rushdie suggests a political literature; when Orwell suggests the whale, Rushdie suggests a racket: "So, in place of Jonah's womb, I am recommending the ancient tradition of making as big a fuss, as noisy a complaint about the world as is humanly possible. Where Orwell wished quietism, let there be rowdyism; in place of the whale, the protesting wail" (IH, 99). To Rushdie literature is a question of truth, a truth that will always be provisional as it is produced in a cartographic process which may both be political, scientific, and artistic. Consequently, any cartography becomes a matter of positioning or choosing sides in the construction of truth.

The third characteristic of minor literature is that everything has collective value. Any individual enunciation always assumes the quality of being collective because minor literature, by reason of its status as "minor," does not accommodate an excess of talent. As Deleuze and Guattari say: "what each author says individually already constitutes a common action, and what he or she says or does is necessarily political, even if others aren't in agreement. The political domain has contaminated every statement (*énoncé*)" (K, 17). Minor literature is revolutionary per se, it inscribes itself in opposition to the prevailing world picture, in opposition to the dominant language system and to the dominant political power in an abstract sense. In terms of enunciation minor literature takes a peripheral position, from where it establishes a showdown with the centre, just as Rushdie's stereoscopic perspective enables him to destabilise both the English and the Indian language and society from within: "and if the writer is in the margins or complete outside his or her fragile community, this situation allows the writer all the more the possibility to express another possible community and to forge the means for another consciousness and another sensibility" (K, 17).

Minor literature draws new maps of the world by means of the lines of flight it produces in language. In everyday life, the world is presented to us through language: for instance, it is the languages of history books, the visual media (visual images are verbally interpreted by TV hosts), and politicians which tell us what the world looks like. The novel may cast doubt on the commonly accepted images (doxa) which have been determined from the perspective of a central position, by voicing peripheral points of view, toward new consciousnesses and new sensibilities: "The literary machine thus becomes the relay for a revolutionary machine-to-come, not at all for ideological reasons but because the literary machine alone is determined to fill the conditions of a collective enunciation that is lacking elsewhere in this milieu: *literature is the people's concern*" (K, 17-18). In light of this, it is no coincidence, for example, that *Midnight's Children* has been described as a novel that gives voice to an entire continent.

The collective enunciation in *Midnight's Children* is produced through the narrator Saleem. The narrator, that is to say the subject of enunciation, appears at a first glance as the cause of the novel's enunciation, just as the main character Saleem, the subject of statement, seems to constitute the effect of the statements. But in our analysis, the two traditional subject categories, writer and hero, narrator and character, have proved themselves to be unstable entities. They figure as linguistic functions rather than as stable entities who may be linked to specific statements. Deleuze and Guattari say about K in Kafka: "K will not be a subject but will be a general function that proliferates and that doesn't cease to segment and to spread over all the segments. (...) Ultimately, it is less a question of K as a general function taken up by an individual than of K as *a functioning of a polyvalent assemblage of which the solitary individual is only a part*" (K, 84, 85). The position of enunciation in *Midnight's Children* assumes a collective nature despite the insistent individual voice, first of all because the macrocosmic flux flows through the narrator, as for example the political machine, the historical machine, and the gastronomical machine, and secondly because the narrator, through his self-conscious unreliability, orchestrates a universal condition for the position of enunciation: the nomadic monad.[47] Deleuze and Guattari say:

> When a statement is produced by a bachelor or an artistic singularity, it occurs necessarily as a function of a national, political, and a social community, even if the objective conditions of this community are not yet given to the moment except in literary enunciation. (...) The most individual enunciation is a particular case of collective enunciation. (...) the actual bachelor and the virtual community – both of them real – are the components of a collective assemblage (K, 83-84).

Hence, singularity contains universality, individuality contains collectivity, just as the condition of the individual reflects a collective condition: "A writer isn't a writer-man; he is a political man,[48] he is a machine-man, and an experimental man" (K, 7), Deleuze and Guattari say, rejecting literature as *l'art pour l'art* and praising literature as experimental, machinal, and political.

The rhizomatic cartography of human identity renders the tradi-

---

[47] It is of course important to distinguish between the enunciative subject and the stating subject, but rhizomatic identity, the identity of the main character Saleem (the stating subject) as it turns out, only reinforces the assumption of the collective quality of the enunciative subject. Consider for example his status as a "collective voice" when he serves as the communications centre of the Midnight's Children Conference.

[48] The sentence "he is a political man" is missing in the English translation of *Kafka: Toward a Minor Literature* and has been inserted here by the translator of this book, translated from *Kafka: pour une littérature mineure*, Paris: Éditions de Minuit, 1975, p. 15.

tional concept of the subject as a stable organism impossible, instead the rhizomatic subject is defined as flux, as a body without organs and an a-centred entity, swept by machinal assemblages from desire which is not defined as a lack, but as a production of new correlations and connections. It is on this backdrop that Deleuze and Guattari may postulate: "There isn't a subject; *there are only collective assemblages of enunciation*" (K, 18). In the conversational book *Negotiations*, Deleuze elaborates on his theory on the subject of enunciation in the following way: "It's a strange business, speaking for yourself, in your own name, because it doesn't at all come with seeing yourself as an ego or a person or a subject. Individuals find a real name for themselves, rather, only through the harshest exercise in depersonalisation, by opening themselves up to the multiplicities everywhere within them, to the intensities running through them" (N, 6).

Rushdie writes novels in which the English language is deterritorialised as it is forced into new border zones from where it generates metamorphoses and new intensities through an anti-representative technique. Apart from that, Rushdie directly inscribes himself in a political machine as his novels orchestrate a junction between the individual sphere and the political sphere. The political status of his novels does not mean that the novels have one political message in particular, it means that they enter into a sociological-political rhizome. Finally, we have seen how individual voices in Rushdie assume the quality of a collective voice: First, because the individual cannot be perceived as a stable subject, but is rather to be seen as a function of a collective assemblage of heterogeneous flux, of which the private subject is only a small part.[49] Secondly, we may infer a general human condition from the self-conscious unreliability and perspectivism of the position of enunciation in *Midnight's Children*, namely the nomadic and monadic point of view. For this reason, the narrator in the novel becomes a reflection of a collective condition

---

49 In connection with *Midnight's Children*, Rushdie has commented on the mechanisms of the novel as individual and collective property, respectively: "I do feel that it's no longer my property. The reaction to it in India has been so enormous that it belongs to hundreds of thousands of people, and in a way my view of it is now no more or less valuable than anyone else's" (Haffenden, 36).

despite his insistently individual voice, through which collectivity may be seen as embedded in individuality. Linda Hutcheon may suitably close this sub-chapter with an observation that supports this idea: "To elevate 'private experience to public consciousness' in postmodern historiographic metafiction is not really to expand the subjective; it is to render inextricable the public and the historical and the private and biographical" (Hutcheon, 94). Hutcheon is going to be one of the main figures in the next sub-chapter because of her notion of postmodern literature as historiographic metafiction.

HISTORIOGRAPHIC METAFICTION

> "My position is that texts are worldly, to some degree they are events, and, even when they appear to deny it, they are nevertheless a part of the social world, human life, and of course the historical moments in which they are located and interpreted."
> – Edward Said: *The World, the Text, and the Critic*

In the following I will elaborate on some of the themes we have already looked at through a determination of Rushdie's novels as historiographic metafiction, thus drawing a rounded picture of the poetics and aesthetics of his writings. In *Poetics of Postmodernism* Linda Hutcheon designates postmodern literature as historiographic metafiction: "What I want to call postmodernism in fiction paradoxically uses and abuses the conventions of both realism and modernism, and does so in order to challenge their transparency, in order to prevent glossing over the contradictions that make the postmodern what it is: historical and metafictional, contextual and self-reflexive, ever aware of its status as discourse, as a human construct" (Hutcheon, 53). Accordingly, the figure that characterises postmodern literature is paradox, given that this literature contains two strong components, namely a historical context (historiography) and a self-reflective intratext (metafiction). Speaking of metafiction, Patricia Waugh's definition of the concept in her exemplary *Metafiction* is also inescapable: "*Metafiction* is a term given to fictional writing which self-consciously and systematically draws attention to its status as an artefact in order to pose questions about the relationship between fiction and reality. In providing a critique of their own methods of construction, such writings not only examine the fundamental structures of narrative fiction, they also explore the possible fictionality of the world outside the literary fictional text" (Waugh, 2). In this way postmodern literature highlights concepts like the past, history, memory, subject, narrativity, fiction, reality, language, and representation.

Historiographic metafiction does not deny the existence of the past and history, but our access to the past is inescapably mediated by discourses which may be verbal or nonverbal: "Historiographic metafiction acknowledges the paradox of the *reality* of the past but its *textualized accessibility* to us today" (Hutcheon, 114). In *Midnight's Children* we find the following passage, supporting the idea that memory and language are our only doorways to the past: "for the first time, I fell victim to the temptation of every autobiographer, to the illusion that since the past exists only in one's memories and the words which strive vainly to encapsulate them, it is possible to create past events simply by saying they occurred" (MC, 443). Consequently, language plays a significant role in the construction of the past, but at the same time Rushdie underlines the ability of language to create false chains of events, which the reader may or may not be suspicious of, depending on the authority of enunciation. Saleem admits the falsity of his construction in a typical Rushdian one-liner: "To tell the truth, I lied" (MC, 443).

Rushdie is not an extreme constructivist, though, as he never really denies that the past actually existed. On the contrary, he problematises the status of the past as an innocent product by calling attention to how we can know anything about the past and what we may know about the past: "Historiographic metafiction does not deny that reality *is* (or *was*), as does this kind of radical constructivism (according to which reality is only a construct); it just questions how we *know* that and how it is (or was)" (Hutcheon, 146), Hutcheon points out.

In *Postmodernist Fiction* Brian McHale argues that the distinction between modernism and postmodernism is determined by the shift that takes place from epistemology as the dominant of modernism to ontology as the dominant of postmodernism; at the same time he stresses that it is of course impossible to separate epistemology and ontology from each other. According to McHale, this shift is made emphatically clear in William Faulkner's *Absalom, Absalom!* (1936) which largely places itself in the modernist epistemological genre, but changes its dominant concern in one particular place in the novel. *Absalom, Absalom!* is centred on epistemological themes such as the accessibility and circulation of knowledge, different configurations of the "same" knowledge in the minds of different people, and the problem of the limits of knowledge and its feasibility at all. These epistemological themes are orchestrated through usual modernist techniques, such as the juxtaposition of several perspectives and the focalisation of knowledge through one central consciousness (Quentin Compson), and finally the epistemological dominant is conveyed to the reader through, for instance, interrupted chronology and retained information, activating the reader in the task of (re-)construction.

In *Absalom, Absalom!* the epistemological question of the status of knowledge is dominant, but in chapter eight there is a shift of focus to an ontological question of various modes of being: "In short, Ch. 8 of *Absalom, Absalom!* dramatizes the shift of dominant from problems of *knowing* to problems of *modes of being* – from an epistemological dominant to an *ontological one*. At this point Faulkner's novel touches and perhaps crosses the boundary between modernist and postmodernist writing" (McHale, 10). In chapter eight Quentin and Steve thus begin constructing the course of the past, but the construction is to a great extent produced by the two narrators giving way to imagination, thus delineating several possible models of the course of events in and around the Sutpen family. Accordingly, in chapter eight, the novel concentrates more on the shapes of the past than on the possibility of accessing the past. In Rushdie we have seen examples of an ontological "flicker" in the narrator's orchestration of a polyphony in connection with *Shame*, for instance, in which it is most visible in the indeterminacy between the male and female discourses.

Historiographic metafiction incorporates both an ontological and an epistemological element as it examines exactly how we can know the past while at the same time investigating the status of the past (and the present): "The epistemological question of how we know the past joins the ontological one of the status of the traces of that past" (Hutcheon, 122), Hutcheon says. Her point is that postmodernism does not constitute a radical break with modernism. Rather, it incorporates the techniques of modernism as part of a movement between use and misuse, respect and parody.

Like *Absalom, Absalom!*, *Midnight's Children* contains all the well-known epistemological themes. Noticeably, it revolves around the function of memory as a filter between past and present, which Rushdie has explicitly commented on in "'Errata': Or, Unreliable Narration in *Midnight's Children*":

> When I began the novel (...) my purpose was somewhat Proustian. Time and migration had placed a double filter between me and my subject, and I hoped that if I could only imagine vividly enough it might be possible to see beyond those filters, to write as if the years had not passed, as if I had never left India for the West. But as I worked I found that what interested me was the process of filtration itself. So my subject changed, was no longer a search for lost time, had become the way in which we remake the past to suit our present purposes, using memory as our tool (IH, 23-24).

The quotation points to the epistemological focus in the novel, Rushdie's motive changing from a wish to describe the past as it was to a wish to illuminate the actual filters. Apart from that, the novel orchestrates a poly-perspectivism in several places through secondary narrators which are, in turn, drawn together in a central consciousness (Saleem's), and, finally, the reader is also activated in the epistemological process as the novel superimposes the chronological string by means of digressions and pro- and analepsis, involving the reader in a reflective process where "how" and "why" are often more important than "what".

However, *Midnight's Children* also examines the ontology of the past. The epistemological question of how we can know anything about the past is inseparably connected with the ontological question of what the status of the past is: "Historiographic metafiction asks both epistemological and ontological questions. How do we know the past (or the present)? What is the ontological status of that past? Of its documents? Of our narratives?" (Hutcheon, 50), says Hutcheon. The traces of the past in *Midnight's Children* have primarily been created by Rushdie (and Saleem) through memory, but in working with the novel Rushdie has also gathered information from history books, newspapers and photo archives. The historical material has helped Rushdie creating a mimetic element in the novel. Bombay is vividly and realistically portrayed in great detail, as we may experience London in Dickens's novels for instance. Accordingly, Rushdie's novels are characterised by a very strong referentiality which refrains from rejecting reality, the past, and history as pure illusion and anchors the universe of the novel in a recognisable environment. Yet at the same time, our access to the past and reality is problematised by their mediation through memory and language. In this way, historiographic metafiction explores the limits of mimesis. Memory can never return the past to us in an unadulterated form, just as language can never bring us an unmachined form of "reality": we are dealing with ontological borders which are only partially penetrable. Rushdie acknowledges the fragility of any project of reclamation:

> It may be that writers in my position, exiles or emigrants or expatriates, are haunted by some sense of loss, some urge to reclaim, to look back, even at the risk of being mutated into pillars of salt. But if we do look back, we must also do so in the knowledge – which give rise to profound uncertainties – that our physical alienation from India almost inevitably means that we will not be capable of reclaiming precisely the thing that was lost; that we will, in short create fictions, not actual cities or villages, but invisible ones, imaginary homelands, Indias of the mind (IH, 10).

Conditioned by memory, Saleem is deemed to project the past in fragments and in an altered state through what Deleuze and Guattari call childhood blocks: "Memory brings about a reterritorialisation of childhood. But the childhood block functions differently. It is the only real life of the child; it is deterritorialisation; it shifts in time, with time, in order to reactivate desire and make its connections proliferate; it is intensive and, even in its lowest intensities, it launches a high intensity" (K, 78-79). Childhood blocks are not caught by a regressive, nostalgic oedipal desire, on the contrary, they work as catalysts of new connections by a reactivation of desire because they change in and with time. It is for this reason that the narrator in *Midnight's Children* emphasises his unreliability and his fragmented point of view as opposed to an untainted, duplicating projection of a pure past. The past plays a part in shaping Saleem, it cannot be rejected as pure illusion, but at the same time he cannot return to the past as it once was.

In this way, the past and history become discursive, provisional constructions marked by being events rather than essentially determined.

Discourse analysis focuses on the circumstances of the creation of the discourse, such as who speaks, from where does he/she speak, when does he/she speak, and what motivates the speech? Accordingly, discourse is situationally determined, the situation being permeated by forces that strive to motivate the discourse in one way or another. This is suggested in the following passage from *Shame*, inspired by Darwin and Foucault:

> History is natural selection. Mutant versions of the past struggle for dominance; new species of fact arise, and old, saurian truths go to the wall, blindfolded and smoking last cigarettes. Only the mutations of the strong survive. The weak, the anonymous, the defeated leave few marks: field-patterns, axe-heads, folk-tales, broken pitchers, burial mounds, the fading memory of their youthful beauty. History loves only those who dominate her: it is a relationship of mutual enslavement (S, 124).

Language is never neutral, it reflects ideological struggles. Certainty is perceived as positional, which is to say that it derives from a complex network of local and contingent conditions.[50] The provisional status of history and the past is not an expression of nihilism, refuting thinking as superfluous; quite the opposite, thinking is activated by the scepticism one may adopt in response to direct representations of the past and history: "If we accept that all is provisional and historically conditioned, we will not stop thinking, as some fear; in fact, that acceptance will guarantee that we never stop thinking – and rethinking" (Hutcheon, 53).

What postmodernism does is to cast doubt on the possibility that we may ever know the past in its pure form. Postmodernism sets the stage for the notion that the social, historical, and existential reality of the past is a discursive reality when used for purposes of referentiality in

---

50   "In the computer age, the question of knowledge is now more than ever a question of government" (Lyotard, 9), it says in Lyotard's *The Postmodern Condition*. Lyotard goes on to elaborate on the situational determination of enunciation: "A self does not amount to much, but no self is an island; each exists in a fabric of relations that is now more complex and mobile than ever before. Young or old, man or woman, rich or poor, a person is always located at 'nodal points' of specific communication circuits, however tiny these may be" (*ibid.*, 15).

art. Therefore, the only true historicity is the one that openly acknowledges its discursive and contingent status. The past as referentiality is not erased, quite the reverse, it is incorporated and processed.

Postmodernism and historiographic metafiction acknowledge the permeation of language by power relations which are latently upheld and endorsed even by everyday language. Power and metaphysics in language are underpinned in a perpetual process of naturalisation, giving rise to forms of oppression in language in even "innocent" representations. Edward Said's analysis of the Occidental discourse on the Orient, "orientalism," is an example, for instance, of a Eurocentric metaphysics sustained in and by language. Likewise, Rushdie inscribes himself in a tradition that seeks to deconstruct the prevailing metaphysics through a new language, which we have already dealt with before.

In the "realist" novels of the nineteenth century, language was often perceived as a transparent medium, in which everyday language reflected an unproblematic common sense in relation to reality. Metafiction does not deny the existence of objective facts in reality, but it counterwrites the use of language in the so-called realist novel that sanctions a positivist and straightforward approach to reality. The meta-level in historiographic metafiction is necessary precisely because it is through this level that the mimetic illusion is shattered: it is through the meta-level that the relation between the world of fiction and the world outside fiction may be examined and elucidated. Simultaneously, by drawing our attention to its own principles of construction, the novel draws attention to the principles behind the construction of reality in other forms of discourse, be it historical writing, journalism, law, etc.

In *Shame* the narrator reflects on the outcome if he was writing a realist novel: then he would not write about Bilquìs and her fear of the Loo-wind, but about the illegal installations of subterranean water pumps in the Defence district in Karachi, with which the lawns were kept green while the city was suffering from a shortage of water; he would write about the club in the city which still had a sign forbidding the entrance of women and dogs; and he would analyse the subtle logic of the country's industrial plans which necessitate the development of nuclear reactors, but not refrigerators. "How much real-life material might become compulsory!" (S, 69), the disheartened narrator exclaims. Apart from the fruitless and problematic mimesis of the world, there are other more palpable incentives for writing a new kind of realism:

> By now, if I had been writing a book of this nature, it would have done me no good to protest that I was writing universally, not only about Pakistan. The book would have been banned, dumped in the rubbish bin, burned. All that effort for nothing! Realism can break a writer's heart.
>
> Fortunately, however, I am only telling a sort of modern fairy-tale, so that's all right; nobody need get upset, or take anything I say too seriously. No drastic action need be taken, either.
>
> What a relief! (S, 70).

The narrator's attempt to undermine the role of fiction is of course ironic, not least because *Shame* to a great degree functions as a *roman à clef* in which some of the characters are based on real people (Raza Hyder and Iskander Harappa share certain features with Zia Ul-haq and Zulfikar Ali Bhutto respectively). Rushdie often exploits the possibilities of this genre to create a recognisable referentiality, but at the same time the autonomy of the fictive universe is underscored.

In *Midnight's Children* Saleem reflects on the relation between fiction and reality in the following passage about Pakistan: "in a country where the truth is what it is instructed to be, reality quite literally ceases to exist, so that everything becomes possible except what we are told is the case; and maybe this was the difference between my Indian childhood and Pakistani adolescence – that in the first I was beset by an infinity of alternative realities, while in the second I was adrift, disoriented, amid an equally infinite number of falsenesses, unrealities and lies" (MC, 326). Rushdie may seem radical in this passage ("reality quite literary ceases to exist"), but in regard to dictatorial states, in which reality is constructed to an extreme degree in an attempt to control the people, the postulation is perhaps only slightly hyperbolic. In another place in *Midnight's Children*, Saleem notes the incongruity between news headings and reality in relation to the border war between India and Pakistan: "Divorce between news and reality" (MC, 334). Saleem expands on the discrepancy: "That much is fact; but everything else lies concealed beneath the doubly hazy air of unreality and make-believe which affected all goings-on in those days, and especially all events in the phantasmagoric Rann... so that the story I am going to tell, which is substantially that told by my cousin Zafar, is as likely to be true as anything; as anything, that is to say, except what we were officially told" (MC, 335). Here Saleem leans on his cousin Zafar's story about the events in Rann of Kutch, but in spite of Zafar's presence in Rann the events are marked by ontological uncertainty whereby the truth may actually accommodate any description except from the official version. However, Saleem is conscious about the demand for facts in historical writing: "Important to concentrate on good hard facts. But which facts?" (MC, 338), he says despairingly. "Nothing was real; nothing certain" (MC, 340), he continues, and in order to increase uncertainty he also incorporates a mythical discourse: "Aircraft, real or fictional, dropped actual or mythical bombs" (MC, 341). The above clearly demonstrates Rushdie's preoccupation with the nature of fiction, reality, and myth as linguistic constructions. Rushdie does not regret this state of things because this is exactly where he sees the motive of art: art is to create alternative versions of reality as counter-images to official versions. In light of this, I will now move on to Rushdie's employment of the historical episode of the satanic verses.

*

Rushdie's use of the satanic verses must be viewed principally in extension of both the examination above of the generic characteristics of historiographic metafiction and the examples of discursive formations of the past in *Midnight's Children* and *Shame*. As we have seen, Hutcheon argues that postmodernism is a blend of historiography and metafiction and, as will be shown below, *The Satanic Verses* is very historiographic indeed.

The affair of the satanic verses ensues from a much-discussed episode in the origin of Islam.[51] The Koran comprises the revelations of the Prophet Muhammad which he received through the archangel Gabriel at

---

51   I base my informative historical recount of the affair in 616 primarily on Jakob Skovgaard-Petersen's enlightening and mediating article "Hvad er de sataniske vers?" ("What are the Satanic Verses?") from the Danish anthology *Satanisk, guddommeligt – og såre menneskeligt (Satanic, Divine – And Simply Human)* which was published in connection with the tenth anniversary of the fatwa.

the beginning of the seventh century. In the beginning Muhammad and his few disciples had great difficulties establishing Islam and the monotheistic faith in Allah as the supreme religion in Mecca, Muhammad's birthplace. The Meccans had no intention of giving up their polytheism and therefore, according to some historical sources, Muhammad was compelled to make a compromise, declaring through a revelation that al-Lat, al-Uzza, and Manat, the three favourite Meccan goddesses, could be considered as heavenly intercessories en route to Allah: "*al-Lat, al-Uzza, and Manat are the transcendent swans, in whose intercessory prayer (with Allah) one dares put one's trust!*" (Skovgaard-Petersen cites Frants Buhl's *Muhammeds Liv (Muhammed's Life)* from 1903. Buhl relies on the (pseudo)historian ibn Ishaq who died in 767 and whose works have been lost). Apparently this compromise attracted a great deal of enthusiasm in Mecca, but Gabriel immediately reproached Muhammad for the revelation and thought it to be an insertion from Satan. The verses were replaced by a revelation that turns down the idea of God being able to beget children, especially daughters, as meaningless. Sûra 53 opens with an assurance of the Prophet Muhammad's unselfish intentions and infallibility. Verses 1-6 go like this, for example: "By the declining star, your compatriot is not in error, nor is he deceived! He does not speak out of his own fancy. This is an inspired revelation. He is taught by one who is powerful and mighty." Verses 17-19 make up the replacement of the former verses of compromise: "Have you thought on Al-Lât and Al-'Uzza, and on Manât, the third other? Are you to have the sons, and He the daughters? This is indeed an unfair distinction!"

Accordingly, the satanic verses, that is, Muhammad's compromise with the Meccans resulting in the acceptance of the three goddesses as Allah's daughters, is not to be found in the Koran, they have been given to us by Muslim historians and their authenticity is doubtful: "In short, the affair has been passed on to us by early Muslim historians, but not by the earliest. And on the basis of the sources, it is impossible to say whether this is because later historians, like ibn Hisham, have removed them or because the story only comes about at this late stage" (Skovgaard-Petersen, 46). Nevertheless, it is not important in this connection whether the satanic verses did exist in the Koran or not. The very fact that the episode is mentioned by historians makes it possible to call

Muhammad's reliability into question and, with that, the dependability of the Koran as such, which is exactly the optics Rushdie is toying with in *The Satanic Verses*.

Skovgaard-Petersen's merit is that he brings in Rushdie's overt and deliberate use of Muhammad-images from a Western anti-Islamic tradition, in which Muhammad, prior to the Enlightenment, was represented as the devil's instrument and a false prophet. From the nineteenth century onwards, a more scientific approach to Islam started portraying Muhammad as a person who had founded a religion for personal reasons and hence could be held morally responsible. As a replacement for the polemical Christian image of Muhammad, the West strove to demean the image of the Prophet by questioning his honesty as a human being. Was he an opportunist obsessed with power? Did he believe in the revelations himself? Was he sick? The most widespread diagnosis from the angle of Victorian psychology was that Muhammad was epileptic which caused him to believe that he was receiving revelations. It is in connection with this, and in this period from about 1860, that importance was added to the affair in biographies of Muhammad: "The idea that Muhammad perceived something he wanted as a revelation was seen as a crucial symptom of mental disturbance. The affair of the satanic verses becomes a *locus classicus* of a psychological interpretation of Muhammad" (*ibid.*, 49). In a later anti-Islamic tradition the affair is used as proof of the argument that the Koran has been manipulated and edited. Rushdie exploits most of the register of the Western anti-Islamic tradition as it is suggested in the novel that 1) Muhammad is a false prophet, 2) he is the instrument of the devil (the use of the name Mahound), 3) his motives are at times pragmatic-egotistic, and, finally, 4) Rushdie's project is precisely to manipulate the original recitation through fiction.

It may sound strange that Muslim historians mention the affair if it never occurred. What would be their interests in defaming Muhammad? May their very mentioning of the affair not function as evidence of the truth of the affair? According to Skovgaard-Petersen, the English critic John Burton changes the focus from Sûra 53 to Sûra 22 which is also mentioned by Frants Buhl. To Muhammad's further assurance, he receives a revelation in Sûra 22, verse 53, saying that Allah removes anything that Satan may insert: "But God abrogates the interjections of Satan and confirms His own revelations." This verse is central to the theory of *naskh*, Burton points out, in which verses may be cancelled by other verses. Accordingly, some of the rules in the Koran are no longer valid as they have been annulled by other verses (e.g. the prohibition of and the permission to drink wine, which are both to be found in the Koran, in which it is the chronology of the time of the revelation (not the chronology of the Koran) that validates the former), but in extension to this there was also an interest in asserting that certain rules applied which were no longer to be found in the Koran (e.g. the punishment of adultery which was believed to be too mild in the existing version). "Accordingly, the story of the satanic verses is said to be an obvious example of a verse that had to be removed in order to bolster the theory that other verses existed which had to be included. Altogether a way of relativising the corpus of Koranic law" (*ibid.*, 51), Skovgaard-Petersen concludes on John Burton's theory. The theory answers the question of why Muslim historians would have invented a story which, at a first glance, seems to run counter to their own interests and weaken the Koran: the idea that the verses have been removed is supposed to legitimate the possibility of incorporating new and necessitated regulations that overthrow the existing, but outmoded rules. Burton's theory is rejected by Muslim learned men, however.

Let us take a closer look at Rushdie's use of the story of the satanic verses. The episode of the verses is included in the two chapters about Mahound and Jahilia, chapters II and VI, which appear as Gibreel's dreams. The introduction of chapter II is as fascinating in style and as complex as the opening of the novel. It is described how Gibreel is slipping from a waking state into the inevitable but by now dreaded sleeping state with angelic visions, and on his way into the dream world Gibreel passes his mother who, in addition to calling him an angel, refers to him as Shaitan. The name is a childhood block, relating to the mother's annoyance with Gibreel's boyish pranks as a lunch deliverer, having swapped Hindu and Muslim lunch pails: "mischeevious imp, she slices the air with her hand, rascal has been putting Muslim meat compartments into Hindu non-veg tiffin-carriers, customers are up in arms. Little devil, she scolds, but then folds him in her arms, my little farishta, boys will be boys" (SV, 91). Once again we see that childhood blocks are crucial in constituting the formation of the dream tracks. The quotation explains Gibreel's vacillating self-perception as Shaitan/Little devil or Gabriel/farishta, an indecision and doubt which, apart from the childhood block, is determined by his recent loss of faith.

As in the opening of the novel, and as in the Bible and the Koran, Gibreel "falls and the falling begins to feel like a flight" (SV, 91), alluding to the angels Iblis and Satan, but the fall may also refer to Gabriel's descent to man after his union with God in Heaven: this episode is recounted in Sûra 53 which Rushdie draws on several times. The introduction continues: "In the early dreams he sees beginnings, Shaitan cast down from the sky, making a grab for a branch of the highest Thing, the lote-tree of the uttermost end that stands beneath the Throne, Shaitan missing, plummeting, splat. But he lived on, was not couldn't be dead, sang from hellbelow his soft seductive verses" (SV, 91). Gibreel's dreams are about the stories in the Koran and the stories about the origin of the Koran, but the dreams are informed by a strange subjective logic of interpretation, marked by 1) Gibreel's childhood, 2) his youth readings, 3) his theological Hindu roles, and by 4) the doubt that haunts him and is gradually eating him up.

The seductive verses mentioned in the passage above are the satanic verses and Gibreel dreams about Satan and the three goddesses as rivals to the archangel and Muhammad: "O the sweet songs that he knew. With his daughters as his fiendish backing group, yes, the three of them, Lat Manat Uzza, motherless girls laughing with their Abba, giggling behind their hands at Gibreel, what a trick we got in store for you, they giggle, for you and for that businessman on the hill" (SV, 91). This is where Muhammad/Mahound is mentioned as the "businessman" the first time, which may be referred back to the anti-Islamic tradition of Muhammad-images that Rushdie brings into play. In addition, Rushdie draws on the entire idea of the existence of the satanic verses, fervently rejected by Muslim scholars.[52]

---

52   In the Danish translation of the Koran a footnote has been inserted on verse 21 in Sûra 53 which rejects the episode: "The story about Satan here having whispered something about a hope one could have in the intercessory prayers of the goddesses is clearly a falsification. All of the Sûras evidently and uncompromisingly teach monotheism. The story derives from Wâqidi who is branded as a liar by all

The narrator reflects on the name of the businessman which is a nickname he has adopted himself:

> His name: a dream-name, changed by the vision. Pronounced correctly, it means he-for-whom-thanks-should-be-given, but he won't answer to that here; nor, though he's well aware of what they call him, to his nick-name in Jahilia down below – *he-who-goes-up-and-down-old-Coney*. Here he is neither Mahomet nor MoeHammered; has adopted, instead, the demon-tag the farangis hung around his neck. To turn insults into strengths, whigs, tories, Blacks all chose to wear with pride the names they were given in scorn; likewise, our mountain-climbing, prophet-motivated solitary is to be the medieval baby-frightener, the Devil's synonym: Mahound (SV, 93).

The name Mahound derives from a Medieval Anti-Islamic tradition that regards Muhammad as the devil, but at the same time the reader has to see the motif in light of the novel's overall theme of turning insults into strengths. Mahound is a variation on this theme, like the example of "rivers of blood:" by adopting the name Mahound and carrying it with pride, the name loses its monological status as a derogative term and its satanic essence may be changed into new positive attributes.

We meet Mahound on his forty-fourth birthday on his way up Cone Mountain (the historical Mount Hira) to the cave where he receives the revelations. Whilst there is a festival in Jahilia, Mahound turns to loneliness and asceticism: "A man of ascetic tastes. (What strange manner of businessman is this?)" (SV, 92). The question is part of the project of reclamation mentioned above, the narrator hinting at Mahound's abstinence and unselfish nature as admirable qualities. In addition, it appears as if the term businessman may pass as a relatively undramatic name insofar as Jahilia is a commercial city and most of its citizens do business. On this day Mahound has reached the crisis of his life and one of the novel's recurrent questions is pushing its way through: "*What kind of an idea are you? Man-or-mouse*" (SV, 95).

authorities, or from Tabarî who is described as gullible and an unreliable observer by experts" (Sûra 53, verse 21, footnote 6).

Now the dream shifts its focus from Mahound to the events in Jahilia where we meet Abu Simbel: "The vision yields his name eventually; it, too, is changed by the dream. Here he is, Karim Abu Simbel, Grandee of Jahilia, husband to the ferocious, beautiful Hind" (SV, 96).⁵³ Jahilia is a city built on and of sand with a concentric topography: "the very stuff of inconstancy, – the quintessence of unsettlement, shifting, treachery, lack-of-form, – and [they] have turned it, by alchemy, into the fabric of their newly invented permanence" (SV, 94). The city is a commercial city with games, drinking, fornicating, dance, and poets' competitions, and the centre of the city is perceived by the citizens as the hub of the universe, an axis of rotation with the world "spinning round this point" (SV, 99). The city's state in-between impermanence and permanence may be viewed in part through some of the concepts that have been introduced in connection with Deleuze's theory: "Jahilia has been built in a series of rough circles, its houses spreading outwards from the House of the Black Stone, approximately in order of wealth and rank" (SV, 96). In this way the city reflects both a polytheistic pluralism and a stable hierarchy with a fixed point of rotation, the order of which is determined by wealth and profession. Jahilia is both the exponent of structural ranking, but it is also a society that permits dirty debauchery among its citizens, whereby it might be argued that profanity and sacredness coexist in Jahilia.

Allah ranges as a divinity in Jahilia, but only as one among many and his popularity is not overwhelming: "There is a god here called Allah (means simply, the god). Ask the Jahilians and they'll acknowledge that this fellow has some sort of overall authority, but he isn't very popular: an

---

53   Abu Simbel is based on the historical Abu Sufyan whose real wife was Hind and the greatest rival of Muhammad. Rushdie has chosen to let the name Sufyan appear in connection with the hosting couple in the Shaandaar Café where Hind's name resurfaces, but Abu has been changed to Muhammad. In this way, historical and fictive names are interlaced in a proliferating network, making it impossible to identify any stable centre. In addition, the distinction between dream and reality is erased by means of the names mentioned above, Abu Sufyan and Hind being historical names that feature as Abu Simbel and Hind in the dream track and as Muhammad Sufyan and Hind in the A-line. With its reference to history, the use of the names in the B-line may just as well have a higher priority than the use of these names in the A-line.

all-rounder in an age of specialist statues" (SV, 99). The most cherished and the most powerful gods are the goddesses Uzza, Manat, and Al-Lat, the latter of which is Allah's strongest adversary and the favourite goddess of the poet Baal:

> Abu Simbel and newly perspiring Baal have arrived at the shrines, placed side by side, of the three best-beloved goddesses in Jahilia. They bow before all three: Uzza of the radiant visage, goddess of beauty and love; dark, obscure Manat, her face averted, her purposes mysterious, sifting sand between her fingers – she's in charge of destiny – she's Fate; and lastly the highest of the three, the mother-goddess, whom the Greeks called Lato. Ilat, they call her here, or, more frequently, Al-Lat. *The goddess.* Even her name makes her Allah's opposite and equal. Lat the omnipotent (SV, 99-100).

It is the sharp opposition between Al-Lat and Allah that Mahound is struggling against, but in spite of the citizens' indifference towards Allah, Abu Simbel is worried about Mahound's presence. He tries to persuade Baal to lampoon the Prophet, which Baal initially refuses as he regards the role of the artist as free of political control, but when Abu Simbel resorts to physical violence and lets him know that he is aware of his affair with Hind, Baal submits to the idea. The smear campaign is not the only measure Abu Simbel initiates to protect himself against Mahound. In an attempt to trap the Prophet, Abu Simbel offers Mahound a compromise in which the Prophet has to accept the Meccans' three favourite goddesses in a henotheistic arrangement with Allah as the supreme god.

What is it about the Prophet that so scares Abu Simbel? "For that: one one one, his terrifying singularity. Whereas I am always divided, always two or three or fifteen" (SV, 102). Abu Simbel continues: "*What kind of idea am I?* I bend. I sway. I calculate the odds, trim my sails, manipulate, survive" (SV, 102). As opposed to his unyielding wife Hind, Abu Simbel characterises himself as a flexible man, a pragmatist, and a power monger who counts the odds and acts accordingly; as such he is not a religious idealist, in contrast to both Mahound and Hind.

Having listened to the proposition, Mahound confronts his closest supporters with the idea. "The water-carrier Khalid is there, and some sort of bum from Persia by the outlandish name of Salman, and to complete this trinity of scum there is the slave Bilal" (SV, 101). This passage has incensed and insulted Muslims, but I think that the adjectives must be viewed in the context, whereby the derisive tone does not necessarily express Rushdie's opinion about Mahound's followers. The passage is an example of free indirect discourse in which the narrative voice blends with the general idiom and the general attitude to the Prophet's followers in Jahilia. This is supported by the fact that Baal also calls Khalid, Salman, and Bilal by ugly names immediately after the quotation above: "those *goons* – those fucking *clowns?*" (SV, 101). In preference to a literal translation and the dubiousness of referring the statements back to Rushdie as a person, I find it much more reasonable to read the statements as an ironic critique of disparaging attitudes to immigrants and minorities. Consequently, and in contrast to an offended reading, if Rushdie is present in the statements at all, it is through a sympathetic understanding of Mahound's disciples.

As said, Mahound informs his followers about Abu Simbel's proposition: "He asks for Allah's approval of Lat, Uzza and Manat. In return, he gives his guarantee that we will be tolerated, even officially recognized; as a mark of which, I am to be elected to the council of Jahilia. That's the offer" (SV, 105). The discourse denotes a profane commercial language in which one achieves something in return for something else: Abu Simbel asks a favour, in return he guarantees tolerance and official recognition which is to be marked with Mahound's election to the city council, the offer goes. Mahound, the former businessman, understands this language and is tempted, but Salman, the immigrant, warns him:

> "It's a trap. If you go up Coney and come down with such a Message, he'll ask, how could you make Gibreel provide just the right revelation? He'll be able to call you a charlatan, a fake." Mahound shakes his head. "You know, Salman, that I have learned how to *listen*. This *listening* is not of the ordinary kind; it's also a kind of asking. Often, when Gibreel comes, it's as if he knows what's in my heart. It feels to me, most times, as if he comes from within my heart: from within my deepest places, from my soul" (SV, 106).

With this, Salman indicates the consequences of a compromise. Mahound will appear as a false prophet, a pragmatist, if he returns from Cone Mountain with exactly the kind of revelation he went up there to get. Mahound confesses that his listening on the mountain is just as often a matter of questioning, which is an unambiguous reference to the anti-Islamic image of Muhammad as a utilitarian opportunist who puts the words in the mouth of the Prophet himself. Mahound explicitly indicates that the archangel is no more than the voice of his own heart, that the archangel is merely an instrument in putting forward his own deepest needs. In my view there is no doubt that Muhammad's status as the messenger of uncontaminated divine revelations is questioned in this passage.

Salman, Bilal, and Khalid are divided on the question of a compromise. The mere fact that Mahound is prepared to consider the offer undermines his purity and his unadulterated intentions. What is to be made of the goddesses? Are they devils or archangels? "'Angels and devils,' Mahound says. 'shaitan and Gibreel. We all, already, accept their existence, halfway between God and man. Abu Simbel asks that we admit just three more to this great company. Just three, and, he indicates, all Jahilia's souls will be ours'" (SV, 107). All three disciples are sceptical: "Salman shakes his head. 'This is being done to destroy you.' And Bilal adds: 'God cannot be four.' And Khalid, close to tears: 'Messenger, what are you saying? Lat, Manat, Uzza – they're all *females*! For pity's sake! Are we to have goddesses now? Those old cranes, herons, hags?'" (SV, 107). In the novel the episode of the satanic verses arises from a politician's offer of compromise, a compromise Mahound is tempted to accept. Hence political considerations seem to superimpose religious idealism, which is a distortion of the way Islam understands itself: in Islamic communities religion sets the agenda of society. Rushdie's distortion is a clear insinuation that the religious discourse surrounding the creation of the Koran may not have been all that innocent, pure, and divinely motivated.

Gibreel dreams that Mahound consults the archangel on the mountain, and on one of the novel's complex levels of enunciation, Gibreel dreams about his own dream, flinching from his role as the archangel: "who, me? *I'm* supposed to know the answers here? I'm sitting here watching this picture and now this actor points his finger out at me, who ever heard the like, who asks the bloody audience of a 'theological' to solve the bloody plot? – But as the dream shifts, it's always changing form, he, Gibreel, is no longer a mere spectator but the central player, the star" (SV, 108). In his dream Gibreel oscillates between a passive role as a dreamer and an active role as the archangel while Mahound demands an answer and revelation from him. Gibreel is terrified by the thought of playing the archangel, a role loaded with heavy responsibility: "*Mahound comes to me for revelation, asking me to choose between monotheist and henotheist alternatives, and I'm just some idiot actor having a bhaenchud nightmare, what the fuck do I know, yaar, what to tell you, help. Help*" (SV, 109).

Gibreel's experience of his relation with Mahound partly confirms Mahound's perception of things, namely that it is Mahound who controls Gibreel's revelation:

> But when he has rested he enters a different sort of sleep, a sort of not-sleep, the condition that he calls his *listening*, and he feels a dragging pain in the gut, like something trying to be born, and now Gibreel, who has been hovering-above-looking-down, feels a confusion, *who am I*, in these moments it begins to seem that the archangel is actually *inside the Prophet*, I am the dragging in the gut, I am the angel being extruded from the sleeper's navel, I emerge, Gibreel Farishta, while my other self, Mahound, lies *listening*, entranced, I am bound to him, navel to navel, by a shining cord of light, not possible to say which of us is dreaming the other. We flow in both directions along the umbilical cord (SV, 110).

The focal point moves from Mahound's experience of "*listening*" to the archangel Gibreel's feelings of being inside the Prophet, and this double focalisation is united in the dreamer Gibreel who thus has a feeling of being both the archangel and the Prophet. Gibreel is left in painful doubt, but he listens to "the listening-which-is-also-an-asking" (SV, 110) in which Mahound tells him of his hardship, about his miracles which have convinced no one and, finally, Mahound asks what to recite and if the goddesses are really angels. When Gibreel refrains from answering, Mahound's internal dialogue continues, displaying him as a man of insight as he doubts his own motives and considers the possibility that they be latent vanity, arrogance, weakness, and greed for power: "Is Allah so unbending that he will not embrace three more to save the human race? – I don't know anything. – Should God be proud or humble, majestic or simple, yielding or un–? *What kind of idea is he? What kind am I?*" (SV, 111).

In this half-sleeping/half-waking state, Gibreel is reminded of his indignation and anger at Allah for having deserted him during his illness. Allah still does not reveal himself, instead the Prophet keeps turning up, haunting and terrifying Gibreel with his greatness, and suddenly the revelation begins:

> It happens: revelation. Like this: Mahound, still in his notsleep, becomes rigid, veins bulge in his neck, he clutches at his centre. No, no, nothing like an epileptic fit, it can't be explained away that easily: what epileptic fit ever caused day to turn to night, caused clouds to mass overhead, caused the air to thicken into soup while an angel hung, scared silly, in the sky above the sufferer, held up like a kite on a golden thread? The dragging again the dragging and now the miracle starts in his my our guts, he is straining with all his might at something, forcing something, and Gibreel begins to feel that strength that force, here it is *at my own jaw* working it, opening shutting; and the power, starting within Mahound, reaching up to *my vocal cords* and the voice comes.
>
> *Not my voice* I'd never know such words I'm no classy speaker never was never will be but this isn't my voice it's a Voice.
>
> Mahound's eyes open wide, he's seeing some kind of vision, staring at it, oh, that's right, Gibreel remembers, me. He's seeing me. My lips moving, being moved by. What, whom? Don't know, can't say. Nevertheless, here they are, coming out of my mouth, up my throat, past my teeth: the Words.
>
> Being God's postman is no fun, yaar.
>
> Butbutbut: God isn't in this picture.
>
> God knows whose postman I've been (SV, 112).

In this passage the narrator turns down the theory of epilepsy as a true miracle seems to emerge with the change of weather, but as in Gibreel's tropicalisation of London this may turn out to be a hallucination. Once again focal points seem to coincide ("his my our") in which the positions of enunciation fuse and Mahound's will urges Gibreel to recite. Gibreel's powerlessness and status as a detached spectator is elucidated by the fact that Gibreel does not speak the language of the revelation. The miracle of this episode is repeated in one of the even-numbered chapters where we experience the dreaming and delirious Gibreel through Allie. Gibreel's speech turns out to be Arabic, a language he neither speaks nor understands, and when Allie shows her phonetic transcripts to an imam, his hairs stand on end as Gibreel's recitation turns out to be the satanic verses. Moreover, we see how the perspective assumes the quality of a *mise en abyme* in the quotation above in the scene where Gibreel sees Mahound see Gibreel. The three finishing lines form Gibreel's comment on his role as the archangel, a comment which secularises the relation between God and archangel/prophet, but there is also a suggestion as to who may actually be behind the verses insofar as God does not feature in the footage of the dream: the verses are infused by Satan, Gibreel acting as his messenger through his doubt.

When Mahound returns to Jahilia he proceeds straight to the market place instead of sticking to his usual practice of returning to the camp of his followers. The market place is a symbol of the popular spirit which is why Mahound chooses it as the site to recite his revelation, to be more specific in the poets' tent, linking the satanic element with art. The recitation is a repetition of Sûra 53 from the contemporary Koran, but the verses acknowledging the three goddesses have been inserted: "'Have you thought upon Lat and Uzza, and Manat, the third, the other?' - After the first verse, Hind gets to her feet; the Grandee of Jahilia is already standing very straight. And Mahound, with silenced eyes, recites: 'They are the exalted birds, and their intercession is desired indeed'" (SV, 114). Cheers and devotions to Al-Lat ensue, but Abu Simbel and Hind's gesture of bending their knee to Allah gives rise to the crowd's acceptance of Allah as well, and the great event is celebrated in Jahilia all through the night.

Yet another part of the novel has provoked many Muslims, notably the section in which Mahound wakes up in Hind's bed the morning after the compromise and the phantasmagorical night of madness, murder, and pleasure. Mahound's uneasiness about not being able to recall how he has ended up in her bed, and his apparent wish to get away (two possibly sympathetic and condoning elements), quickly leads the conversation onto a track of irreconcilability, Hind refusing the idea of Al-Lat submitting to Allah and Mahound demanding that Allah reign supreme. The quarrel develops into a fight between sand and water and, as has been said about Jahilia at an earlier stage, it is a city whose wealth is founded on the power of sand. But with Mahound (and later on with the Imam) sand is challenged by the force (and purity) of water. The incident between Mahound and Hind ends with the following exchange: "'You are sand and I am water,' Mahound says. 'Water washes sand away.' 'And the desert soaks up water,' Hind answers him. 'Look around you'" (SV, 121). In my view, this is an almost emblematic image of Rushdie's aesthetics as it incorporates the processuality, the open-endedness, the sharply drawn lines of antagonism, and the inclusive disjunctive synthesis that does not synthesise elements as in dialectics, but allows both sub-elements to retain their distinctive status. Finally, the passage illustrates the paradoxical nature of meaning, in which sand may suck up water, on the one hand, and water may wash away sand on the other.

After the confrontation with Hind, Mahound returns to the mountain, but this time with a wish to revoke the verses. Upon a week-long wrestle, in which Mahound and Gibreel fuse once again, and in which Mahound's will controls Gibreel once more, the prophet falls into a deep sleep as usual, but this time he awakes earlier than usual and realises that the devil had been at work the last time:

> "It was the Devil," he says aloud to the empty air, making it true by giving it voice. "The last time, it was Shaitan." This is what he has *heard* in his *listening*, that he has been tricked, that the Devil came to him in the guise of the archangel, so that the verses he memorized, the ones he recited in the poetry tent, were not the real thing but its diabolic opposite, not godly, but satanic. He returns to the city as quickly as he can, to expunge the foul verses that reek of brimstone and sulphur, to strike them from the record for ever and ever, so that they will survive in just one or two unreliable collections of old traditions and orthodox interpreters will try and unwrite their story, but Gibreel, hovering-watching from his highest camera angle, knows one small detail, just one tiny thing that's a bit of a problem here, namely that *it was me both times, baba, me first and second also me*. From my mouth, both the statement and the repudiation,

verses and converses, universes and reverses, the whole thing, and we all know how my mouth got worked (SV, 123).

Mahound's revelation tells him that the verses had been inserted by Satan, but the dreamer Gibreel knows that the earlier verses as well as the new ones all came from his mouth. A drama of doubt has played out in Gibreel's mind: the drama of the authenticity of the satanic verses as an open work.

As soon as he returns to Jahilia, Mahound removes the satanic verses and inserts the new ones, rejecting the idea of God having daughters while man has sons. Subsequently, Mahound finds his innocent wife murdered and he isolates himself for several weeks, during which Abu Simbel and Hind in particular institute tight sanctions against the followers of the new religion who are now also assaulted with physical violence, arson, and spit: "And, by one of the familiar paradoxes of history, the numbers of the faithful multiply, like a crop that miraculously flourishes as conditions of soil and climate grow worse and worse" (SV, 125). Islam has been born, but the Muslims are forced into exile in Yathrib, from where Mahound does not return until twenty-five years later.

The chapter may end on a note of rehabilitation on the part of Mahound as Khalid thinks that the Prophet has shown his followers a deeper truth by showing them the work of the devil and his defeat by the righteous and the faithful. "'It was a wonderful thing I did. Deeper truth. Bringing you the Devil. Yes, that sounds like me'" (SV, 125), is Mahound's bitter-ironic answer. I think that the above is useful in defending Rushdie against the most one-sided allegations of him drawing a blasphemous portrait of Muhammad. The novel orchestrates an internal struggle in Mahound between compromise and obduracy, and after accepting Abu Simbel's offer Mahound realises his mistake and chooses the "right" way. Is it not a sign of strength to doubt but to end up making the right decision? Does the fact that Mahound has a choice not make him more reliable and sincere as a person? At least that is one way of viewing the affair.[54] Yet the fact that the entire chapter is also thoroughly marked by

---

54   Rushdie himself has supported this reading in a recent essay: "I felt the story humanized the Prophet, and therefore made him more accessible, more easily com-

a questioning of the authenticity of the Koran is inescapable, but this is one of Rushdie's deliberate moves.

*

In the course of the twenty-five years Mahound lives in exile, Jahilia slowly falls into disrepair because of changes in the hierarchical field of trade routes. Trade by sea becomes easier than trade by land/sand, which may be said subtly to indicate Islam's takeover of power in Hind's polytheistic Jahilia. In chapter VI it is the poet Baal and the immigrant and scribe Salman in particular who are in the spotlight. When Baal sees a tear of blood drop from the eye of Al-Lat in the beginning of the chapter, he knows that Mahound is on his way back. Baal is sought out by Salman who has fled from Yathrib, having manipulated with the revelations in his transcriptions. The once so vital and intoxicating city of Jahilia has now become a poor and prosaic place, Baal has turned fifty, Mahound sixty-five, in exile, and both have changed, while Hind, at sixty, rules Jahilia with a rod of iron and feigns the illusion of greatness and permanence. The time is ripe for Mahound's return.

The chapter consists of Gibreel's six dreams about 1) Salman's atrocity, 2) Jahilia's surrender, 3) Mahound's response to his newly gained power, 4) Baal's hiding place in the bordello, 5) the bordello's disintegration, and, finally, 6) Mahound's death.

In the first dream, Salman tells Baal about the growing dissatisfaction with Mahound's leadership. Mahound seems to have become increasingly obsessed with law and regulations, introducing more and more rules against people's behaviour and conduct, "so that Salman the Persian got to wondering what manner of God this was that sounded so much like a businessman" (SV, 364). As such, Salman's testimony carries several of the anti-Islamic images that the novel has drawn of Mahound so far. He goes on posing the rhetorical question: "Mahound – or should one say the Archangel Gibreel? – should one say Al-Lah?" (SV, 363). As Salman sees it, Mahound makes up his mind about things to be done

prehensible to a modern reader, for whom the presence of doubt in a human mind, and human imperfections in a great man's personality, can only make that mind, that personality, more attractive" (SA, 230).

during confrontations with legal matters of everyday life, and only then does he turn to the archangel to have his decisions confirmed in "endlessly proliferating rules" (SV, 365). But as usual the novel does not lend unchallenged authority to single voices, such as Salman's, as it is suggested that there may be selfish motives behind Salman's defamation of Mahound, Salman being disappointed and bitter about a lack of recognition in connection with his heroic actions in an earlier war between Yathrib and Jahilia.

Apart from being outraged by Mahound's pragmatic relation to the archangel, whom he refers to as the "practical angel" (SV, 366), Salman decries the change of women's social position in Yathrib. It used to be an almost matriarchal society, the women were powerful, but now they are compelled to be "docile or maternal" (SV, 367). At one point, having dreamt about himself as Gibreel or Shaitan (there is no end to the variations on and proliferation of dreams and echoes) hovering above Mahound, Salman gets the idea to test Mahound's sincerity:

> After that, when he sat at the Prophet's feet, writing down rules rules rules, he began, surreptitiously, to change things.
>
> "Little things at first. If Mahound recited a verse in which God was described as *all-hearing, all-knowing*, I would write, *all-knowing, all-wise*. Here's the point: Mahound did not notice the alterations. So there I was, actually writing the Book, or re-writing, anyway, polluting the word of God with my own profane language. But, good heavens, if my poor words could not be distinguished from the Revelation by God's own Messenger, then what did that mean? What did that say about the quality of the divine poetry?" (SV, 367).

Salman's distrust turns out to be well-founded as the Prophet does not notice the alterations, not even when Salman writes Jew instead of Christian. Salman's manipulation escalates until one day when he sees Mahound knitting his brows before giving his approval of the transcription. At that moment Salman knows that he has reached a limit and he decides to make his escape. Baal encourages Salman to disclose his knowledge, but Salman's knowledge is useless as no one will believe him. Mahound is still vested with the power and credibility that turns everything he says into truth just by saying it: "making it true by giving it voice" (SV, 123). Since Mahound's victory seems unpreventable, there is just one question that concerns Baal: "How do you behave when you win?" (SV, 369). In Gibreel's second dream, Abu Simbel surrenders Jahilia to Mahound and converts to Submission. At the same time a provisional answer to Baal's question is indicated as Mahound spares the people.

The third dream is about the entry of the Muslims into Jahilia where all statues of former gods and goddesses are destroyed. During the conversion in the tent, Hind also kneels to Mahound's feet, covered by a veil, in a manner that frightens Mahound. "Can compromise be hoped for from the uncompromising, pity from the pitiless?" (SV, 371), Hind had asked her husband after his conversion before her, with the antagonism between water and sand in mind, thus indicating that Hind is hardly sincere about her submission; she is still uncompromising and she regards Mahound as being so too.

Hence Mahound's entry into Jahilia is largely gentle without any incidents of vindictiveness or hostility. Yet Mahound wants to find Salman who is hiding and when he succeeds, he pronounces the often cited sentence which has assumed a prophetic quality in the light of the Rushdie Affair: "Your blasphemy, Salman, can't be forgiven. Did you think I wouldn't work it out? To set your words against the Words of God" (SV, 374). Two interesting problems crop up: Can we read the Salman in the novel as Salman Rushdie? Is Mahound convincing as a prophet after all, since he has obviously discovered Salman's blasphemous work?

The last question almost answers itself: I think that it is also legitimate to allow for this possibility, meaning that Mahound may actually be said to recover his credibility, if not completely then at least in part. In his confrontation with Salman, Mahound is once again portrayed as a very generous and honourable man. In my opinion, it is possible to complicate the first question, although it may not be complex at all; likewise it may be made too simple which it is not either. A simplification of the question implicates an equation of the writer with the character, but the novel's enunciation, composition, and theme of human identity are far too complex to make this possible. It is naïve to think that the "message" of *The Satanic Verses* may be referred back to one character who even features in only two out of nine chapters. The other way round, to wander off into too much theory may lead to a dilution of the novel's ideological universe by making everything optional, arbitrary, and, ultimately, of no consequence. There are many similarities between Salman in the novel and Salman Rushdie – but similarities between writer and character are frequent in Rushdie's novels – and the ideological weight behind Salman's statements may also be said to be heavy. What Salman does in the novel corresponds to what Salman Rushdie does with the novel, and the state of doubt that succeeds Salman's painful loss of faith is one of the great recurrent themes of the novel as well. The conclusion is that Salman occupies a central position in the hierarchy of voices in the novel's enunciation, but he does not carry the message of the novel alone. Added to this, we must point to the fact that the message, or the aesthetics of the novel, cannot be ascribed to characters' statements, but are also to be searched for in the novel's way of composing and combining elements in its overall aesthetic form.

So, Mahound spares Salman's life (possibly because Salman offers him Baal: apparently, Mahound has not given up his business talents of negotiation), and the narrator sums up Mahound's answer to the question of the victor's rule after his conquest: "O generosity of Submission! Hind has been spared; and Salman; and in all Jahilia not a door has been smashed down, not an old foe dragged out to have his gizzard slit like a chicken's in the dust. This is Mahound's answer to the second question: *What happens when you win?*" (SV, 375). Yet, the reader may perceive an ironic undertone in the narrator's voice, which issues from an expectation that Mahound still wants to revenge himself on Baal who used to lampoon Mahound in his poetry in the past. After that, the dream ends: "Jahilia settled down to its new life: the call to prayers five times a day, no alcohol, the locking up of wives" (SV, 376).

*

As an echo of Flapping Eagle in *Grimus*, Baal takes refuge in the city's bordello, the Hijab which means curtain or veil. Whereas the name of the bordello in *Grimus*, The House of the Rising Son, indicated "the son" Flapping Eagle's revolt against "the father" Grimus, the name Hijab suggests the general state of secrecy and masquerade in the bordello in *The Satanic Verses*, but it also refers to specific maskings, such as the eternal cover of the matriarch of the bordello, Madam of the Curtain, behind a curtain and Baal's disguise as a eunuch.

Baal hides in the bordello for more than two years, feeling safe in the beginning, but beginning to sense impermanence and his own death drawing closer after the news of the destruction of Al-Lat's temple whom Baal had believed in his entire life. The feeling does not scare him, on the contrary: "After a lifetime of dedicated cowardice he found to his great surprise that the effect of the approach of death really did enable him to taste the sweetness of life, and he wondered at the paradox of having his eyes opened to such a truth in that house of costly lies. And what was the truth? It was that Al-Lat was dead – had never lived – but that didn't make Mahound a prophet. In sum, Baal had arrived at godlessness" (SV, 378-79). By rising above the idea of gods, rulers, and laws, Baal realises that his life is inexorably intertwined with Mahound's, all of which is slowly giving shape to a plan: "People fantasize more about what they can't see" (SV, 380), Baal thinks in connection with the untapped potential of the Hijab. Baal continues his contemplations and a comparison of the number of Mahound's wives with the number of women in the bordello comes to mind: "How many wives? Twelve, and one old lady, long dead. How many whores behind the Curtain? Twelve again; and, secret on her black-tented throne, the ancient Madam, still defying death. Where there is no belief, there is no blasphemy" (SV, 380). Consequently, the Hijab is transformed into a surrogate for Mahound's harem and each of the prostitutes adopts an identity corresponding to one of Mahound's wives, identifying so strongly with their roles that they cannot remember their original names and identities when the bordello is eventually closed down.

In consultation with Abu Simbel, "Mahound, most pragmatic of Prophets, had agreed to a period of transition" (SV, 381). And while Mahound resides in Yathrib, the bordello flourishes, tripling its business after the girls have adopted their new names and even picked up the behavioural patterns and tempers of Mahound's wives. Rushdie explores the dangerous cocktail of sex and religion in which the forbidden is desirable and the hidden is rousing. The story of the bordello is possibly the part of the novel that has provoked the most enraged responses among Muslims. Their indignation may be hard to understand for a Western reader, probably because nothing appears to be sacred or tabooed in the West anymore. But to a Muslim, Rushdie has broken the greatest of taboos. The accusation is to the effect that Rushdie depicts Mahound's wives as whores, although his defenders have argued the contrary, that Rushdie actually depicts Mahound's wives as virtuous. There is no ignoring the fact that the actual mirroring of Mahound's harem in the prostitutes is problematic seen from a Muslim-Islamic perspective. Hence, the question is not whether Rushdie has insulted Muslims and definitely not if he has done so on purpose.[55] The question is whether Rushdie has the right to insult Muslims. I should think so, and at the same time I want to underline that the unrelentingly confrontational style in which he does so probably contributes to further division of the parties rather than bringing them any closer to each other. The violence of "the attack" will always remain a problem of degree.

After a while the girls in their new roles as wives are beginning to miss a husband and they persuade Baal and Madam to have Baal marry them, giving him Mahound's role as the head of the harem: "Be the boss" (SV, 384), the old-fashioned prostitutes demand of Baal, thus becoming, like the women in Yathrib, "docile or maternal." Baal's new role suits him fine as "The poetry that came was the sweetest he had ever written" (SV, 384). He recovers the pleasure of writing, inspired by the muses of love rather than the lampooning verses. In a characterisation of his own aesthetics, Baal charts a poetics which seems to correspond to the overall aesthetics of the novel, just like the passage about the mutual dependence of water and sand:

> The landscape of his poetry was still the desert, the shifting dunes with the plumes of white sand blowing from their peaks. Soft mountains, uncompleted journeys, the impermanence of tents. How did one map a country that blew into a new form every day? Such questions made his language too abstract, his imagery too fluid, his metre too inconstant. It led him to create chimeras of form, lionheaded goatbodied serpenttailed

---

55 Rushdie says: "*He did it on purpose* is one of the strangest accusations ever levelled at a writer. Of course I did it on purpose. The question is, and it is what I have tried to answer: what is the 'it' that I did?" (IH, 410).

impossibilities whose shapes felt obliged to change the moment they were set, so that the demotic forced its way into lines of classical purity and images of love were constantly degraded by the intrusion of elements of farce (SV, 370).

The poetry of Baal and Rushdie forms a cartography with the evanescence of the desert sand as its raw substance, perpetually creating new landscapes in which the journeys of nomads remain incomplete and their tents provisional. In a cartographic activity like that, the popular and the high-flown, love and farce coexist in a chimerical form. Here is Rushdie's own description of the novel:

> *The Satanic Verses* celebrates hybridity, impurity, intermingling, the transformation that comes of new and unexpected combinations of human beings, cultures, ideas, politics, movies, songs. It rejoices in mongrelization and fears the absolutism of the Pure. *Mélange*, hotchpotch, a bit of this and a bit of that is *how newness enters the world*. It is the great possibility that mass migration gives the world, and I have tried to embrace it. *The Satanic Verses* is for change-by-fusion, change-by-conjoining. It is a love-song to our mongrel selves (IH, 394).

After two years and a day, Baal is recognised by Salman, and following a night of long discussions, in which Baal is shocked by Salman's growing bitterness about Mahound, Salman returns home to Persia. Baal, in turn, has woken up from his long sleep, a sleep owing to the isolation of the bordello. Soon after, Mahound returns from Yathrib and declares the end of the transition, which, among other things, results in the forced shutting down of the bordello, the arrest of the whores, and Madam's suicide.

Gibreel dreams his fifth dream in which Baal – awake from his sleep – nails his newly composed verses of tribute to his twelve wives to the prison wall, revealing the secret of their adopted names. The former admiration among the population for the beauty of the verses is replaced by anger and Baal is taken to court where he recounts the entire story of the bordello in front of Mahound. In spite of the blasphemous nature of the story, the listeners cannot help laughing, but Mahound sentences Baal to death (in yet another passage with a prophetic sound to it). Baal's response to his death sentence is: "'Whores and writers, Mahound. We are the people you can't forgive.' Mahound replies, 'Writers and whores. I see no difference here'" (SV, 392). The poets cleared out of the way, both Salman and Baal are gone now, the scene is set for a purely intra-religious showdown between Mahound and Hind who has spent the two years and two months since Mahound's entry into Jahilia in self-imposed isolation in her tower room, preparing herself for the final confrontation. Magic and witchcraft are her weapons.

In Gibreel's last dream Mahound is ill and close to death, and – having seen and been offered Paradise – he chooses God's kingdom. In his last hour Mahound sees a figure which he thinks at first is the angel of death Azraeel:

> But Ayesha heard a terrible, sweet voice, that was a woman's, make reply: "No, Messenger of Al-Lah, it is not Azraeel."
>
> And the lamp blew out; and in the darkness Mahound asked: "Is this sickness then thy doing, O Al-Lat?"
>
> And she said: "It is my revenge upon you, and I am satisfied. Let them cut a camel's hamstrings and set it on your grave."
>
> Then she went, and the lamp that had been snuffed out burst once more into a great and gentle light, and the Messenger murmured, "Still, I thank Thee, Al-Lat, for this gift" (SV, 394).

Ayesha, Mahound's chief wife, says to the grieving wives: "If there be any here who worshipped the Messenger, let them grieve, for Mahound is dead; but if there be any here who worship God, then let them rejoice, for He is surely alive" (SV, 394). Thus the dream ends the chapter. The ending does not leave any unequivocal explanations of the meaning of Mahound and Hind's conversation. I do not see this as the end of the battle between sand and water, rather the battle has been interrupted without us knowing the final result. Hind may be said to prevail, inasmuch as she has her revenge, but revenge is a word that makes sense only to her. Mahound may be said to prevail inasmuch as he thanks Hind for having shown him the path to Allah, thus proving that Allah is the ultimate being, but this insight has value only to Mahound as Hind does not understand it. Hind and Mahound are irreconcilable oppositions, but at the same time they cannot exist without each other's counter-image. Al-Lat meaning the goddess in Arabic and al-ilah the god, the unresolved battle between Hind and Mahound symbolises the equality of the masculine and the feminine. Hence, the novel seems implicitly to launch a criticism of Islam's oppressive view on women, which has also been suggested through Bilal's exclamation about the acceptance of female goddesses implied in the compromise and through the resultant divine correction of the satanic verses, a correction that is informed by chauvinist argumentation.

*

I will now try to summarise what I think is Rushdie's overall project with the episode of the satanic verses. It is erroneous to see the episode as something unprecedented in Rushdie's historiographic novels, but in many ways it appears emblematic of his writings, which is also noted by Martine Hennard Dutheil: "In the novel, the episode becomes the paradigm of the confusion of opposites (God and Satan, fiction and history, prophetic and poetic languages) that takes place at the origin and constitutes the very condition of discourse" (Dutheil, xxxv). By using the creation of a religion and historical sources as his point of departure, Rushdie calls attention to concepts like authenticity, origin, and permanence. The Koran is perceived as a direct and unadulterated transcription of Allah's words, which is pointed out in the foreword of the Danish translation: "The Qur'ân contains only God's revelation through *His own spoken word* to the Prophet. This is the safest form of revelation. (...) That the Qur'ân, in its present form, word for word, is identical with the version Muhammad passed on to his disciples, is a fact that all analysts – believing and non-believing – entirely agree on" (Koranen (The Koran, Danish translation), XI). Nevertheless, we have seen how Rushdie in various ways throws doubt on this self-identity.

First, the episode of the satanic verses points to an internal difference within divinity itself, namely Satan's presence together with the archangel Gabriel. The difference leads all the way back to the main character Gibreel Farishta's names. He is baptised Ismail Najmuddin,[56]

---

[56] Najmuddin means the star of faith, and the title of Sûra 53 is al-Najdm, meaning star (and plant without a stem).

people refer to him as both angel and devil, and he calls himself Gabriel Angel (farishta). In addition, he plays a number of roles as Hindu divinities in theological movies. The co-existence between angel and devil, and between good and evil, is in this way pointed out again and again throughout the novel. Hence, meaning is never essentially determined, but is always referred to through a contextual relation. Rushdie questions the idea of the imperviousness of the Koran by insinuating that its contents have to some extent been determined by political and economical interests at the time of its creation.

What is more, the episode of Salman's satanic verses also point to the difference that is immanent in repetition. The translation of the revelation from God/Satan to Gabriel, from Gabriel to Mahound, and finally from Mahound to Salman represents the transition from 1) a divine logos to 2) thought, onwards from thought to 3) speech, eventually ending up as 4) the written word. As we have seen before in Rushdie's writings, this translation prompts a process of gain and loss. The basis of Lars Erslev Andersen's article "At sætte lethed mod tyngde" ("Pitting Levity against Gravity") is precisely the difference between the written and the spoken word, a difference that has been examined by Walter J. Ong who has inspired both Andersen, Dutheil, and others. Andersen sees Rushdie's overall project as deconstruction:

> Rushdie's novel may be read simply as a destruction of the discourse(s) that operate(s) in terms of purity and untaintedness as positive conditions, leading to their disintegration and the simultaneous formation of a discourse that operates in terms of hybrid forms, mongrels as positive qualities. The point is that this process can only be brought about by making the detour of destroying the narrative and rhetorical patterns that structure the ways in which we use language and, with that, the ways in which we see (read) the world (Andersen, 1991, 59).

The destructive element in Rushdie's novels "simply consists in a desacralisation of the linguistic formations we call ideology, and the technique is a matter of allowing them to be appropriated by literature, that is, to turn them into fictions" (*ibid.*, 58). By repeating a religious context in a fictive context, one also inscribes a difference determined by the new context whereby the truth value of the original, uncorrupted religious context is undermined. The transfer causes a slide from logos to simulacrum, a slide which is illustrated by the weighting in religious discourse of the spoken word and the written nature of fictive discourse in which language can never be pure presence and self-identity, as Derrida has pointed out. In writing, discourse is to some degree separated from its originator whereby the circulation of meaning is liberated and opens to interpretation. In contrast, the spoken word has a presence and a direct contextual relation, causing meaning to appear more evident. The slide from direct representation to interpretation determined by difference is orchestrated through Salman and the revelations lose their authenticity; at the same time, repetition in fiction creates difference, just as simulacrum creates difference in the hierarchy of copies.

Accordingly, Rushdie's overall project is to illustrate how the creative premises of fiction are created on the basis of historical constructions in an interplay between repetition and difference, in which fictionalisation indicates the fragility of the status of the original source as immanent self-identity as the source itself will always be contaminated with difference in order to exist at all.

Are there any limits in art as to what can be said? Is it possible to apply the brakes on thought? Can art function as a medium between the sacred and the profane? What is art? These questions set the stage for a more general and abstract discussion of art than the specific discussion above on *The Satanic Verses*. I believe that art is to open new doors in our minds, and in order for it to do so, it has to expose the insufficiency of existing ideas, perhaps even destroy them. Art is iconoclastic, but the distinctly sabotaging performance of art must be followed by a cartographic activity in which the world is drawn in new colours and forms. If art is confined by dogmas, the development of the world and man's opportunity to experience new affects and percepts are hampered. It is illusive to believe that thought may be brought to a standstill (for long), and it is wrong to think that something once thought may be unthought. The possible is the driving force of art: "And as for risk: the real risks of any artist are taken in the work, in pushing the work to the limits of what is possible, in the attempt to increase the sum of what it is possible to think" (IH, 15). The *raison d'être* of art is not to produce confirming copies (doxa), quite the contrary, it is to produce invalidating-confirming simulacra (paradoxa) whose differential perspectives force their way out into the possible and extend the world to an *open totality*. In Rushdie's essay "The Location of *Brazil*" we are encouraged to construct reality and to play: "*Play. Invent the world.* The power of the playful imagination to change for ever our perceptions of how things are has been demonstrated by everyone from Laurence Sterne, in *Tristram Shandy*, to a certain Monty Python in his *Flying Circus*. Our sense of the modern world is as much creation of Kafka, with his unexplained trials and unapproachable castles and giant bugs, as it is of Freud, Marx or Einstein" (IH, 123). Consequently, it is not only technological breakthroughs within the field of science that change the world. Art appeals to the human intellect and can change man's understanding of the world as well by creating new affects and percepts. Art only exists as an expansion of the world, hence Pound's decree "Make it New!": in that way art is always modern.

*

I will now take a closer look at the political aspects of the Rushdie Affair and its various lines of reasoning, with an aim to estimate the latter on the basis of our analysis of the novel. *The Satanic Verses* was released on 26 September 1988 and Khomeini's fatwa on 14 February 1989 marked the culmination of several months of rioting. The furore started in India where a Muslim member of parliament protested against the novel's blasphemy. On 5 October 1988 the book was banned. When this news reached England, photocopies of the provocative passages in the novel were distributed to Islamic organisations. Merely three days after the Indian ban a Muslim newspaper condemned Rushdie and shortly after that a Muslim journal published some of the novel's "sensitive" passages. In December the book was burned in Bolton, Lancashire, but it was no great media event. In January 1989 the book was destroyed in flames once again, this time in Bradford, and the event was broadcasted on national television. Two weeks later 8.000 people marched in London. In the course of all this, Rushdie tried to defend himself by claiming that the novel was not anti-religious but dealing with migration.[57] The ball was rolling, however,

---

57   Already before Rushdie was necessitated to defend himself and lift the veil

and in Islamabad in Pakistan passages of the book were read aloud on street corners. On 12 February 1989 a group of Muslims stormed the American culture centre and five demonstrators were shot. The day after, in Kashmir, one person died and more than sixty people were injured. These events were shown on Iranian television and Ayatollah Khomeini is supposed to have seen the pictures. Khomeini called a secretary and dictated the wording of the fatwa which was broadcasted on Iranian radio on 14 February 1989, on Valentine's Day.

In India the ban of the novel on 5 October 1988 must be seen as a largely political manoeuvre on the part of Rajiv Gandhi as India was facing an election in which the more than 100 million Muslim votes could be decisive of the outcome. Rushdie responded to the ban of his book with a letter to Gandhi already the day after it had been issued, in which he said about the Muslim opposition leaders: "You know, as I know, that Mr Shahabuddin, Mr Khurshid Alam Khan, Mr Suleiman Seit and their allies don't really care about my novel one way or the other. The real issue is, who is to get the Muslim vote?" (Appignanesi and Maitland, 36). The growing Muslim outrage against the novel in India was more or less personified by Syed Shahabuddin and his article in *Times of India* on 13 October: "Yes, I have not read it, nor do I intend to. I do not have to wade through a filthy drain to know what filth is" (*ibid.*, 39).

Likewise the banning of the novel in Pakistan must be viewed in terms of politics as fundamentalist Muslims exploited the novel to put an enormous pressure on the inexperienced but reform minded Benazir Bhutto. Bhutto was caught in a bind: she would probably be happy to ban the book, given that she was the model of Virgin Ironpants in *Shame*, but, on the other hand, she also represented the first democratically elected government in Pakistan in ten years. Here too, the banning of the novel was without a doubt infiltrated in a tactical political game which Bhutto

---

on his intentions, he had – before the novel was even released – stated in interviews that its theme was migration: "What I think the novel is also conceptually about is the act of migration, and of hybridisation, of the way in which people become combinations" (Tripathi and Vakil, 84), says Rushdie in 1987. In this regard the argument of migration cannot be said to have been invented for the occasion; it was already there as a real drive in the process of the novel's creation.

could only succumb to if she wanted to maintain her position as the country's leader.

In England social indignation among Muslim minorities overshadowed the hurt feelings about the book itself. Among other things, anger resulted from a disproportionately high unemployment rate among ethnic minorities, in addition to political tax reforms that fell heaviest on the underprivileged, and the perhaps well-intentioned feminist criticism of the position of Muslim women had also hit the Islamic communities hard. Finally, the legislation on blasphemy in England may be mentioned as a source of offence among Muslims because it only took account of blasphemy in relation to Christianity. The irony of the Muslim riots in England, culminating with the book burning in Bradford on 14 January 1989, is that it was probably this group of the population that Rushdie had the greatest sympathy with and felt most emotionally connected with. The core of the novel's characters is occupied by Muslim immigrants and these characters are mostly portrayed with genuine compassion and empathy, supported by the personal experiences Rushdie had gained through his voluntary work with and for London's minorities.

In Iran the issuing of Khomeini's fatwa was also politically motivated.[58] The book had provoked a worldwide outrage among Muslims, but why did Khomeini not respond with the fatwa until 14 February 1989? There is little doubt that domestic politics were at work. First of all, Khomeini had just had to swallow a bitter pill, being forced to sign a peace treaty with the dictator of Iraq, Saddam Hussein. Iran's war against Iraq was part of the worldwide holy war that Khomeini and Islam felt obligated to carry on. The war had been started when the internal struggles for power among the revolutionaries, succeeding the flight of the Shah and the Islamic revolution in 1979, had come to an end. The

---

58   The actual concept of *fatwa* has been the subject of much discussion in connection with the Rushdie Affair. Some observers have argued that it is invalid in relation to established Islamic case law, but regardless of whether it is legally valid or not, the death sentence has practical validity: "Basically a fatwa is a small thing, simply a statement by a learned Muslim on the religious position on a given matter. Fatwas are issued by the thousands every single day. And they may very well contradict each other. For that reason, they cannot really be annulled" (Andersen and Skovgaard-Petersen, 1999, 11).

clerical wing of the revolutionaries had taken power with little difficulty due to a much more carefully conceived plan and programme. The war against Iraq was a most welcome assignment for Khomeini, which could unite the Iranian people, but as the war did not proceed as intended, the Iranian people started feeling powerless and might even have begun to doubt the ideas of the revolution. Forced to assert himself internationally and forced to take action domestically in an attempt to make the Iranian people feel as one people once again, Khomeini (in my opinion, and seen from an Iranian perspective too, I would argue) made an exaggerated and politically unwise move in issuing the death sentence against Rushdie. What Iran needed at this time, apart from an immediate union of the Iranian people, was a closer cooperation with the West with the aim of straightening up the country's disastrous economy. This possibility was destroyed with Khomeini's fatwa, which is also pointed out by Claus V. Pedersen: "Khomeini's fatwa and the time it was issued may be seen as a useless and ill-considered measure, considering the subsequent consequences of Iran's foreign policy and their effect on Iran's domestic situation" (Pedersen, 96). Apart from regenerating an enormous focus on Islamic ideology, the fatwa meant that Khomeini left behind a problematic will for his political and religious successors in Iran: in addition to being perhaps the greatest foreign political impediment to normalised relations with the West, which had been in the making with the ceasefire agreement with Iraq and the new constitutional initiatives, the fatwa was, to quote Lars Erslev Andersen, a "Gordian knot" in terms of domestic politics (Andersen, 1999, 127). Finally, it may be added that the argument of the fatwa as politically motivated is supported by the fact that the novel had already been reviewed in Iran without giving cause to any attention worth mentioning.

*

Generally speaking, the fatwa was met with both fanatic support and urgent condemnation, which was to some extent also the case with the novel. In the West (among non-Muslims) the death sentence was unanimously condemned whereas the response to the novel was divided into defenders who admired it and saw no problems with it and a group of critics who disapproved of its disrespectful treatment of Islam, thus recognizing the cause of Muslim fury.⁵⁹ In the Arab countries it is possible to distinguish between three groups of critical voices (cf. Ziadeh, 78-84): The first group condemned the death sentence and defended the right to write disrespectfully, a right that was even regarded as necessary in the struggle against intellectual stagnation. Within this group one does not find a state, nor a political party, nor any important religious people, instead one finds intellectuals like Edward Said and Sadek al-Azm. The other group, by far the greatest of the three groups, condemned the death sentence as an exaggerated reaction and politically motivated manoeuvre, but at the same time it took offence at the novel's disrespect and was doubtful about the writer's sincerity: "On the one hand they condemned Khomeini's fatwa as un-Islamic and legally invalid, and they maintained that Khomeini did not represent Islam or Muslims. On the other hand, they condemned the traditional Western hostility towards and prejudice against Islam" (Ziadeh, 80). Within this group one finds most governments, faithful Muslim writers and intellectuals in addition to the mass media. The third group condemned Rushdie and his book and many people supported the death sentence or felt that the writer ought to be punished. Within this group we find the most fundamentalist Islamic groups who were behind the book burning in England, for instance, and who, in Iran, gave their backing to Khomeini's fatwa.

Understandably, perhaps, there has been a tendency to view the Affair as an insurmountable condition of antagonism between Western freedom of speech and Islamic fundamentalism (which is very much due to the fatwa), but fortunately this is a tendency many people have tried

---

59   Moreover, there was a group of voices in the West who tried to exploit the polarising tendency of the Affair. This applies to Jean-Marie le Pen in France, for example, who used the Affair in a racist campaign against Muslims. Rushdie has tried several times to give expression to an approach that mediates between East and West, criticising the Orientalist one-sidedness in the Western view of Islam: "It needs to be said repeatedly in the West that Islam is no more monolithically cruel, no more an 'evil empire,' that Christianity, capitalism or communism. The medieval, misogynistic, stultifying ideology which Zia imposed on Pakistan in his 'Islamization' programme was the ugliest possible face of the faith, and one by which most Pakistani Muslims were, I believe, disturbed and frightened. To be a believer is not by any means to be a zealot" (IH, 54).

to problematise in recent years, for example in the Danish book *Satanisk, guddommeligt – og såre menneskeligt* (*Satanic, Divine – and Simply Human*) which declares its unreserved support of Rushdie, but at the same time points to and maps the Western, at times, imperialist, colonial, and condescending way of viewing Islamic culture.[60]

Just as the initial Muslim outrage had often been more about politics than religious ideals, Lars Erslev Andersen shows in a study of the volatile course of the German and Danish policies towards Iran from 1989 to 1992 that the opposing, parochial Western focus on freedom of speech was equally superimposed by (security) political and economical interests: "That alone shows that the Rushdie Affair is not only about freedom of speech, about saving an author's life, about guarding fundamental traits of European culture, or about defending international law, including national sovereignty. The Affair is also about these things, but apparently only as long as they do not clash with general economical objectives and security interests" (Andersen, 1999, 133). After 1992 the new EU adopted a so-called "critical dialogue" towards Iran which failed to put an end to the erratic course of European relations with the country in spite of everything. In 1995 the Iranian government promised orally that it would do nothing to carry out the death threat, but later on when the Danish foreign minister at the time, Niels Helveg-Petersen, asked for a written confirmation the Iranians refused to pass it. In 1996 Denmark and particularly the Danish government, headed by Prime Minister Poul Nyrup Rasmussen, faced a political storm when Rushdie was denied an entry permit into Denmark, rather clumsily, by the Prime Minister's Office because it was believed that his safety could not be guaranteed. Rushdie, who was going to Copenhagen, the 1996 Culture City of Europe, to receive the Aristeion Award for *The Moor's Last Sigh*, accused Denmark of indirectly supporting Iran and the prestige Denmark had gained in connection with Helveg-Petersen's efforts in 1995 and the Iranian responsiveness and oral withdrawal of the death sentence was lost. In 1997

---

60   Whereas the Affair may be viewed as a conflict between East and West, there are also many things that make it plausible to view it as a conflict between Shia and Sunni Muslims, which the tension in March 1989 at a conference in OIC (Organization of the Islamic Conference) attests to (cf. Petersson, 201).

the German government was involved in some fishy intelligence affairs with Iran, which provoked an outrage in the USA and Israel.

As mentioned, the election of the reform-minded president Mohammad Khatami led to a relaxation in the relations between the West and Iran and the fatwa has been officially withdrawn by the government. However, there are still a number of private fundamentalist funds and initiatives that threaten Rushdie. Upon this review of the political motives behind the Affair and the general reactions to the fatwa and the novel, let us sum up what has actually been said about the novel.

Rushdie has been accused by Muslims of blasphemy and of being a spokesman in a Western anti-Islamic campaign, the purpose of which it is to swamp the East with a decadent Western culture through a capitalist mechanism of propagation.[61] In his mediating article "Reading the Crisis: The Polemics of Salman Rushdie's *The Satanic Verses*," Amin Malak enumerates the offensive elements in the novel as being the description of Mahound as a businessman, the designation of Islam as submission, and the reference to Jahilia as ignorance; in addition, the episode of the satanic verses compromises the sanctity of the Koran; and finally Malak thinks that the brothel scenes may be the most offensive parts of the book to Muslims. Malak concedes that the furore may be hard to understand for the Western reader, but that is why he tries to explain the

---

61   I will mention only a few negative reactions against Rushdie. I quote from Ziadeh, page 74: for example, a university professor by the name of Barqawi accuses Rushdie "of infantile behaviour, ignorance, narrowmindedness and stupidity." A leading critic by the name of Raja al-Naqash writes that the novel provides western readers with an image of of Muslims as people "who live in isolation, backwardedness, inclined to a Beduin life style and with a hatred of progress and civilisation." A journalist, Ahmad Baha Ad-Din, writes "that the book is disgusting, the product of a sick soul who has consented to its own westernisation by selling its spirit and tradition." Furthermore, the critic Abdallah al-Husseini claims that "the dimensions of the Zionist conspiracy reveals itself in the enormous efforts Western and Zionist circles have made to make preparations for this book, in translating it into various languages and in publishing it as quickly as possible in the farthest corners of the world, as well as in the generous financial support the book receives from powerful capitalists." Added to this, Ziadeh mentions that a study carried out by a journal showed that only two out of thirteen Egyptian writers, critics, and learned men who had condemned or attacked the book had actually read it.

significance Muhammad has to a Muslim: he represents the only fixed centre they have in a modern, erratic world. The offensiveness, which Malak also traces back to a Western anti-Islamic tradition, causes many Muslims to regard Rushdie as a "witness for the Western prosecution" as his depiction of Islam does not correspond to Muslim self-perception. Hence, Rushdie is considered as an apostate, a lapsed Muslim who has turned traitor by launching pitiless, Orientalist attacks on Islam.

In response to Malak's points, which we have already dealt with in the analysis of the novel, I want to say that Rushdie's use of the term businessman is not necessarily to be interpreted as dramatically as Malak does. First of all because the most common occupation in Jahilia was commerce, which is not treated as a dubious trade in the novel, and, secondly, the analysis of the novel's use of free indirect discourse furnishes us with a more nuanced picture of the novel's enunciation: the term businessman is employed in, for instance, Salman's direct speech (who must be regarded as an unreliable secondary narrator) whereby the term gets to circulate in a blend of narrator and narrated person in other situations. In regard to the use of the terms ignorance and submission, it is hard to see the offence as these are merely translations of the Arabic words Jahilia and Islam. Yet, it is plausible that Rushdie's insistent use of these translations may have a confrontational objective. As concerns the episode of the satanic verses, we have concluded that Rushdie is evidently making use of an anti-Islamic tradition, and the employment of the episode is without doubt problematic in relation to Islamic self-perception. If we are to talk about a "conciliating" element in this connection, it may be argued that Rushdie actually recovers the purity of the Koran and Mahound's integrity by letting Mahound reject the verses, but of course his initial acceptance and inclusion of the verses undermines any original purity. Regarding the brothel scenes, there is little doubt about their offensive content. The episode is an example of the fictive discourse's play between repetition and difference, Mahound's wives being repeated with the difference that they are now enacted by prostitutes. Rushdie's defenders have pointed out that there is no violation of Mahound's wives just because the prostitutes have adopted their names: his wives are nowhere portrayed in a compromising manner (with the exception perhaps of a single ambiguous episode with Ayesha).⁶²

The Western defence of the novel has concentrated on the freedom of speech and the freedom of art to be offensive, in addition it is often noted that many Muslim critics have not even read the book (which actually applies to some of its defenders as well). In this way, the Affair has often been marked by a discussion of universal and abstract concepts, leaving the novel to recede into the background. I would like to stay a bit with the fact that few of its critics have read the novel, as I see this as a great and central problem.

As a literary genre, the novel is a highly complex, primarily Western product of art and because of this it may be problematic to demand of a non-specialist that he be able to read a novel like *The Satanic Verses*. Skovgaard-Petersen argues against the strenuous and elitist view that does not recognise the right to feel offended if one has not read the book: "But is it reasonable to demand that people have knowledge of a bourgeois literary culture before they are in a position to feel shocked and hurt about things they have heard about a book? No, that is not reasonable. It is both an elitist and a naïve point of view. It serves to disqualify these people's right to be offended" (Skovgaard-Petersen, 64). I think this argument is problematic. I partly agree with Skovgaard-Petersen's observation of actual psychological mechanisms, but when he speaks of the right to be offended, he moves from an actual state to an ideal practice. I can *understand* the outrage to a certain extent, but I will not defend people's *right* to feel offended. The ideal practise I am talking about is based on a culture of academic integrity and enlightenment that strives towards the greatest possible relevancy and accuracy of the information

---

62   Rushdie summarises his defence in the following way: "What does the novel dissent from? Certainly not from people's right to faith, though I have none. It dissents most clearly from imposed orthodoxies *of all types*, from the view that the world is quite clearly This and not That. It dissents from the end of debate, of dispute, of dissent. Hindu communalist sectarianism, the kind of Sikh terrorism that blow up planes, the fatuousnesses of Christian creationism are dissented from as well as the narrower definitions of Islam. But such dissent is a long way from 'insults and abuse.' I do not believe that most of the Muslims I know would have any trouble with it" (IH, 396-97).

that is passed on. Accordingly, a great deal of responsibility is placed on the expert in this ideal practice and at the same time the expert enjoys a great deal of respect from the non-specialist.

A positive consequence of an ideal practise would be that *The Satanic Verses* would be studied for what it is, namely a complex, linguistic statement, and not an anti-religious manifesto in which individual sentences may be cut out and be said to represent the writer's opinion. Another consequence would be that an attempt might be made to add at least as much importance to the literary scholar's overall analysis as to that of the mullah. There is a regrettable tendency in cultural relativism to dismiss the insights that can be found in the fields of for instance linguistics and comparative literature that contribute to an understanding of the novel's complexity compared with for example a legal document (which of course has its own unique difficulties). To the question of integrity and complete readings, Skovgaard-Petersen says: "I would hate to feel an obligation to finish reading a book before assessing it and putting it down. This is not an excuse to desist from understanding the issues one criticises. However, it is an argument against branding other people's offendedness as illegitimate because they have not read, refuse to read, or even cannot read a book" (*ibid.*, 64). I do not read all books from end to end either, even if I may use them for an academic piece of work. Skovgaard-Petersen also thinks that one has to familiarise oneself with the things one considers or criticises. But his attempt to legitimise readings based on isolated statements fails to respect one of the most time-honoured principles of art acquisition, that is, the principle that a work of art must be read, seen, experienced, or listened to in its entirety. Hopefully, my analysis of the novel has shown how significant the very composition of individual parts into a larger – but not summary – whole is to an understanding of the novel's distinctiveness.

I distinguish between an actual and an ideal practice with an aim to bridge the defence and the accusations. The actual situation makes it impossible to expect that a great number of people have read or are reading the novel, and that does not only pertain to the Arab countries. In addition, in the actual situation opinions are naturally spread across, along, from above, and from below in society, and this does not only pertain to the Arab countries either. The ideal practice, however, aims to limit the circulation of untrained and half-performed formations of opinion and has a, perhaps naïve, faith in whatever the experts say. Is it then only literary scholars who are allowed to comment on novels? No, of course not. But a minimum requirement for those who comment on a novel, perhaps even sentence a man to death because of a novel, may be that they have read it.

I hope that I have managed to display some of the incredible complexity of the Rushdie Affair. We have seen how the episode of the satanic verses forms a much discussed event in the research of Islam and we have seen how Rushdie incorporates it with the purpose of emblematising the deconstructive game of fiction between repetition and difference, in which concepts such as origin, authenticity, and genuineness are problematised and acquire new meanings through the simulacrum-operation of writing. Moreover, we have seen how the novel has been criticised, a criticism which has been both absurdly "unscientific," but also a criticism which has been reasonable and more or less understandable. However, it is important for me to emphasise that the reasonable and understandable criticism in no way means that I dispute Rushdie's right to do what he did. In this connection, our analysis has admitted to the blasphemous and offensive elements of the novel, but at the same time we have pointed to the ambiguous nature of these elements. Finally, we have made an outline of the political aspects that surround the novel and the fatwa throughout the 1990s. In the next and final sub-chapter before the epilogue and the conclusion we will turn our focus on the way in which the three novels generate open endings.

THE OPENNESS OF TOTALITY

> "A whole is what has a beginning and middle and end. A beginning is that which is not a necessary consequent of anything else but after which something else exists or happens as a natural result. An end on the contrary is that which is inevitably or, as a rule, the natural result of something else but from which nothing else follows; a middle follows something else and something follows from it. Well constructed plots must not therefore begin and end at random, but must embody the formulae we have stated."
> – Aristotle: *Poetics*

In this sub-chapter we will take a closer look at the significance and status of the novels' endings. I will show that Rushdie consistently finishes his novels in either a contingent, hence an anti-Aristotelian manner, or in a non-conclusive way where the last sign is the question mark rather than the full stop. This relates to the subjacent processual ontology where any ending always implies a new beginning and things are persistently located in the middle.

Midnight's Children
One of the leading structural principles in *Midnight's Children* is the parallel between Saleem's acts of narration and chutnification: while writing a chapter he simultaneously mixes a pickle-jar of chutney. Accordingly the thirty chapters of the novel have each their parallel in the form of a pickle-jar with the same heading:

> Twenty-six pickle-jars stand gravely on a shelf; twenty-six special blends, each with its identifying label, neatly inscribed with familiar phrases: "Movements Performed by Pepperpots," for instance, or "Alpha and

> Omega," or "Commander Sabarmati's Baton." Twenty-six rattle eloquently when local trains go yellow-and-browning past; on my desk, five empty jars tinkle urgently, reminding me of my uncompleted task. But now I cannot linger over empty pickle-jars; the night is for words, and green chutney must wait its turn (MC, 384).

While the act of narration is in this way connected with a gastronomical machine, the passage also metaphorically enhances the status of literature as a collective act of communication as Saleem is writing by a window looking on to power chords and railway tracks: electricity and train traffic functioning as symbols of communication and global networks.

When Saleem returns to Bombay with his son and Picture Singh, he tastes a grasshopper-green chutney after a snake charmers' competition in the Midnite Confidential Club:

> On the thali of victory: samosas, pakoras, rice, dal, puris; and green chutney. Yes, a little aluminium bowl of chutney, green, my God, green as grasshoppers... and before long a puri was in my hand; and chutney was on the puri; and then I had tasted it, and almost imitated the fainting act of Picture Singh, because it carried me back to a day when I emerged nine-fingered from a hospital and went into exile at the home of Hanif Aziz, and was given the best chutney in the world... the taste of the chutney was more than just an echo of that long-ago taste – it was the old taste itself, the very same, with the power of bringing back the past as if it had never been away (MC, 455-56).

This event turns out to be Saleem's Proustian moment. Through the involuntary, violent encounter with the chutney-sign, Saleem is brought back to the Bombay of his childhood, just as Marcel is brought back to Balbec through the Madeleine cookie (note also the alliterations between the names of the characters Marcel and Saleem and the city names Balbec and Bombay, the latter is of course just a coincidence).[63] In *Proust*

---

63 The catalyst behind the novel in the real world was Rushdie's encounter with his old childhood home during a visit to Bombay: "It is probably not too romantic to say that that was when my novel *Midnight's Children* was really born; when I realized

and Signs Deleuze comments on the necessity of the violent encounter with the sign:

> What forces us to think is the sign. The sign is the object of an encounter, but it is precisely the contingency of the encounter that guarantees the necessity of what it leads us to think. The act of thinking does not proceed from a simple natural possibility; on the contrary, it is the only true creation. Creation is the genesis of the act of thinking within thought itself. This genesis implicates something that does violence to thought, which wrests it from its natural stupor and its merely abstract possibilities. To think is always to interpret – to explicate, to develop, to decipher, to translate a sign. Translating, deciphering, developing are the form of pure creation (PS, 97).

Through the formation of violent encounters art gives us an immanent image of thought. Art orchestrates a direct image of the genesis of the act of thinking within thought itself, it places the reader directly on the plane of immanence of thought where thought is nothing, or about nothing, but its own genesis. Deleuze criticises the tradition that considers thought as something that comes naturally to the philosopher. On the contrary, creative thought only occurs in the violent encounter with an Outside where man directly enters the plane of immanence of thought.

Contingency creates a sheer childhood block for Saleem, a transversal connection between the past and the present. Tasting the chutney becomes an "Open Sesame," bringing him on the scent of his old ayah, Mary Pereira, who now owns a pickles factory in which, as we know, Saleem is later installed as the creative chef of production due to his olfactory super-skills:

> My special blends: I've been saving them up. Symbolic value of pickling process: all the six hundred million eggs which gave birth to the population of India could fit inside a single, standard-sized pickle-jar;

how much I wanted to restore the past to myself, not in the faded greys of old family-album snapshots, but whole, in CinemaScope and glorious Technicolor" (IH, 9-10).

six hundred million spermatozoa could be lifted on a single spoon. Every pickle-jar (you will forgive me if I become florid for a moment) contains, therefore, the most exalted of possibilities: the feasibility of the chutnification of history; the grand hope of the pickling of time! I, however, have pickled chapters. Tonight, by screwing the lid firmly on to a jar bearing the legend *Special Formula No. 30: "Abracadabra,"* I reach the end of my long-winded autobiography; in words and pickles, I have immortalized my memories, although distortions are inevitable in both methods. We must live, I'm afraid, with the shadows of imperfection (MC, 459).

With reference to Deleuze, each chapter and each jar may be said to comprise a block of sense perceptions in which percepts and affects are severed from subjective perceptions and affections and are immortalised as autonomous images of thought. Several times in the novel Saleem indicates his physical and mental disintegration, cracking skin, bone cancer, and lapses of memory, through which he is reciprocally related to the novel and the jars: the further they progress, the more he cracks. Saleem's becoming-imperceptible, his becoming-anonymous and his becoming-art are inscribed in the chutnification process.

As we have seen earlier, it is impossible to separate the narrator from the hero as two subjects, a subject of enunciation and a subject of statement, because this would be the same as connecting the novel with a traditional system of subjectivity. As Deleuze points out in connection with Proust: "There is less a narrator than a machine of the Search, and less a hero than the arrangements by which the machine functions under one or another configuration, according to one or another articulation, for one or another purpose, for one or another production" (PS, 181). In Salman-Saleem-Sinai-Rushdie's becoming-imperceptible, in his becoming-machine and becoming-assemblage, the novel is elevated from an individual to a collective level in a language-machine which the reader may hook on to in his or her own becoming-other.

The chutney jars are signs that enfold and unfold childhood blocks and becomings in a pure state of *durée*. Having filled thirty jars and written thirty chapters, the thirty-first jar remains empty: "The proces of revision should be constant and endless" (MC, 460). The immortality represented in the chutney jars, and hence that of the percepts and affects too, is indicated through the process of chutnification: "In the spice bases, I reconcile myself to the inevitable distortions of the pickling proces. To pickle is to give immortality, after all: fish, vegetables, fruit hang embalmed in spice-and-vinegar" (MC, 461). The distortion that the production process entails is underlined together with the permanence it creates through the adding of spices and their subsequent effect. The end of the novel points to the immortality and permanence of art and chutney whereas the mixture of spices and the fallibility of memory point to the distortions that art and chutney lead to and, finally, chapter and jar number thirty-one point to an endless revision of what is preserved, an open ending, the eternal reactualisability of art and, at the same time, the ambiguity and the degree of fictionality of history.

The novel's openness and unfinishedness are further emphasised by its ending in which the centrifugal forces finally make themselves felt. *Midnight's Children* reflects a colourful and diverse India, in which Saleem himself is eventually scattered to the winds. Despite the excessive use of the connecting *leitmotifs*, such as the perforated sheet and the spittoon, he has to give up the attempt of bringing together all the stories in a closed entity.

Shame

Whereas *Midnight's Children* seems to strike an optimistic tune, among other things through Saleem's firm belief in his son's generation, *Shame* appears, to a far greater extent, to end in the minor key. The last chapter of the novel, entitled "Judgment Day," carries strong Biblical connotations not only through its title, but also through the language use in general. Rushdie's circular constructions involve a promise of hopeful rebirth in both *Grimus* and *Midnight's Children*, but the circularity in *Shame* does not suggest any positive outlook, at least not on the level of events. However, contemplating the possibilities of escaping the dead ends of sheer disintegration, on the one hand, and a new dictatorial regime on the other, the narrator reflects on the future of Pakistan: "The third option is the substitution of a new myth for the old one. Here are three such myths, all available from stock at short notice: liberty; equality; fraternity. I recommend them highly" (S, 251). Among other things, it is passages like this one that assume a monological nature.⁶⁴ The proclamation appears one-sided and narrow-minded if seen in isolation, yet it must be kept in mind that the narrator and Rushdie have projected a highly complex cartography through the overall construction of the novel. Thus, individual statements also attain a greater complexity insofar as they are read in the light of a greater contextual configuration.

Still, the narrator admits in a disheartened voice that the three myths of liberty, equality, and fraternity, which origin from the French Revolution of 1789, are superimposed instead by the myth Virgin Ironpants is in the process of creating of her father, Iskander Harappa: "The fall of God, and in his place the myth of the Martyr Iskander" (S, 276). Once again the narrator touches on the theme of inversion and degradation in a passage that reminds us of Deleuze's reading of catechism, in which man is created in God's image and resembles Him whereas today man continues to be an image of God, but has ceased to look like Him. From moral beings (aspiring to a metaphysical idea about the good), we have changed into aesthetic beings (that is, a spectrum of existential possibilities without any essential moral plan), which is illustrated in *Shame* through the endless number of inversions and degradations the novel contains. For example in the way that Omar forms a bad, but autonomous image of the poet Omar. Likewise, Omar's birth in a deathbed may be mentioned as well as the inversion of the traditional relation between centre and periphery, exemplified, for instance, in the female discourse which also forms an exposure of the collapse of hierarchies and their conventional status of arbitrarity.

Despite the pessimist note that may be traced at the end of *Shame*, an insistence on open-endedness may still be identified.⁶⁵ For instance,

---

64   "In terms of politics *Shame* contains certain political criticisms, which makes it didactic in that sense. If you're going to write about politics it is almost impossible to escape having a view about it. I have a simple view: I believe military dictatorships to be bad and that it's desirable to end them" (Haffenden, 45), says Rushdie to Haffenden.

65   Cundy is of another opinion as she insists on the closedness of the novel: "*Shame* is a model of closed construction" (Cundy, 1996, 44). Moreover, she points out: "*Shame* is aware of its narrative trajectory from the outset" (*ibid.*, 44). Cundy identifies a cyclical pattern in the novel through its use of motifs (e.g. the recurrent

we hear of Omar's thoughts of the world just before he is confronted with Sufiya: "He persisted in his belief that the world was changing outside, old orders were passing, great structures were being cast down while others rose up in their place. The world was an earthquake, abysses yawned, dream-temples rose and fell, the logic of the Impossible Mountains had come down to infect the plains" (S, 274). The logic Omar has in mind is the logic of inversion that he has been infected with since birth when he saw the world turned upside down for the first time.

Nishapur, which has functioned as a metaphor of Pakistan's isolation, stagnation, timelessness, and closedness throughout the entire novel, suddenly turns into a labyrinth in movement, containing, in the eyes of Omar, "the sum of all his possibilities" (S, 275). "Stories end, worlds end; and then it's judgment day" (S, 277), says the narrator before the novel ends in a nuclear explosion like a Biblical apocalypse. Rushdie has commented on the ending of the novel himself in the David Brooks interview: "But what happens at the end of *Shame*... well, I'm not really sure about that explosion. I don't know what it is, or signifies. I don't think it necessarily means anything as simple as the end of the world. It's a kind of question mark. I suppose it implies a cleansing of the stables" (Brooks, 67).

The Satanic Verses

Since the novel runs along three lines there are several endings in *The Satanic Verses*. We have already dealt with the end of the last chapter: the atypical ending in Rushdie where Saladin is united with Salahuddin and a blissful future with Zeenat Vakil is more than hinted at. Another ending is that of the B-line in which Mahound hears Hind just before he dies. This is an open ending as the fight between the two rivals ends without a resolution. Hind introduces the female element as an equal, yet an-

umbilical chords, nooses, etc.), through which she projects a predetermination in the entire project. However, the technique of using leitmotifs, prolepsis, and analepsis are also present in *Midnight's Children* which to an equal degree reflects a consciousness that remembers the entire novel all at once. I do not consider *Shame* as a closed novel, but it does have a more monological character than Rushdie's other novels.

tagonistic counterpart to the masculine element in Islam. No harmonic balance is struck as both parties think they have gained the upper hand. This line finishes as a both-and, or, rather, as an *inclusive* disjunctive synthesis of either-or.

We still need to look at the ending of the C-line about the villagers' pilgrimage to Mecca. There are several echoes in the C-line from the other two lines, for instance, the antagonistic relation between Mirza Saeed and Ayesha in which the theme of compromise and inflexibility reappears. Mirza Saeed is a sceptical, secular and rational man, inspired by Western science and technology. He follows the villagers in a big, air-conditioned Mercedes Benz, "the station wagon of scepticism" (SV, 481). In contrast, Ayesha is an uneducated peasant girl who all of a sudden receives Allah's revelations through the archangel Gabriel who, with a typically Rushdian twist of irony, sings the revelations to her to the tunes of popular hits. Mirza Saeed tries to make a compromise with Ayesha, offering her and a select few a flight to Mecca, including Mishal, Mirza's cancer-stricken wife: "His offer had contained an old question: *What kind of idea are you?* And she, in turn, had offered him an old answer. *I was tempted, but am renewed; am uncompromising; absolute; pure*" (SV, 500). We have come across Ayesha's intransigence several times in the novel: Mahound represents it to some degree, but especially Hind Simbel, the Imam and the hijacker Tavleen are symbols of obduracy and irreconcilability. Ayesha's unbendingness is the result of a revelation that corroborates her belief: "Gibreel says the sea is like our souls. When we open them, we can move through into wisdom. If we can open our hearts, we can open the sea" (SV, 501).

As the villagers are wading into the sea, Mirza witnesses how the thousands of butterflies that have accompanied them on their journey form a giant creature above the ocean, but none of the coincidental bystanders see the miracle. The narrator continues: "Within minutes the entire village was in the water, splashing about, falling over, getting up, moving steadily forwards, towards the horizon, never looking back to shore" (SV, 502). The episode by the sea is surrounded by ontological indefiniteness and the narrator tries to explain the irrationality of the incident: "Human beings in danger of drowning struggle against the water. It is against human nature simply to walk forwards meekly until the sea swallows you up. But Ayesha, Mishal Akhtar and the villagers of Titlipur subsided below sea-level; and were never seen again" (SV, 503). In this way it is suggested that the villagers may have experienced a miracle when acting against human nature. After the episode, the survivors, Mirza Saeed, Osman, the Sarpanch, Mrs Qureishi and Srinivas, are questioned by the police who consider pressing charges against them: "The authorities were considering the feasibility of charging the survivors of the Ayesha expedition with attempted illegal emigration" (SV, 504). The interrogations produce an inconsistent evidence as all survivors of the expedition except Mirza Saeed actually saw the ocean part, thus leaving the possibility of a spiritual miracle despite the fact that the bodies of the drowned pilgrims wash up on the shore in the days following the episode.

When Mirza Saaed returns alone to Titlipur he is met by a deserted, dilapidated and destroyed village. The draught has made farming impossible and ruined the villagers who stayed behind. Mirza finds snakes, frogs, and dust all over his house, and the symbolic fig tree, under which Titlipur used to grow and lead a sheltered life, has died. The end of the C-line is more characteristic of Rushdie's novels than the ends of the other two lines as the symbolic tree explodes: "On the last night of his life he heard a noise like a giant crushing a forest beneath his feet, and smelled a stench like a giant's fart, and he realized that the tree was burning. He got out of his chair and staggered dizzily down to the garden to watch the fire, whose flames were consuming histories, memories, genealogies, purifying the earth, and coming towards him to set him free" (SV, 506). The carnivalistic theme of death and rebirth is repeated once more and Rushdie reuses the apocalyptic discourse to end his story: "He saw the tree explode into a thousand fragments, and the trunk crack, like a heart" (SV, 506). During his death struggle Mirza Saeed suddenly experiences that his mouth is full of butterflies, that he is in the water next to Ayesha who tries to get him to open up his heart, and when he finally permits himself to be overpowered by her will he sees the ocean part. Is this a true miracle? Or is it a result of starvation and hallucinations? The novel allows for the concurrence of both possibilities. It allows for both either and or.

EPILOGUE:
THE GROUND BENEATH HER FEET

> "I think that one will finally realise that the artist creates the possible at the same time as the real when he produces his work of art."
> - Henri Bergson: "The Possible and the Real"

With the novel *The Ground Beneath Her Feet* from 1999 Rushdie expands the geographical cartography he has thus far drawn in his novels. He consolidates and continues his migratory movement as the fictive canvas in this novel engages with the American continent as a weighty and concrete scene. Having explored the Indian subcontinent through India, Pakistan, and Bangladesh in *Midnight's Children* and *Shame* and expanded to the British Isles in *The Satanic Verses*, it is only symptomatic of the migration writer Rushdie that the space of *The Ground Beneath Her Feet* is global. Bombay and India still function as important elements together with London and England, but the novel's geography is enlarged with New York and America as well as other both rural and urban localities. Succeeding a brief paraphrase of the novel, the analysis in this chapter will take up the three angles on literature that made up the structure of the chapter on Deleuze: first, the novel's world view will be analysed through assertions found on the level of the story; secondly, I will try to identify the novel's perception of art through the ways in which it operates, that is, on the level of enunciation; finally, I will analyse the novel's perception of subjectivity.

The photographer Rai (Umeed Merchant) is the novel's narrator and one of its three protagonists, but the actual focus of the novel is on the relationship between Rai's childhood friends, Ormus Cama and Vina Apsara, a relationship in which Rai only sporadically plays a role as Vina's "backdoor man" and Ormus's companion. The novel deals with both ontological and epistemological issues, examining the status or state of the ground beneath our feet. This ground may be rocked on the ontological level, by love, by migration, by art, and also, literally, by the planet's geological processes. On the epistemological level, it is the recurrent question of the nature of memory that determines the condition of the ground.

The Ground Beneath Her Feet is Rushdie's homage to rock music and, as a result, also a portrait of several generations, starting back in Bombay in the 1940s and 1950s and leading the reader onwards to the New York of the 1980s and 1990s over the London of the 1960s and 1970s. The myth of Orpheus and Eurydice and its thematic triangle of love, art, and death functions as a subjacent base of resonance throughout the entire novel: "Death is more than love or is it. Art is more than love or is it. Love is more than death and art, or not. This is the subject. This is the subject. This is it" (GB, 202).[66] Ormus, the Indian child prodigy, whose fin-

---

66   Whereas Vina may be perceived as a modern parallel to Eurydice, the Orpheus-figure is divided between Ormus and Rai who both have works of art to create and may be seen as modern Orphic lyre players, accordingly: Ormus is a musician whereas Rai is photographer, narrator, and poet. The myth of Orpheus and Eurydice contains, as Maurice Blanchot has shown in "The Gaze of Orpheus," an entirely paradoxical structure between elements such as absence-presence, impatience-patience, desire-loss, light-darkness, day-night, which may be each other's opposites, but also turn into each other's necessary reciprocal counterparts. Blanchot writes about Orpheus: "He loses Eurydice because he desires her beyond the measured limits of the song, and he loses himself too, but this desire, and Eurydice lost, and Orpheus scattered are necessary to the song, just as the ordeal of eternal worklessness is necessary to the work" (Blanchot, 439). In the same way Rai may be said to write his novel on the basis of the present absence that Vina constantly represents for him; she is the novel's initiator, its blind spot which Rai keeps trying to make visible. Both Rai and Ormus lose Vina, and, like Orpheus, they also lose themselves along the way, but the lost Vina and the destroyed heroes are necessary for the creation of the novel. At times Rai and Ormus are also situated in the borderland that Blanchot calls worklessness, which is necessary for the work, a borderland where death and non-literature are the last resort, but where these zero points incessantly form the basis that makes literature possible at all; literature lives on turning its gaze into the unsayable, into death, into the night, into the forbidden, as it is from here it draws its inspiration, but at the same time this inspiration results in the impossibility of the work: "Orpheus' gaze is Orpheus' ultimate gift to the work, a gift in which he

gers move by guitar chords at birth, and Vina, the American wildcat with the velvety voice, fall in love when they meet in a record store in Bombay. Vina has moved from Chickaboom, USA, where her mother killed all her children, except Vina, and then killed herself. Now Vina, at thirteen, lives in Bombay with the Doodhwhala family who are distant relatives. When Vina and Ormus's love is discovered by the foster family, a bruised and red-eyed Vina turns up at Rai's home and his family immediately adopts her into their idyllic circle. Vina and Rai become friends and Rai falls headlong in love with Vina who is a bit older than him and does not reciprocate his feelings. Accordingly, Rai remains a peripheral hero throughout the novel, often placed outside the centre of events, or usually with the photographer's ability to invisibly register central scenes: "I had learned the secret of becoming invisible, of disappearing into the work" (GB, 213). He tells his story and writes his book because he wants to give Vina peace wherever she may be found: "I have chosen to tell our story, hers and mine and Ormus Cama's, all of it, every last detail, and then maybe she can find a sort of peace here, on the page, in this underworld of ink and lies, that respite which was denied her by life. So I stand at the gate of the inferno of language, there's a barking dog and a ferryman waiting and a coin under my tongue for the fare" (GB, 21).

Ormus and Vina start a career as musicians, but are abruptly separated when Vina is suspected of having stolen jewellery from Rai's mother and burned the house of the Merchants down to the ground, which all causes her to take flight back to the USA. In Bombay Ormus desperately searches for new Vinas while Vina continues her career as a singer in the USA, without any success though. Later on Ormus moves to London where he works at a radio station. After a serious car accident he winds up in a coma and does not awake from his sleep of death until Vina turns up. After that, they get together again and form the super group VTO which turns into a world famous rock band. When Vina disappears during an earthquake in Mexico on Valentine's Day in 1989, Ormus once again sets out on a hunt for her copy. Rai is selected as the man who is to seek out

rejects the work, in which he sacrifices it by moving towards its origin in the boundless impulse of desire, and in which he unknowingly still moves towards the work, towards the origin of the work" (*Blanchot*, 440).

the chosen one and he falls in love with Vina's mirror image, Mira, who turns out to have her own distinct identity, however. VTO is reformed, but Ormus is shot dead in front of the entrance of his apartment in New York. The novel ends on a hopeful note, not unlike *The Satanic Verses*, where Rai seems to have reconciled with Vina's death, picturing a future for himself with Mira and her little daughter.

*

Jan Kjærstad claims that all writers are searching for the "main metaphor" of the epoch in which they live:

> You are looking for a kind of model, a reduction, which combines crucial traits of reality to form a coherent whole. The surprising thing about such a model of the original, a main metaphor, is that it may shed more information about the original than the original may divulge about itself. In a way it is the copy that makes us able to see the original as it really is. Consequently, a metaphor like this is not a copy of reality, but an uncovering of the form of things (Kjærstad, 31).

This idea may easily be applied to Rushdie's writing. In *Midnight's Children* the main metaphor, or at least one of them, is the perforated sheet which becomes a kind of model or a reduction of crucial traits of reality; the perforated sheet functions as a metaphor of the narratological technique of the novel (the tension between covering and uncovering) and of a general epistemological point which indicates that we are deemed to sense and recognise the world in fragments. In *The Satanic Verses* the main metaphor is migration which is seen as a metaphor of the nomadic condition of human life and the incessant mutations and metamorphoses of forms.

In *The Ground Beneath Her Feet* the main metaphor is the earthquake: "Geology as metaphor" (GB, 203). The metaphor of the earthquake has an ontological point which we may refer back to the ontological affinity between Rushdie and Deleuze delineated at the beginning of this book. When Deleuze writes that modern art and the modern novel is a simulacrum-art, it means that the modern novel disallows eternal hierarchies and truths while constantly inventing the world anew in a constructivist process. As has been noted, Deleuze creates a synonym of the concept of simulacrum which is interesting in the case of *The Ground Beneath Her Feet*: simulacrum-literature is *effondement* which means that it is both foundation and collapse, it is both earth and earthquake, territorialisation and deterritorialisation. In other words, the modern novel is both form and vitalism, it is vitalistic form, in constant movement and without any stable centre or central perspective. But how is this ontology expressed on the level of the story?

The Ground Beneath Her Feet starts with a description of an apocalyptic scenario, namely an earthquake in Téquila in the central part of the western highlands of Mexico. At first Vina escapes but is caught up by it in Puerto Vallarta on the Pacific coast, after which no one ever sees her alive. It is characteristic of Rushdie's writing that opposing tendencies are present at the same time: the novel begins with a double ending, so to speak, the apocalypse and the death of the heroine, which, once again, emphasises the mutual exchangeability of any beginning and end. Besides, the date of the earthquake is not without significance: Valentine's Day 1989, or, to put it differently, 14 February 1989, which was the day the fatwa against Rushdie was issued, or the day of his personal earthquake. What we have here is a decisive point. Like *Midnight's Children* and *The Satanic Verses*, the novel opens with a state of in-betweenness: In *Midnight's Children* the simultaneous birth of India and Saleem indicates the transition in-between two states of being, a point that is further underlined by the symbolic nature of the midnight hour. In *The Satanic Verses* airspace and the fall at the beginning of the novel function as intensifying symbols of a metamorphic zone in-between. And in *The Ground Beneath Her Feet* it is the earthquake that is employed as a symbol of the becoming of and the passage into something new, just as the date marks a personal point of intersection for Rushdie. Apart from that, the year of the novel's publication, 1999, contains apocalyptic undertones and stands out as an intermezzo of the transition to a new millennium.

Rai is present in Téquila and immediately begins photographing the chaotic set-up. In the following passage, he reflects on the metamorphic consequences and implications of the earthquake:

> Here was the eternal silence of faces and bodies and animals and even nature itself, caught – yes – by my camera, but caught also in the grip of the fear of the unforeseeable and the anguish of loss, in the clutches of this hated metamorphosis, the appalling silence of a way of life at the moment of its annihilation, its transformation into a golden past that could never wholly be rebuilt, because once you have been in an earthquake you know, even if you survive without a scratch, that like a stroke in the heart, it remains in the earth's breast, horribly potential, always promising to return, to hit you again, with an even more devastating force (GB, 13).

The quotation exemplifies one of these liminal situations between the new and the old which Rushdie's universe is teeming with. Man and nature are caught in a situation emblematic of the general conditions of life, that is, in the middle of metamorphosis and becoming. The vitalistic impulse of life is present in the description where life as faces, bodies, animals, and nature are caught within an intermezzo, within the sheer immanence of becoming. Hence, the passage gives expression to the metamorphic ontology, life as a "messy ocean" of unruly and contingent forces and processes. The existential condition that the novel professes, accordingly, is also expressed later on in the novel in the following mode of proclamation: "Our world has lost its moorings. (...) The universe seemed to lose shape and meaning. The earth trembled" (GB, 136, 172). We are far from the world of roots where cosmos revolves around an immovable axis in a movement that guarantees the eternal return of the same. Instead, the survivors of the earthquake develop an experience of a permanently potential tremor which results in the fact that the ground beneath the human condition can only be one of provisional stability.

Just as we find examples of an earthquake-ontology on the level of the story, we also come upon examples of a complimentarity-ontology on this level. The formal articulation of the latter may be referred to Deleuze's concept of the inclusive disjunctive synthesis (the inclusive logic of either-or), which draws on both Nietzsche's perspectivism and Bohr's quantum physics. This poly-ontology is expressed in several places in the novel. For example, at one point it is stated that "Realities are in conflict" (GB, 325) and, in extension to this, Rai says about the girl Maria, who has difficulties comprehending the seeming incongruity of the modern world: "She looks back to a utopian golden age in which there were no quakes, for the world was at peace, there were no conflicting versions, the earth lacked its present tragic quality of irreconcilability" (GB, 327).[67]

Rushdie projects a parallel universe in the novel, which, with small variations, differs from the "actual" narrated universe. In this way the novel runs along two lines, *"two variations of the same world"* (GB, 325), which are both constructed and fictive, with one line, however, constituting the "primary" universe of the novel. Characteristically, both universes manipulate the official truths of history as the narrated universes in the novel come to serve as two parallel and alternative universes in relation to reality. Accordingly, Lou Reed has become a woman, U2 has become Vox Pop, Andy Warhol is called Amos Voight, Kennedy survives Oswald's assassination in Dallas, and in India a young exquisitely beautiful boy writes Dylan's great songs years before Bob takes up his pen. Elvis's manager Tom Parker has been promoted to Tom Presley whereas Elvis Aaron Presley himself has received the Colonel's surname and his stillborn twin's first name, winding up as Jesse Garon Parker. Hence, the theme of variation makes up an allegory of the role of art as a co-creator of reality, and at the same time the fragility of custom-made, complete versions of reality is underscored. Accordingly, it is in view of a strong mimetic referentiality, which is almost always present in Rushdie's novels, that it becomes possible to outline variations in a constructivist creatio. Creatio presupposes mimesis, one might say, and hence the effect of construction becomes all the greater as recognition is required as a launching pad for difference and becoming.

So, the earthquake may be said to be the novel's ontological metaphor of a capricious world, and, as has also been shown, of how the novel's parallel worlds relate to a constructivist practice that does not accept the meaning of the world as self-evident. In a beautiful passage elsewhere in the novel Rai presents a tribute to art which also contains traces of a normative poetics and a vitalistic view of the world:

67 Gonzalez describes the technique like this: "a composite chaos of contradiction summed up by the offensive collocation of incompatible frames of reference" (Gonzalez, 147).

> The world is not cyclical, not eternal or immutable, but endlessly transforms itself, and never goes back, and we can assist in that transformation.
>
> Live on, survive, for the earth gives forth wonders. It may swallow your heart, but the wonders keep on coming. You stand before them bareheaded, shriven. What is expected of you is attention.
>
> Your songs are your planets. Live on them but make no home there. What you write about, you lose. What you sing, leaves you on the wings of song.
>
> Sing against death. Command the wildness of the city.
>
> Freedom to reject is the only freedom. Freedom to uphold is dangerous.
>
> Life is elsewhere. Cross frontiers. Fly away (GB, 146).

Rai explicitly postulates that the world is not subjected to the eternal return of the same, but is constantly changing and man participates actively in this process of transformation. The same thought is at work when Deleuze's ontology is perceived as a pragmatics: the creative performance, the creation of the new, and, with that, art as such, is an inevitable part of life understood as becoming. Moreover the passage says that our songs are planets we may inhabit, but at the same time the passage warns us against settling down on these planets as that would be a betrayal of life. The planets, or art, require reinvention, revision, and to be reactivated in new ways which do not just form a mere reflection of the world as change, but change the world and open new doors of perception. Art must cross borders and produce lines of flight.

To return to the predominant theme of the novel, the earthquake, we may identify yet another indication of the weight of the theme: "earthquakes are the new hegemonic geopolitics" (GB, 554), Rai decides towards the end of the novel. The following passage supports the idea of the hegemonic character of the earthquake, but at the same time it is underlined that pure vitalism has an antipole: "Earthquakes, scientists say, are common phenomena. Globally speaking there are around fifteen thousand tremors a decade. Stability is what's rare. The abnormal, the extreme, the operatic, the unnatural: these rule. There is no such thing as normal life. Yet the everyday is what we need, it's the house we build to defend us against the big bad wolf of change. If, finally, the wolf is reality, the house is our best defence against the storm: call it civilization" (GB, 500). The antipole of extremity and abnormality comprises the habits of our everyday lives and our ability to construct metaphorical and literal houses and defences against inner and outer chaos. Civilisation is a form that enables us to resist chaos and, with that, our own downfall. However, the structure of the constructed (transcendent) model and the subjacent (immanent) force and process which characterises Deleuze's philosophy also comprises the structure of Rushdie's novel: "The laws of the universe may be changing. Such transformations may – incredibly, horrifyingly – become normal" (GB, 391). The primary layer is change, whereas forms and identities are only temporary effects. "In a time of constant transformation (...) All that is solid melts into fucking air" (GB, 353, 351), it also says. Earlier on in the novel, the condition of modernity is expressed in a concluding and summarising passage: "We all have to deal with the uncertainty of the modern. The ground shivers, and we shake" (GB, 62).[68]

In the above I have dealt with the novel's worldview as it is expressed on the level of the story. I have briefly touched on a nascent poetics celebrating the transgression of borders and the production of lines of flight, but so far this poetics has only been implied on the novel's level of the story. So, up until now, we have mainly dealt with what the novel says and less with what it does. The immediate worldview of the novel may be generated through an analysis of the explicit assertions we meet on the level of the story whereas its pragmatics (its latent worldview, one might say) will have to be analysed through the way the novel works, that is on the level of discourse. Hence, we will now move from the question of what the novel says to how it says it, in an attempt to elucidate the novel's perception of art.

68   Gonzalez touches on the same idea when she writes: "The creed of Heisenbergian uncertainty, espoused early on in Rushdie's career is developed as the ethos behind this fictional project, announcing the necessary relativity of all knowledge and creating a dubious fictional space where the text can only shadowbox itself into a schizoid metaphysics reflected by the constant switching and mixing of registers and styles, not only within the text as a whole, but within the unit of the sentence or even the 'single' word" (Gonzalez, 43).

*

The Ground Beneath Her Feet explicitly postulates that the world is in constant change and, at the same time, that man may assist in this process of transformation through the creation of iconoclastic art. But it is one thing for art to assert metamorphosis and quite another matter to make it happen. How does the novel practice and administer its normative messages, such as "Fly away" and "Cross frontiers"? Where are we to look for the Dionysian blood in the Apollonian veins? If the novel is about how the existential conditions of modernity may be compared with an earthquake-like situation on its thematic level, then this Dionysian force will also have to show on the formal and stylistic level?

The eternal imbalance between chaos and form, between immanence and transcendence, or between vitalistic becoming and formalistic articulation may be located more precisely in the novel's *becoming-form*. The form that manifests itself after its meeting with chaos may punctuate heterogenesis in a certain way, but if the form may be brought to contain remnants of its own becoming, the discrepancy between life and form is partially dissolved. The becoming of form in art is orchestrated through the breaking of frames, for example through the destruction of illusions, changes of perspectives, or ontological level-changes (Deleuze's lines of flight). Through the breaking of frames connections are drawn back to the chaotic and heterogeneous reality and thrust ahead to a lasting and final, yet always only transitory form; the territories that are charted by art are deterritorialised and reterritorialised in a perpetual process. Madelena Gonzalez puts it this way:

> The culmination of a search for a language of fiction to represent an ever more complex, contradictory and painfully problematic experience of being-in-the-world characterizes especially *The Moor's Last Sigh* and *The Ground Beneath Her Feet*. It is the working-out before our eyes of the realization of the impossibility of transcendence, as creation becomes an endless process of redundant reformulation, defeated by a late postmodern reality which mocks authenticity, wherever it may be sought. Organized around a syntax of disorientation, impermanence, evanescence and inmixing, Rushdie's post-fatwa universe is a world where spiritual and moral homelessness are the norm" (Gonzalez, 32).

I have already mentioned the shift of ontological levels between the novel's two parallel universes in the above. The narrator carefully builds up a universe only to "break it down" again, a new world being constructed alongside the old one. Within this constant reciprocity between the construction and destruction of frames, the novel contains remnants of its own becoming and thus it contains traces of its own methods of construction. With a poly-ontology like this (the coexistent and often incompatible versions of the world), the novel's morphogenetic element (the birth of form) is emphasised and, as a result, so are the metamorphic and earthquake-like ploys of operation that Rushdie makes use of in his novel. Apart from the indecisiveness and openness of the text, the novel's ontological doubt, its ontological flicker, also leaves a remnant of the origin of the forms and the fictive universe. The technique is a consequence of a pronounced and recurrent imperative throughout the novel which goes like this: "*The only people who see the whole picture are the ones who step out of the frame*" (GB, 203). The imperative states the idea of making one's perspective differential, to turn it into a generator of differences, that is, to make it singular, ex-centric, immanent, and mobile: "construction work never stops completely" (GB, 79). Is there a more appropriate motto for Rushdie's art?

The frame breaks, the destruction of illusions, and the shifts between ontological levels occur in several places in the novel. In addition to the two parallel universes, there is, for example, the dichotomy between a worldly reality and an Underworld which Vina might sink into during the earthquake, and which might be the place she emerges from towards the end of the novel to take Ormus along with her into the realm of the dead in order for them to be finally united in eternity. There is also an irreconcilable ontology between urban and rural India, the nature of reality completely changing in the passing from one sphere to the other:

> City dwellers were constantly told that village India was the "real" India, a space of timelessness and gods, of moral certainties and natural laws, of the eternal fixities of caste and faith, gender and class, landowner and sharecropper and bonded labourer and serf. Such statements were made as if the real were solid, immutable, tangible. Whereas the most obvious lesson of travelling between city and the village, between the

crowded street and the open field, was that reality shifted. Where the plates of different realities met, there were shudders and rifts. Chasms opened (GB, 238).

In addition, one may point to the differences in the projection of the three metropoles Bombay, London, and New York (Manhattan). Whereas Bombay is partly connected with the rootedness of childhood and the sphere of family through the term "*Wombay*," and whereas London is partly captured in idyllic and nostalgic images of the heyday of the imperial past, America is represented as the place of virtualitity par excellence: "I want to be in America, America where everyone's like me, because everyone comes from somewhere else. All those histories, persecutions, massacres, piracies, slaveries; all those secret ceremonies, hanged witches, weeping wooden virgins and horned unyielding gods; all that yearning, hope, greed, excess, the whole lot adding up to a fabulous noisy historyless self-inventing citizenry of jumbles and confusions" (GB, 252). With this, the reader is presented with a – perhaps a bit clichéd – image of the American melting pot where rootedness and structure have been replaced by a network of roots and transgressions of boundaries, of the freedom of not belonging anywhere and of being without deep roots and where the Americans are presented as a people that has always believed in composing their own personal stories and their own lives. This is one of the reasons why Rushdie is fascinated with the American continent as an expansion of potentialities. In Deleuze's terminology the USA is a body without organs, sheer vitalism, and free of determining coordinates, which is why the USA offers the favourite conditions for rebirth.

The ontological shifts mentioned above between (often) incompatible universes – between the two parallel universes and between these universes and "reality," between the worldly world and the Underworld, between rural and urban India, England, and America, and between Bombay, London, and New York – these shifts are all examples of frames which are constructed and torn down, the technique of enunciation supplementing the assertions about processuality and the becoming of form on the level of the story.

The fifth and last example of the breaking of frames and ontological flicker in the novel that I want to mention are the "slices in the screen"

(GB, 348) produced by metafictive passages. For instance, when the narrator exclaims: "Damn it, there are things I can't remember" (GB, 64), and when he says: "I must briefly halt my runaway bus of a narrative" (GB, 86), or: "Now my story begins to strain in opposite directions, backwards, forwards" (GB, 101), then the novel implies that the narrated universe is a constructed discourse, pointing onwards to the consequence that any story is constructed and, thus, human, fragile, and fallible. Accordingly, our access to reality is mediated by filters like language and memory which are neither neutral nor reliable; hence the need for the discourse of art as an alternative cartographic performance to the "official" creation of images.

Another quotation indicating the constructedness of the universe sounds as follows: "All these alibis, all these alternative story lines, that we must abandon!" (GB, 198), and what is more: "These stories float, now, in the limbo of lost possibilities" (GB, 198). Here the narrator points indirectly to the composition of the novel's frames, letting the reader know that something is included whereas other things have had to be left out of the narrated universe. It is also in passages like these that the form of the novel reveals traces of its own becoming. To Rai the conclusion is that he realises how the work of the artist is always provisional and incomplete: "First to create an illusion, then to show that it *is* an illusion, then finally to destroy the illusion: this, I began to see, was honesty" (GB, 447-48). The last passage I want to cite wraps up the points above as it links an ontological assertion with a poetological and metafictive technique: "There. Now I've removed my mask, and you can see what I really am. In this quaking, unreliable time, I have built my house – morally speaking – upon shifting Indian sands. *Terra infirma*" (GB, 244).

The above has shown us how Rushdie's novel both asserts a vitalistic worldview (story) and *performs* the metamorphosis (discourse). Accordingly, the ontological point is present on the level of narrative and on the level of narration, in the projected universe and in the practice of projection. As a closing entry, we will now turn our gaze on the novel's gallery of characters in order to establish a picture of the novel's perception of human identity.

*

In our optics, subjectivity is to be examined for its capability of tackling chaos and producing forms, or as I have mentioned earlier, for its positioning between root and rootlessness or belonging and flight. To a great extent *The Ground Beneath Her Feet* relates to the forms of identity and experience articulated in the earlier novels. Rushdie's universe is conspicuously constructed by repetitions with small variations, and *The Ground Beneath Her Feet* easily lends itself to be read as a kind of culmination of or, rather, a summation of Rushdie's oeuvre.[69]

In order to get a foretaste of the problematisation of identity in the novel, we may return to the opening earthquake scene where we get the following reflection on the human reaction to catastrophes: "This is how people behave when their dailiness is destroyed, when for a few moments they see, plain and unadorned, one of the great shaping forces of life. Calamity fixes them with her mesmeric eye, and they begin to scoop and paw at the rubble of their days, trying to pluck the memory of the quotidian – a toy, a book, a garment, even a photograph – from the garbage heaps of the irretrievable, of their overwhelming loss" (GB, 16). The passage captures man in the middle of metamorphosis, in an intensified kind of transformation where the old is destroyed and the new constructed. The narrator observes people through his camera eye with a mixture of cynicism and compassion: at one and the same time there is the inevitability of standing face to face with the force of life, which in a way wrenches people out of their established subjectivity and causes the understandable reaction in a situation like this of clinging to the past, habits and memory in an attempt to preserve a continuity of identity.

In regard to continuity, the narrator notes in one place: "In spite

---

69   Yet, in a way this is contradicted by Madelena Gonzalez who sees a "mutation" in Rushdie's body of writing where there seems to be a stronger tendency to examine negativity after the fatwa, and, moreover, according to Gonzalez, there seems to be a kind of "disappearance of the real" where the political disappears in favour of a more introvert examination of language as an aesthetic means of expression: "self-parody and even self-pastiche become the dominant mode of the post-fatwa fiction as Rushdie 'does' Rushdie" (Gonzalez, 4, 18). I think her thesis is interesting, but I am not sure that I fully agree. Negativity is notably at issue in both *Midnight's Children*, *Shame*, and *The Satanic Verses* which are resplendent with self-parody and self-pastiche. What may be at stake is differences of degree.

of all the evidence that life is discontinuous, a valley of rifts, and that random chance plays a great part in our fates, we go on believing in the continuity of things, in causation and meaning. But we live on a broken mirror, and fresh cracks appear in its surface every day" (GB, 30-31). In spite of man's attempt to establish a form of consistency, all pointers indicate that life in its pure form is a matter of discontinuity.

One may find a counterpart of the way in which the opening scene brings matters to a head at the beginning of *The Satanic Verses* where the two main characters, Gibreel Farishta and Salahuddin Chamchawalla, fall from the exploded aircraft and miraculously land unharmed on the English coast. In this scene air space comprises an intensified symbol of the conditions, practices, and consequences of migration where the migrant is perceived as a person who has conquered the force of gravity and learned to fly, exactly as a counterbalance to the idea of roots as a conservative myth invented to tie people down in one place.

We may also get an idea of the problem of human identity by looking at the fate of the three main characters. Vina was born as Nissa Shetty in the USA where she was abandoned by her father and at a later point her mother kills her new husband and all her children, except Vina, and then proceeds to commit suicide. Vina/Nissa is the one who finds the butchered family: "Literally selfless, her personality smashed like a mirror, by the fist of her life. Her name, her mother and family, her sense of place and home and safety and belonging and being loved, her belief in the future, all these things had been pulled out from under her, like a rug. She was floating in a void, denatured, dehistorised, clawing at the shapelessness, trying to make some sort of mark. An oddity" (GB, 121). Evidently this is a portrayal of one of Rushdie's extreme characters. Vina has been thrown into chaos, so to speak, into the formless, deprived of all the traditional coordinates that determine identity, like family, name, place, home, love, belonging, and future: "She was a rag-bag of selves, torn fragments of people she might have become" (GB, 122). But Vina pulls through and she learns to embrace instability as a condition of life and starts to make up her own ground rules. At one and the same time, a shimmer of tragedy and affirmation pervades Vina as the freedom of inventing one's own rules also involves a distrust of the love that ties us together.

We also counter this problem, that love and freedom are antagonistic, in connection with Ormus who is freed from his family through the lack of love: "Such were the factors that detached Ormus Cama from the ordinary ties of family life. The ties that strangle us, which we call love. Because of the loosening of these ties he became, with all the attendant pain of such becoming, free" (GB, 53). In Ormus's case, we are told that he was simply born into the world as an ex-centric person without any strong attachments: "*born not belonging*, who come into the world semidetached, if you like, without strong affiliation to family or location or nation or race" (GB, 72-73). The novel celebrates Ormus's nature of the rebel and the mole who undermines conventions and takes on the "taboos against rootlessness" (GB, 73).

Just as the opening scene of the novel may remind us of the opening scene of *The Satanic Verses*, we come across another scene which may even have a more direct connection with the latter, the description of Ormus's journey and arrival in London: "As the plane lifts from his native soil, so his heart lifts also, he sheds his old skin without a second thought, crosses that frontier as if it didn't exist, like a shapeshifter, like a snake" (GB, 250). The quotation explicitly suggests the transformative nature of migration as Ormus casts off his skin; transformation occurs all the way through to a molecular level: "a mutation is occurring at the level of the cell, of the gene, of the particle" (GB, 253). Up in air space the plane seems to strike a membrane which is of course a symbol of the passage itself, and having passed through the membrane Ormus starts his new life: "He has passed through the membrane. His new life begins" (GB, 255). The experience of standing on foreign soil calls upon the migrant's cartographic activity and power of imagination as he is compelled to reinvent the world for every step he takes. The absence of the ground beneath his feet is the consequence of migration, a consequence that Ormus is confronted with in Heathrow airport:

> As his foot alights upon Heathrow, he succumbs to the illusion that nothing is solid, nothing exists except the precise piece of concrete his foot now rests upon. (...) His footprints are the only fixed points in his universe. (...) Everything must be made real, step by step, he tells himself. This is a mirage, a ghost world, which becomes real only beneath

our magic touch, our loving footfall, our kiss. We have to imagine it into being, from the ground up (GB, 268).

The quotation supports my earlier claim that the world is not presented as a predefined entity, but that human activities contribute to its creation. Hence, there is a clearly positive appraisal of the migrant as he/she is inevitably equipped with new angles on reality.

The last person we will take a closer look at is the narrator of the novel. Rai grows up in Bombay in a well-heeled and healthy family as an only child, until the family decides to adopt Vina after her unsuccessful stay with the Doodhwhalas. But Rai also experiences family tragedy when his mother dies from a brain tumour after which his father hangs himself. With this, his bonds of belonging are loosened and, like Vina and Ormus, he becomes a floating person: "Detachment, a weakened sense of affiliation, was simply in my nature. (...) I'm not over-attached to history, or Bombay. Me, I'm the under-attached type" (GB, 76, 78). But Rai also admits that roots can be rewarding and comforting: "So this is what they feel like, I thought: roots. Not the ones we're born with, can't help having, but the ones we put down in our own chosen soil, the you could say radical selections we make for ourselves" (GB, 414). The quotation refers to Rai's situation in New York where he, for the first time since the death of his parents, feels that he has managed to build a home on fairly solid ground, a home that is also the home of his artistic development as a photographer. This also indicates a movement away from the idea of man as a tap root to the idea of man as a network of roots, that is, with roots in several places in constant horizontal proliferation: "Yet I myself am a discontinuous being, not what I was meant to be, no longer what I was. So I must believe – and in this I have truly become an American, inventing myself anew to make a new world in the company of other altered lives – that there is thrilling gain in this metamorphic destiny, as well as aching loss" (GB, 441). This conclusion hits the nail on its head in Rushdie's universe as the passage points out both the contingent, constructivist, and discontinual nature of human identity while at the same time it is established that metamorphosis involves both loss and gain; metamorphosis is the existential condition of being, be it fast or slow, painful or pleasant. It is in view of this insight that Rai is able to say at the end of the novel: "I'll stand my ground, right here" (GB, 575), knowing that this ground will have to be invented over and over again, because it is a *"Terra infirma"* (GB, 244).

So far there may have been a tendency to glorify the seemingly chaotic state of reality and to focus on lines of flight, but the novel also incorporates a recognition of the fact that man needs form to survive: "The world is irreconcilable, it doesn't add up, but if we cannot agree with ourselves that it does, we can't make judgements or choices. We can't live" (GB, 351). Incompatibility and the lack of final answers are conditions that man has to struggle with, but the quotation also says that, in our daily lives, we have to abstract from this irreducibility and live according to a logic of identification that generalises and establishes connections in order to be able to voice judgements and make choices (moral being): "in our functioning we follow the dictates of our need for form" (GB, 380). Love is also perceived as a counterbalance to chaos in the novel: *"Love is the attempt to impose order on chaos, meaning on absurdity"* (GB, 422). In this way, the theme of chaos-form is repeated in the problem of subjectivity, once again with the result that focus is concentrated on becoming per se and the provisionality of form.

The end of the novel carries the same hopeful and optimistic note that also leaves its mark on the end of The Satanic Verses. The reason for this is the force of love Rai experiences in the company of Mira. The Phoenix motif, which we have seen repeat itself many times in all of Rushdie's novels, that "death" always involves a new "birth," is also to be found at the end of The Ground Beneath Her Feet where Vina's death and Rai's love for her is slowly and painfully replaced by Rai's new love for Mira: "a new love had been born out of the ashes of the old" (GB, 563). In addition, Rai notes that the relationship between him, Mira, and her daughter annuls the usual biological coordinates in favour of a logic of chance: "another family relationship forged by circumstance rather than biology" (GB, 568). Besides, the motifs of rebirth and de-hierarchisation are emphasised by Rai telling us that the English manor inhabited by Ormus' mother in her old age is burning at the end of the novel, along with a number of more than two-hundred-year-old oak trees belonging to the estate. We already discovered the Phoenix motif of the burning trees in *Grimus* as a symbol of process, becoming, and the subversion of logos.

*

Before I reach a final conclusion, I would like briefly to sum up the points of the three levels that I have used as a framework and angle of entrance to both this epilogue on *The Ground Beneath Her Feet*, but also throughout the book in general. The ontological affinity between Rushdie and Deleuze comprises a perception of the world and life as becoming which means that life constantly ejects singular events that cannot adapt to transcendent determinations as these would generalise the specific and thus make it universal. When the world is in constant transformation, it also becomes impossible to maintain any definitive truth about the world, and hence truth has to be relentlessly reinvented; truth is not re-presentation, but production. Art plays an important part in this constructivist activity, as it creates new, perhaps even better, images of the world than the ones that are at our disposal at any given point in time. *The Ground Beneath Her Feet* and Rushdie's other novels wrestle with the immediate tension between the chaotic and the formalistic through an extreme focus on the becoming of form, that is, the point where the ascension from the heterogeneous matrix of reality also results in a formalistic articulation. In Rushdie this happens specifically through the breaking of frames that take the form of, for instance, fractures between the narrated level and the level of narration as this is where we may trace remnants from the morphogenesis; indications, to be specific, of how the form has come about and how it has been constructed. Likewise, we have seen how human identity is determined by the tension between chaos and form where metamorphosis with its duality of loss and gain is a condition of man's survival, just as it is the inevitable condition of form in general.

CONCLUSION

> "But dawn broke and morning overtook Shahrazad, and she lapsed into silence. Then Dinarzad said, 'sister, what a lovely story!' Shahrazad replied, 'What is this compared with what I shall tell you tomorrow night? It will be even better; it will be more wonderful, entertaining, and delectable if the king spares me and lets me live.' The king was all curiosity to hear the rest of the story and said to himself, 'By God, I will not have her put to death until I hear the rest of the story.'"
> - *Arabian Nights*

In this book I have drawn a picture of Salman Rushdie's novels as rhizomes. We have seen how Deleuze characterises the rhizome as a liquid work of art determined by lines rather than by points, and in which any attempt to establish any stable, point-based centrism is annulled by the work's lines of flight. In a rhizome, simulacrum prevails as a subjacent force, constantly causing the collapse of any hierarchies or stable stratifications, yet only with the purpose of creating new, but always provisional foundations. Accordingly, the rhizome may most precisely be described as metamorphic and processual inasmuch as it is defined by an imbalance between vitalistic becoming and formalistic articulation. The rhizome is a vitalistic form or a becoming-form. It may be designated as a system, but it is an open system in which multiplicity is in constant movement and in which openness produces the possibility of creating newness.

Rushdie's compositional strategy generally proves to undermine stable points like beginning and end. They are illusory, illustrated in the interaction between contingency and necessity. Moreover, we have seen how any beginning in Rushdie's universe always emanates from a previous ending, and any ending seems to contain the seeds of a new beginning. Hence, the novels may generally be determined as intermezzo, always spreading out from a position in-between things, which is also motivated by their consistent and constant circling about threshold situations.

Enunciation in the novels turns out to support the idea of a missing centre in Rushdie's universes as enunciation in Rushdie is elusive, unstable, and minoritory. The instance of enunciation is a variable linguistic function, making use of differential perspectives and generating new percepts and affects, rather than a stable entity which may be led back to a fixed subject. The novels contain myriads of languages, discourses, foci, and perspectives which rarely refer back to a central point, orchestrating instead a nomadic distribution that makes it possible for complementary worlds to coexist.

The nomadic principle reappeared in our examination of Rushdie's characters. They are migrants, which, incidentally, we all are according to him. Human identity, as it turns out, is suspended between the two poles of rootedness and rootlessness, through which Rushdie creates an endless number of variations. The principal "philosophy" in Rushdie's perception of human identity celebrates hybridity, metamorphosis, and processuality, but instead of flatly rejecting the conservative myth of roots, Rushdie sees people as networks of roots with their feet planted in several places at the same time. As a consequence of this a new form of genealogy is projected which allows the existence of a-parallel, impure (r)evolutions, graftings, and transversal communications, in place of the old genealogy running along pure, vertical lines of provenience.

The conjunctive and disjunctive styles of the novels, which coordinate the divergent series of the novel through a both-and logic and distributes them through an inclusive logic of either-or, secure mobility within the novels' multiplicity. We have seen how becoming in the novels is prompted by a metaphorical technique which is basically a metamorphic technique. In bringing together two heterogeneous fields of meaning, the metaphor gives rise to a conflictual collision that produces a surplus of meaning, making it possible for newness to enter the world; at the same time, the meaning of each semantic field is also changed as each of them deterritorialises the other.

The deterritorialisation of language is brought about by setting the linguistic system in motion, and Rushdie may be said to destabilise the (official) English language especially by giving voice to minorities in writing metamorphically and in squeezing language out of its dualistic nature. Deterritorialising language is a political act as it undermines the hidden metaphysics of the dominant language, determining our images of the world. Accordingly, it is the most distinguished task of literature to chart new (and better) maps of reality.

The cartographic process is activated in Rushdie by means of an interaction between historical referentiality and intratextual self-referentiality. The novels constitute provisional, but still durable maps, rewriting historical discourse and revealing the extent of its fictionality and constructedness. At the same time, the novels expose their own constructedness through intratextual self-criticism, emphasising the necessity of reactualisation, revisionism, and creativity.

*

Salman Rushdie is a reverse Shahrazad as the only way for him to earn the mercy of the "king" is to stop telling stories: "By God," Khomeini said to himself, "I will put him to death before I hear the rest of his story." With the fatwa Rushdie's person became so translucent and exposed that he had to seek refuge in the artificial night of hiding in order to evade the eternal dawn and, with that, the termination of storytelling. At times he managed to create the vital nocturnal mood in his peripheral, underground position, postponing the break of day and enabling him to continue writing his novels. Rushdie's novels are "wonderful, entertaining, and delectable," and they draw inspiration from the Oriental tradition of storytelling in which stories only end temporarily to be resumed the following night from the point where the narrator and the listener left them. At this time of my narrative, I see dawn breaking like Shahrazad, and hence I will lapse into silence.

BIBLIOGRAPHY

By Salman Rushdie
Grimus (1975). London: Vintage, 1996.
Midnight's Children (1981). London: Vintage, 1995.
Shame (1983). London: Vintage, 1995.
The Jaguar Smile: A Nicaraguan Journey (1987). London: Picador, 1997.
The Satanic Verses (1988). New York: Viking, 1989.
Haroun and the Sea of Stories (1990). London: Granta Books, 1991.
Imaginary Homelands. Essays and Criticism 1981-91 (1991). London: Granta Books, 1992.
The Wizard of Oz (1992). London: British Film Institute, 1998.
East, West (1994). London: Jonathan Cape, 1994.
The Moor's Last Sigh (1995). London: Vintage, 1994.
The Ground Beneath Her Feet (1999). New York: Henry Holt and Company, 1999.
Fury (2001). London: Jonathan Cape, 2001.
Step Across This Line: Collected Nonfiction 1992-2002 (2002). New York: Random House, 2002.
Shalimar the Clown (2005). London: Jonathan Cape, 2005.

On Salman Rushdie
Books
Andersen, Lars Erslev and Jacob Skovgaard-Petersen (eds.). *Satanisk, guddommeligt – og såre menneskeligt (Satanic, Divine – And Simply Human)*. Copenhagen: Gyldendal, 1999.
Appignanesi, Lisa and Sara Maitland (eds.). *The Rushdie File*. Syracuse, NY: Syracuse University Press, 1990.
Brennan, Timothy. *Salman Rushdie and the Third World: Myths of the Nation*. London: Macmillan, 1989.
Cundy, Catherine. *Salman Rushdie*. Manchester: Manchester University Press, 1996.
Dutheil de la Rochère, M.H. *Origin and Originality in Rushdie's Fiction*. Bern: Peter Lang, 1999.

Fletcher, M.D. (ed.). *Reading Rushdie: Perspectives on the Fiction of Salman Rushdie*. Amsterdam: Rodopi, 1994.

Gonzalez, Madelena. *Fiction After the Fatwa: Salman Rushdie and the Charm of Catastrophe*. Amsterdam: Rodopi, 2004.

Goonetilleke, D.C.R.A. *Salman Rushdie*. London: Macmillan, 1998.

Grant, Damien. *Salman Rushdie*. Plymouth: Northcote House, 1999.

Harrison, James. *Salman Rushdie*. New York: Twayne Publishers, 1992.

Kirpal, V. (ed.). *The New Indian Novel in English: A Study of the 1980s*. New Delhi: New Asia Books, 1990.

Kuortti, Joel. *Fictions to Live In: Narration as an Argument for Fiction in Salman Rushdie's Novels*. Frankfurt a.M.: Peter Lang, 1998.

Parameswaran, Uma. *The Perforated Sheet: Essays on Salman Rushdie's Art*. New Delhi: Affiliated East-West Press, 1988.

Petersson, Margareta. *Unending Metamorphoses: Myth, Satire and Religion in Salman Rushdie's Novels*. Lund: Lund University Press, 1996.

Rao, M. Madhusudhana. *Salman Rushdie's Fiction: A Study*. New Delhi: Sterling, 1992.

Reder, Michael R. (ed.). *Conversations with Salman Rushdie*. Jackson: University Press of Mississippi, 2000.

Ruthven, Malise. *A Satanic Affair*. London: Chatto & Windus, 1990.

Sanga, Jaina C. *Salman Rushdie's Postcolonial Metaphors: Migration, Translation, Hybridity, Blasphemy, and Globalization*. Westport: Greenwood Press, 2001.

Taneja, G.R. and R.K. Dhawan (eds.). *The Novels of Salman Rushdie*. New Delhi: Indian Society for Commonwealth Studies, 1992.

Articles

Afzal-Khan, Fawzia. "Myth De-Bunked: Genre and Ideology in Rushdie's *Midnight's Children* and *Shame*." *South Asian Review* 17, no. 14 (1993).

Andersen, Lars Erslev. "At sætte lethed mod tyngde" ("Pitting Levity Against Gravity"). *Slagmark* 18 (1991).

Andersen, Lars Erslev. "Khomeinis besværlige testamente" ("Khomeini's Problematic Will"). In *Satanisk, guddommeligt – og såre menneskeligt (Satanic, Divine – And Simply Human)*.

Aravamudan, Srinivas. "'Being God's Postman is no Fun, Yaar.'" In *Reading Rushdie: Perspectives on the Fiction of Salman Rushdie*.

Amanudin, Syed. "The Novels of Salman Rushdie: Mediated Reality as Fantasy." *World Literature Today* 63, no. 1 (1989).

Bader, Rudolf. "Indian Tin Drum." *International Fiction Review* 11, no. 2 (1984).
———. "On Blood and Blushing: Bipolarity in Salman Rushdie's *Shame*." *International Fiction Review* 15, no. 1 (1988).
———. "*The Satanic Verses*: An Intercultural Experiment by Salman Rushdie." *International Fiction Review* 19, no. 2 (1992).
Banerjee, Ashutosh. "A Critical Study of *Shame*." In *The Novels of Salman Rushdie*.
———. "Narrative Technique in *Midnight's Children*." In *The Novels of Salman Rushdie*.
Bardolph, Jacqueline. "Language is Courage." In *Reading Rushdie: Perspectives on the Fiction of Salman Rushdie*.
Batty, Nancy E. "The Art of Suspense: Rushdie's 1001 (Mid-)Nights." *Ariel* 18, no. 3 (1987).
Bhatt, Indira. "*Shame*: A Thematic Study." In *The Novels of Salman Rushdie*.
Birch, David. "Postmodernist Chutneys." *Textual Practice* 5, no. 1 (1991).
Booker, Keith M. "*Finnegans Wake* and *The Satanic Verses*: Two Modern Myths of the Fall." *Critique* 32, no. 3 (1991).
Bramming, Pernille. "Et billede af skabelsen af et billede" ("An Image of the Creation of an Image"). In *Satanisk, guddommeligt – og såre menneskeligt (Satanic, Divine – And Simply Human)*.
Brennan, Timothy. "*Shame*'s Holy Book." In *Reading Rushdie: Perspectives on the Fiction of Salman Rushdie*.
Chandra, Suresh. "The Metaphor of *Shame*: Rushdie's Fact-Fiction." In *The Novels of Salman Rushdie*.
Chaudhuri, Una. "Imaginative Maps." *Turnstile* 2, no. 1 (1990).
Close, Anthony. "The Empirical Author: Salman Rushdie's *The Satanic Verses*." *Philosophy and Literature* 14, no. 2 (1990).
Cook, Rufus. "Cultural Displacement and Narrative Duplicity." *The Centennial Review* 41, no. 2 (1997).
———. "Place and Displacement in Salman Rushdie's Work." *World Literature Today* 68, no. 1 (1994).
Corcoran, Marlena G. "Salman Rushdie's Satanic Narration." *The Iowa Review* 20, no. 1 (1990).
Cundy, Catherine. "'Rehearsing Voices': Salman Rushdie's *Grimus*." *The Journal of Commonwealth Literature* 27, no. 1 (1992).
Davies, J.M.Q. "Aspects of the Grotesque in Rushdie's *The Satanic Verses*." *Aumla* 85 (1996).
Dingwaney, Anuradha. "Author(iz)ing *Midnight's Children* and *Shame*: Salman Rushdie's Constructions of Authority." In Nelson, Emmanuel (ed.).

Durix, J.P. "The Artistic Journey in Salman Rushdie's *Shame*." *World Literature Written in English* 23, no. 2 (1984).

———. "Magic Realism in *Midnight's Children*." *Commonwealth* 8, no. 1 (1985).

———. "Salman Rushdie's Declaration of Kaleidoscopic Identity." In Sampietro, Luigi (ed.). *Declarations of Cultural Independence*. Novara: D'Imperio Editore, 1989.

Ferrell, Robert. "Sympathy for the Devil: Salman Rushdie's *The Satanic Verses*." *South Asian Review* 16, no. 3 (1992).

Finney, Brian. "Demonizing Discourse in Salman Rushdie's *The Satanic Verses*." *ARIEL* 29, no. 3 (1998).

Flanagan, Kathleen. "The Fragmented Self in Salman Rushdie's *Midnight's Children*." *Commonwealth Novel in English* 5, no. 1 (1992).

Fletcher, M.D. "Introduction: The Politics of Salman Rushdie's Fiction." In *Reading Rushdie: Perspectives on the Fiction of Salman Rushdie*.

———. "Rushdie's *Shame* as Apologue." In *Reading Rushdie: Perspectives on the Fiction of Salman Rushdie*.

Fokkema, Aleid. "Post-modern Fragmentation or Authentic Essence?: Character in *The Satanic Verses*." In Barfoot, C.C. and Theo D'haen (eds.). *Shades of Empire – In Colonial and Post-Colonial Literatures*. Amsterdam: Rodopi, 1993.

Grewal, Inderpal. "Salman Rushdie: Marginality, Women, and *Shame*." In *Reading Rushdie: Perspectives on the Fiction of Salman Rushdie*.

Hewson, Kelly. "Opening Up the Universe a Little More: Salman Rushdie and the Migrant as Story-Teller." *SPAN* 29 (1989).

Huggan, Graham. "The Postcolonial Exotic: Salman Rushdie and the Booker of Bookers." *Transition* 64 (1994).

Hussain, Nasser. "Hyphenated Identity: Nationalistic Discourse, History, and the Anxiety of Criticism in Salman Rushdie's *Shame*." *Qui parle* 3, no. 2 (1989).

Ismail, Quadri. "A Bit of This and a Bit of That: Rushdie's Newness." *Social Text* 9, no. 4 (1991).

Johansen, Ib. "The Flight From the Enchanter: Reflections on Salman Rushdie's *Grimus.*" *Kunapipi* 7, no. 1 (1985).

Juan-Navarro, Santiago. "The Dialogic Imagination of Salman Rushdie and Carlos Fuentes: National Allegories and the Scene of Writing in *Midnight's Children* and *Cristóbal Nonato.*" *Neohelicon* 20, no. 2 (1993).

Jussawalla, Feroza. "Beyond Indianness: The Stylistic Concerns of *Midnight's Children.*" *Journal of Indian Writing in English* 12, no. 2 (1984).

———. "Post-Joycean/Sub-Joycean: The Reverses of Mr. Rushdie's Tricks in *The Satanic Verses.*" In *The New Indian Novel in English: A Study of the 1980s.*

———. "Resurrecting the Prophet: The Case of Salman, the Otherwise." *Public Culture* 2, no. 1 (1989).

Kern, Susan. "'His Word Against Mine': An Exploration of Bakhtinian Polarity in Salman Rushdie's *The Satanic Verses.*" *South Asian Review* 16, no. 3 (1992).

Kerr, David. "Migration and the Human Spirit in Salman Rushdie's *The Satanic Verses.*" *Commonwealth Review* 2, no. 1-2 (1990-91).

King, Bruce. "Who Wrote *The Satanic Verses?*" *World Literature Today* 63, no. 3 (1989).

Kortenaar, Neil Ten. "*Midnight's Children* and the Allegory of History." *ARIEL* 26, no. 2 (1995).

Krishnaswamy, Revathi. "Mythologies of Migrancy: Postcolonialism, Postmodernism and the Politics of (Dis)Location." *ARIEL* 26, no. 1 (1995).

Leer, Martin. "Spejlvendte verdener" ("Inverted Worlds"). In *Satanisk, guddommeligt – og såre menneskeligt (Satanic, Divine – And Simply Human).*

Lewis, Bernard. "Behind the Rushdie Affair." *American Scholar* 60, no. 2 (1991).

Lipscomb, David. "Caught in a Strange Middle Ground: Contesting History in Salman Rushdie's *Midnight's Children.*" *Diaspora* 1, no. 2 (1991).

Malak, Amin. "Reading the Crisis: The Polemics of Salman Rushdie's *The Satanic Verses.*" *ARIEL* 20, no. 4 (1989).

Mann, Harveen S. "'Being Borne Across': Translation and Salman Rushdie's *The Satanic Verses.*" *Criticism* 37, no. 2 (1995).

Masse, Sophie. "Language versus Language in *The Satanic Verses.*" *Commonwealth* 20, no. 1 (1997).

Mathur, O.P. "Sense and Sensibility in *Shame.*" In *The Novels of Salman Rushdie.*

Mazrui, Ali A. "Is *The Satanic Verses* a Satanic Novel?: Moral Dilemmas of the Rushdie Affair." *The Michigan Quarterly Review* 28 (1989).

Merivale, Patricia. "Saleem Fathered By Oskar: *Midnight's Children*, Magic Realism, and *The Tin Drum.*" In Zamora, Lois, and Parkinson (eds.).

Magical Realism: Theory, History, Community. Durham: Duke University Press, 1995.

Mishra, D.S. "Narrative Techniques of Salman Rushdie's *Shame*." *Research Bulletin* 18, no. 1 (1987).

Mishra, Vijay. "Postcolonial Differend: Diasporic Narratives of Salman Rushdie." *ARIEL* 26, no. 3 (1995).

Moka-Dias, Brunda. "The Stuff That Dreams Are Made of: Interpreting Dreams in Salman Rushdie's *The Satanic Verses*." *Journal of the Fantastic in the Arts* 7, no. 4 (1996).

Mookerjea, Sourayan. "Irradiations of History: The Author, Cosmopolitanism and *The Satanic Verses*." *World Literature Written in English* 32-33, no. 2-1 (1992-93).

Moss, Stephanie. "The Cream of the Crop: Female Characters in Salman Rushdie's *Shame*." *International Fiction Review* 19, no. 1 (1992).

Mufti, Aamir. "Reading the Rushdie Affair: An Essay on Islam and Politics." *Social Text* 9, no. 4 (1991).

——. "Reading the Rushdie Affair: 'Islam,' Cultural Politics, Form." In Burt (ed.). *The Administration of Aesthetics*. Minnesota: University of Minnesota Press, 1994.

——. "*The Satanic Verses* and the Cultural Politics of 'Islam': A Response to Brennan." *Social Text* 10, no. 2-3 (1992).

Mukherjee, Arun P. "Characterization in Salman Rushdie's *Midnight's Children*: Breaking Out of the Hold of Realism and Seeking the 'Alienation Effect.'" In *The New Indian Novel in English: A Study of the 1980s*.

Naik, M.K. "A Life of Fragments: The Fate of Identity in *Midnight's Children*." *Indian Literary Review* 3, no. 3 (1985).

Necef, Mehmet Ümit. "Tilbageblik på den danske Rushdie-debat" ("Looking Back on the Danish Rushdie Debate"). In *Satanisk, guddommeligt – og såre menneskeligt (Satanic, Divine – And Simply Human)*.

Needham, Anuradha Dingwaney. "Author(iz)ing *Midnight's Children* and *Shame*: Salman Rushdie's Constructions of Authority." In Nelson, Emmanuel (ed.). *Reworlding: The Literature of the Indian Diaspora*. Westport: Greenwood Press, 1992.

Needham, Anurandha Dingwaney. "The Politics of Post-Colonial Identity in Salman Rushdie." In *Reading Rushdie: Perspectives on the Fiction of Salman Rushdie*.

Noor, Ronny. "Misrepresentation of History in Salman Rushdie's *Midnight's Children*." *Notes on Contemporary Literature* 26, no. 2 (1996).

———. "Reclaiming 'Mahound': An Intention Misunderstood." *Notes on Contemporary Literature* 22 (1992).
Parameswaran, Uma. "Salman Rushdie's *Shame*: An Overview of a Labyrinth." In *The New Indian Novel in English: A Study of the 1980s*.
Paranjabe, M.R. "Inside and Outside the Whale: Politics and the New Indian English Novel." In *The New Indian Novel in English: A Study of the 1980s*.
Pathak, R.S. "History and the Individual in the Novels of Rushdie." *The Commonwealth Review* 1, no. 2 (1990).
———. "Identity Crisis in the Novels of Salman Rushdie." *Language Forum* 18, no. 1-2 (1992).
Pedersen, Claus V. "Iran, fatwaen og De sataniske vers" ("Iran, the Fatwa and *The Satanic Verses*"). In *Satanisk, guddommeligt – og såre menneskeligt (Satanic, Divine – And Simply Human)*.
Piwinski, David. "Losing Eden in Modern Bombay: Rushdie's *Midnight's Children*." *Notes on Contemporary Literature* 23 (1993).
Pratsch, Th. "Contested Ground: Center and Margin in Rushdie's *The Satanic Verses*." *Philological Papers* 38 (1992).
Rao, M. Madhusudhana. "Quest For Identity: A Study of the Narrative in Rushdie's *Midnight's Children*." *The Literary Criterion* 25, no. 4 (1990a).
———. "Time and Timelessness in Rushdie's Fiction." *The Commonwealth Review* 1, no. 2 (1990b).
Reddy, P. Bayapa. "*Grimus*: An Analysis." In *The Novels of Salman Rushdie*.
———. "*Shame*: A Point of View." In *The Novels of Salman Rushdie*.
Riemenschneider, Dieter. "History and the Individual in Anita Desai's *Clear Light of Day* and Salman Rushdie's *Midnight's Children*." In *The New Indian Novel in English: A Study of the 1980s*.
Rombes, Nicholas D. "*The Satanic Verses* as a Cinematic Narrative." *Literature/Film Quarterly* 21, no. 1 (1993).
Sage, Vic. "The 'God-Shaped Hole': Salman Rushdie and the Myth of Origins." *Hungarian Studies in English* 22 (1991).
Sangari, Kumkum. "The Politics of the Possible." *Cultural Critique* 7 (1987).
Schulze-Engler, Frank. "Riding the Crisis: *The Satanic Verses* and the Silences of Literary Theory." In Stummer, Peter O. and Christopher Balme (eds.). *Fusion of Cultures?* Amsterdam: Rodopi, 1996.
Shepherd, Ron. "*Midnight's Children* as Fantasy." In *The Novels of Salman Rushdie*.
Simonsen, Jørgen Bæk. "Khomeinis dødsdom over Rushdie som ideologisk manøvre" ("Khomeini's Death Sentence Against Rushdie as a Political

Manoeuvre"). In *Satanisk, guddommeligt – og såre menneskeligt (Satanic, Divine – And Simply Human)*.

Skovgaard-Petersen, Jakob. "Hvad er de sataniske vers?" ("What Are the Satanic Verses"). In *Satanisk, guddommeligt – og såre menneskeligt (Satanic, Divine – And Simply Human)*.

Spivak, Gayatri C. "Reading *The Satanic Verses*." In Biriotti, Maurice and Nicola Miller (eds.). *What is an author?* Manchester: Manchester University Press, 1993.

Srivastava, Aruna. "*The Empire Writes Back*: Language and History in *Shame* and *Midnight's Children*." *ARIEL* 20, no. 4 (1989).

Suter, Davis W. "Of the Devil's Party: The Marriage of Heaven and Hell in *Satanic Verses*." *South Asian Review* 16, no. 13 (1992).

Swain, S.P. "Theme of Fragmentation: Rushdie's *Midnight's Children*." *The Literary Half-yearly* 36, no. 2 (1995).

Swan, John C. "*The Satanic Verses*, the Fatwa, and its Aftermath: A Review Article." *Library Quarterly* 61, no. 4 (1991).

Swan, Joseph. "'East is East and West is West'? Salman Rushdie's *Midnight's Children* as an Indian Novel." In *The New Indian Novel in English: A Study of the 1980s*.

Syed, Mujeebuddin. "Warped Mythologies: Salman Rushdie's *Grimus*." *ARIEL* 25, no. 4 (1994).

Taheri, Amir. "Pandora's Box Forced Open." *Index on Censorship* 18, no. 5 (1989).

Thompson, Jon. "Superman and Salman Rushdie: *Midnight's Children* and the Disillusionment of History." *Journal of Commonwealth and Postcolonial Studies* 3, no. 1 (1995).

Tikoo, S.K. "*Shame*: A Modern Comic Epic in Prose." In *The Novels of Salman Rushdie*.

Todd, Richard. "Worlds Apart: Salman Rushdie's 'Privileged Arenas.'" In *Shades of Empire – In Colonial and Post-Colonial Literatures*.

Tyssens, Stephane. "Language is Courage: *The Satanic Verses*." *Commonwealth* 12, no. 1 (1989).

Werbner, Pnina. "Allegories of Sacred Imperfection: Magic, Hermeneutics, and Passion in *The Satanic Verses*." *Current Anthropology* 37 (1996).

Ziadeh, Hanna. "Den sataniske treenighed" ("The Satanic Trinity"). In *Satanisk, guddommeligt – og såre menneskeligt (Satanic, Divine – And Simply Human)*.

Interviews

Ahmed, Akbar. "Salman Rushdie: A New Chapter" (1991). In *Conversations with Salman Rushdie*.

Ball, John Clement. "An Interview with Salman Rushdie" (1988). In *Conversations with Salman Rushdie*.

Banville, John. "An Interview with Salman Rushdie" (1993). In *Conversations with Salman Rushdie*.

Brooks, David. "An Interview With Salman Rushdie" (1984). In *Conversations with Salman Rushdie*.

Crichton, Sarah and Laura Shapiro. "An Exclusive Talk with Salman Rushdie" (1990). In *Conversations with Salman Rushdie*.

Durix, J.P. et al. "Salman Rushdie: Interview" (1982). In *Conversations with Salman Rushdie*.

Grass, Günter and Salman Rushdie. "Fictions Are Lies That Tell the Truth: Salman Rushdie and Günter Grass: In Conversation" (1985). In *Conversations with Salman Rushdie*.

Haffenden, John. "Salman Rushdie" (1983). In *Conversations with Salman Rushdie*.

Hamilton, Ian. "The First Life of Salman Rushdie." *New Yorker*, 25 December 1995.

McCabe, Colin, et al. "Interview: Salman Rushdie Talks to the London Consortium About *The Satanic Verses*." *Critical Quarterly* 38, no. 1 (1996).

Meer, Ameena. "Salman Rushdie" (1989). In *Conversations with Salman Rushdie*.

Morrison, Blake "An Interview with Salman Rushdie" (1990). In *Conversations with Salman Rushdie*.

Pattanayak, Chandrabhanu. "Interview With Salman Rushdie." *The Literary Criterion* 18, no. 3 (1983).

Ross, Jean W. "Salman Rushdie" (1982). In *Conversations with Salman Rushdie*.

Rønning, Helge. "Språk, identitet, litteratur og historie" ("Language, Identity, Literature, and History"). *Samtiden* 93, no. 4 (1984).

Tripathi, Salil. "The Last – and the Best – Salman Rushdie Interview in India!" (1983). In *Conversations with Salman Rushdie*.

Tripathi, Salil and Dina Vakil. "Angels and Devils Are Becoming Confused Ideas" (1987). In *Conversations with Salman Rushdie*.

Webb, W.L. "Salman Rushdie: Satanic Verses" (1988). In *Conversations with Salman Rushdie*.

By Gilles Deleuze

Deleuze, Gilles. *Bergsonism*. New York: Zone Books, 1988.
——. *Cinema 1: The Movement-Image*. New York: Continuum, 1986.
——. *Cinema 2: The Time-Image*. New York: Continuum, 1989.
——. *Difference and Repetition*. New York: Continuum, 2001.
——. *Essays Critical and Clinical*. Minnesota: University of Minnesota Press, 1997.
——. *The Fold: Leibniz and the Baroque*. Minnesota: University of Minnesota Press, 1992.
——. *The Logic of Sense*. London: The Athlone Press, 1990.
——. *Negotiations*. New York: Columbia University Press, 1995.
——. *Nietzsche and Philosophy*. New York: Columbia University Press, 1983.
——. *Proust and Signs*. London: The Athlone Press, 2000.
Deleuze, Gilles and Claire Parnet. *Dialogues*. London: The Athlone Press, 1987.
Deleuze, Gilles and Félix Guattari. *A Thousand Plateaus*. New York: Continuum, 2003.
——. *Anti-Oedipus*. New York: Continuum, 2004.
——. *Kafka: Toward a Minor Literature*. Minnesota: University of Minnesota Press, 1986.
——. *What Is Philosophy?* London: Verso, 1994.

On Gilles Deleuze

Alliez, Eric. *Deleuze: philosophie virtuelle*. Paris: Synthélabo, 1996.
—— (ed.). *Gilles Deleuze: une vie philosophique*. Paris: Synthélabo, 1998.
——. *La signature du monde, ou qu'est-ce que la philosophie de Deleuze et Guattari*. Paris: Cerf, 1993.
Badiou, Alain. *Deleuze: "La clameur de l'Etre."* Paris: Hachette, 1997.
Baudrillard, Jean. "The Precession of Simulacra." In Wallis, Brian (ed.). *Art After Modernism*. New York: Godine, 1984.
Boundas, Constantin V. and Dorothea Olkowski (eds.). *Gilles Deleuze and the Theater of Philosophy*. London: Routledge, 1994.
Buchanan, Ian (ed.). *A Deleuzian Century?* Durham: Duke University Press, 1999.
Busk, Malene. "Tankens passion. Om subjektivitetsproblematikker i Gilles Deleuzes filosofi" ("The Passion of Thought. On the Problematics of Subjectivity in Gilles Deleuze's Philosophy"). In *Flugtlinier. Om Deleuzes filosofi* (*Lines of Flight, On Deleuze's Philosophy*).
Buydens, Mireille. *Sahara: l'Esthétique de Gilles Deleuze*. Paris: VRIN, 1990.
Carlsen, M.S., K.G. Nielsen and K.S. Rasmussen (eds.). *Flugtlinier. Om Deleuzes*

filosofi (*Lines of Flight, On Deleuze's Philosophy*). Copenhagen: Museum Tusculanum Press, 2001.

Colombat, André. *Deleuze et la littérature*. Bern: Peter Lang, 1990.

Foucault, Michel. "Theatrum philosophicum." In *Dits et écrits*. Vol. 2. Paris: Gallimard, 1994.

Goodchild, Philip. *Deleuze and Guattari: An Introduction to the Politics of Desire*. London: Sage, 1996.

Hardt, Michael. *An Apprenticeship in Philosophy: Gilles Deleuze*. London: UCL Press, 1993.

Holland, Eugene W. *Deleuze and Guattari's* Anti-Oedipus: *Introduction to Schizoanalysis*. London: Routledge, 1999.

Hughes, John. *Lines of Flight: Reading Deleuze with Hardy, Gissing, Conrad, Woolf*. Sheffield: Sheffield Academic Press, 1997.

Kaufman, Eleanor and Kevin Jon Heller (eds.). *Deleuze and Guattari: New Mappings in Politics, Philosophy, and Culture*. Minnesota: University of Minnesota Press, 1998.

Lehmann, Niels and Carsten Madsen, et al. (eds.). *Deleuze og det æstetiske* (*Deleuze and the Aesthetic*). Aarhus: Aarhus University Press, 1995.

Madsen, Carsten. "Kræfternes formløse æstetik. Gilles Deleuzes forståelse af tanke og kunst" ("The Formless Aesthetics of Forces. Gilles Deleuze's Understanding of Thought and Art"). In *Flugtlinier. Om Deleuzes filosofi* (*Lines of Flight, On Deleuze's Philosophy*).

Marks, John. *Gilles Deleuze: Vitalism and Multiplicity*. London: Pluto Press, 1998.

Martin, Jean-Clet. *Variations: la philosophie de Gilles Deleuze*. Paris: Payot, 1993.

Massumi, Brian. *A User's Guide to* Capitalism and Schizophrenia: *Deviations from Deleuze and Guattari*. Cambridge, MA: MIT Press, 1992.

Mengue, Philippe. *Gilles Deleuze ou le système du multiple*. Paris: Kimé, 1994.

Olkowski, Dorothea. *Gilles Deleuze and the Ruin of Representation*. Berkeley, CA: University of California Press, 1999.

Patton, Paul (ed.). *Deleuze: A Critical Reader*. Oxford: Blackwell, 1996.

Pearson, Keith Ansell (ed.). *Deleuze and Philosophy: The Difference Engineer*. London: Routledge, 1997.

——. *Germinal Life: The Difference and Repetition of Deleuze*. London: Routledge, 1999.

Ruby, Christian. *Les archipels de la différence: Foucault – Derrida – Deleuze – Lyotard*. Paris: Félin, 1989.

Schérer, René. *Regards sur Deleuze*. Paris: Kimé, 1998.

Stivale, Charles J. "Gilles Deleuze and Félix Guattari: Schizoanalysis and Literary Discourse." *Substance: A Review of Theory and Literary Criticism* 29, (1981).

———. "The Literary Element in *Mille Plateaux*: The New Cartography of Deleuze and Guattari." *Substance: A Review of Theory and Literary Criticism* 13, no. 3-4 (1984).

Tygstrup, Frederik: "Livet og formerne. Efterskrift" ("Life and Forms. Postscript"). In *Flugtlinier. Om Deleuzes filosofi* (*Lines of Flight: On Deleuze's Philosophy*).

———. "Prosaens plan" ("The Plane of Prose. Literary Analysis and Gilles Deleuze's Understanding of Form"). In *Deleuze og det æstetiske* (*Deleuze and Aesthetics*).

Verstraeten, Pierre and Isabelle Stengers (eds.). *Gilles Deleuze*. Paris: VRIN, 1998.

Villani, Arnaud. *La guêpe et l'orchidée: essai sur Gilles Deleuze*. Paris: Belin, 1999.

Zizek, Slavoj. *Organs without Bodies: On Deleuze and Consequences*. New York: Routledge, 2004.

Zourabichvili, François. *Deleuze: une philosophie de l'événement*. Paris: P.U.F., 1994.

General Reading

Ahmad, Aijaz. *In Theory: Classes, Nations, Literatures*. London: Verso, 1994.

Appadurai, Arjun. *Modernity at Large*. Minnesota: University of Minnesota Press, 1996.

Aristotle. *Poetics, Aristotle in 23 Volumes*. Vol. 23. London: William Heinemann, 1932.

Bakhtin, M.M. *The Dialogic Imagination* [1981]. Austin: University of Texas Press, 1981.

———. *Problems of Dostoevsky's Poetics* [1929]. Minnesota: University of Minnesota, 1984.

Barthes, Roland. "The Death of the Author" [1967-68]. In *Image-Music-Text*. London: Fontana Press, 1977.

———. "From Work to Text" [1971]. In *Image-Music-Text*.

Benjamin, Walter. "The Storyteller" [1936]. In *Illuminations*. New York: Schocken Books, 1969.

Bergson, Henri. *The Creative Mind: An Introduction to Metaphysics*. New York: Philosophical Library, 1946.

Bhabha, Homi. *The Location of Culture*. London: Routledge, 1994.

——— (ed.). *Nation and Narration*. London: Routledge, 1990.

Blanchot, Maurice. *The Station Hill Blanchot Reader: Fiction & Literary Essays*. Barrytown, NY: Station Hill, 1999.

Boehmer, Elleke. *Colonial and Postcolonial Literature: Migrant Metaphors*. Oxford: Oxford University Press, 1995.

Booth, Wayne C. *The Rhetoric of Fiction* [1961]. London: Penguin, 1991.

Burke, Seán. *The Death and Return of the Author: Criticism and Subjectivity in Barthes, Foucault, Derrida* [1992]. 2nd edition. Edinburgh: Edinburgh University Press, 1999.

Eco, Umberto. *The Poetics of the Open Work*. Cambridge, MA: Harvard University Press, 1989.

Foucault, Michel. "Qu'est-ce qu'un auteur?" In *Dits et écrits*. Vol. 1. Paris: Gallimard, 1994.

Genette, Gérard. "Discours du récit." In *Figures III*. Paris: Éditions du Seuil, 1972.

Hegel, G.W.F. *The Philosophy of History*. Kitchener: Batoche Books, 2001.

Hutcheon, Linda. *A Poetics of Postmodernism: History, Theory, Fiction*. New York: Routledge, 1988.

Janaway, Christopher. *Images of Excellence, Plato's Critique of the Arts*. Oxford: Oxford University Press, 1995.

Kjærstad, Jan. *Menneskets felt: Essays om litteratur* (*The Human Zone: Essays on Literature*). Copenhagen: Samleren, 1999.

Koranen. (The Koran, Danish translation). Islam International Publications Ltd., Copenhagen: Borgens Forlag, 1989.

Koran, The. London: Penguin, 2003.

Kundera, Milan. *The Art of the Novel* [1986]. London: Faber and Faber, 2005.

———. *Ignorance* [2000], London: Faber and Faber, 2002.

———. *Testaments Betrayed* [1993]. London: Faber and Faber, 1996.

Larsen, Svend Erik. "Om udsigelse" ("On Enunciation"). In *Om litteraturanalyse* (*On the Analysis of Literature*).

Leibniz, G.W. *Discourse on Metaphysics* [1686]. 2nd edition. Chicago: Open Court Publishing Company, 1976.

Lübcke, Poul. "Fænomenologien og hermeneutikken i Tyskland" ("Phenomenology and Hermaneutics in Germany"). In Lübcke, Poul (ed.). *Vor tids filosofi. Engagement og forståelse* (*Philosophy of Our Time. Dedication and Understanding*). Copenhagen: Politikens Forlag, 1982.

Lukács, Georg. *The Theory of the Novel* [1920], London: Merlin Press, 1971.

Lyotard, J.-F. *The Postmodern Condition: A Report on Knowledge* [1979]. Minnesota: University of Minnesota Press, 1999.

McHale, Brian. *Postmodernist Fiction*. New York: Routledge, 1987.

Moretti, Franco. *Modern Epic: The World-System from Goethe to Garcia Marquez*. London: Verso, 1996.
——. *The Way of the World: The Bildungsroman in European Culture* [1987]. 2nd edition. London: Verso, 2000.
Møller, Lis. "Om figurativt sprog" ("On Figurative Language"). In *Om litteraturanalyse (On the Analysis of Literature)*.
—— (ed.). *Om litteraturanalyse (On the Analysis of Literature)*. Aarhus: Systime, 1995.
Orwell, George. *Inside the Whale and Other Essays* [1957]. London: Penguin, 1962.
Plato. *The Republic*. Oxford: Oxford University Press, 1993.
——. *The Symposium*. London: Penguin Books, 2003.
——. *Theaetetus. Sophist*. London: Heinemann, 1961.
Proust, Marcel. *On Art and Literature: 1896-1919*. New York: Carroll & Graf, 1984.
Said, Edward. *The World, the Text, and the Critic*. Cambridge, MA: Harvard University Press, 1983.
——. *Reflections on Exile and Other Essays*. Cambridge, MA: Harvard University Press, 2002.
Spivak, Gayatri C. "Can the Subaltern Speak?" In Williams, Patrick and Laura Chrisman (eds.). *Colonial Discourse and Post-Colonial Theory: A Reader*. New York: Harvester Wheatsheaf, 1993.
The Arabian Nights. New York: W.W. Norton & Company, 1990.
Vološinov, V.N. *Marxism and the Philosophy of Language*. Cambridge, MA: Harvard University Press, 1996.
Waugh, Patricia. *Metafiction: The Theory and Practice of Self-conscious Fiction*. London: Routledge, 1984.
White, Hayden. "The Value of Narrativity." In Mitchell, W.J.T. (ed.). *On Narrative*. Chicago: University of Chicago Press, 1981.

Lightning Source UK Ltd.
Milton Keynes UK
26 January 2011

166433UK00001B/23/P